ROBERT
WAINWRIGHT

ALSO BY ROBERT WAINWRIGHT

Rose: The Unauthorised Biography of Rose Hancock Porteous

The Lost Boy

The Killing of Caroline Byrne

Born or Bred? (with Paola Totaro)

Sheila

The Maverick Mountaineer

Miss Muriel Matters

Rocky Road

Enid

The Scandalous High-Society Life of the Formidable 'Lady Killmore'

ROBERT WAINWRIGHT

ALLEN & UNWIN

First published in Australia in 2020 by Allen & Unwin
This paperback edition published in Great Britain in 2021 by Allen & Unwin

10 9 8 7 6 5 4 3 2 1

A CIP catalogue record for this book is available from the British Library.

Paperback ISBN: 978 1 91163 085 2
E-book ISBN: 978 1 76087 430 8

Printed in Denmark by Nørhaven

Allen & Unwin
An imprint of Atlantic Books Ltd
Ormond House
26–27 Boswell Street
London
WC1N 3JZ

www.allenandunwin.com/uk

For Paola. Always.
Our adventure continues.

CONTENTS

Prologue 1

1 Cawarra 5
2 An independent spirit 14
3 Letter from America 22
4 A birth and a death 31
5 Europe bound 43
6 The transformation 54
7 Caviar Cavendish 64
8 The company of men 76
9 A father and a secret 84
10 Marmaduke 96
11 'He laid the world at my feet' 107
12 Champagny lordy 115
13 A jungle romance 128
14 Crashing the gilded halls 138
15 The sting 150
16 An ultimatum 159
17 La Fiorentina 168
18 Looking-glass world 174
19 Riviera refugees 182

20	Resistance	190
21	Where there's a will . . .	201
22	The fairy queen of Lees Place	211
23	The storekeeper's daughter	221
24	The excessively large gentleman	231
25	The touch of death	240
26	The newsprint knight	250
27	The waiting game	260
28	A lie laid bare	267
29	From the rubble	275
30	Australia	281
31	'Did I really kill them all?'	291
32	The unflappable hostess	303
33	Baron of Waterpark	310
34	A new adventure beckons	320
35	The racing game	329
36	Home	341

Epilogue 347
Afterword and acknowledgements 351
Selected bibliography 355

PROLOGUE

August 1948

She stepped onto the main floor of the Casino de Monte-Carlo, a silver-haired seductress with turquoise eyes.

The action on the tables paused as she glided by, as if carried on a hidden conveyor belt. In a room full of the moneyed, famous and powerful, men and women alike watched in lust or envy as she made her way across the room.

It was not as if she was unknown. The lady had been here many times before and always drew attention, often for her fearless style of play as much as her looks, mature as they were. Legend had it that she had won enough playing chemin de fer, a French baccarat-style card game, one night to buy the most spectacular home on the Côte d'Azur. No one would ever confirm such a story, of course, but neither would anyone deny it in a place that thrived on mystery, splendour and excess.

On this night she was a vision to behold, almost 6 feet tall and dressed in a Molyneux gown of white lace over a pale violet underskirt that clung to her graceful curves like a second skin. Delicate appliquéd flowers adorned the dress, each holding in its centre a diamond that flashed and dazzled, catching the light from the chandeliers that hung in the centre of the room. The effect gave her an ethereal, shining beauty.

At her throat sat a three-tiered diamond necklace while her hair, cut in short, tight waves that accentuated high cheekbones, was crowned with a silver tiara dressed in pink diamonds—a gift from her third husband, Marmaduke the 1st Viscount Furness, to wear at the coronation of an English king.

The usual sounds—gamblers' shrieks of triumph and cries of anguish—dulled for a moment, replaced by whispers of admiration or scorn. The lady divided opinion; a woman whose wealth and prominence was viewed either as well deserved or created by calculated greed. Not that she ever really cared what others thought.

The men at the main table stood as she approached. A chair was fetched and placed next to a portly man in tails. Sir Sultan Muhammad Shah, the third Aga Khan and spiritual leader of 15 million Ismaili Muslims, and one of the richest men in the world, smiled at her arrival.

'My dear Enid, could you not be more discreet with your entrance? Next time please come in black so I might be allowed to get on with the game without the undoubted distraction that your presence at my table is going to create. Allah should have made you a good Muslim and then you would have arrived smothered in veils.'

Lady Kenmare, the former Miss Enid Lindeman of Strathfield in Sydney, smiled quietly and sat down. She was ready to play.

1

CAWARRA

The village of East Gresford, tucked away in the fertile lower Hunter Valley of New South Wales, seems a strange place to begin a story about fame and wealth.

Today its main street, framed by ghost gums and lined with neat lawns and timber-framed houses, wanders up and over a crest, past a small supermarket at the top of the hill, then a cafe, pub and butcher's shop as the road bends left and down into the valley beyond. A church and cemetery with a few dozen worn headstones of long-dead pioneers marks the southern border.

That's it. Don't blink. Population, a few hundred.

Its beauty lies in its tranquillity: nestled into, or perched on the side of, an escarpment, depending on your perspective. Pollution-free skies grant clear views across soft yellow plains to purple hillsides in the distance, disturbed only by the chorus of warbling magpies and the haunting cooee of the common koel.

The pub, Beatty's, and the church, St Anne's, are the only buildings still standing from the nineteenth century when East Gresford and its nearby twin, Gresford, were thriving hamlets built by Europeans who came and transformed the traditional lands of the Worimi, Gringai and Biripi people.

The three clans had each occupied their own sections of the then heavily wooded valleys and hills around a surging river they knew as Kummi Kummi. The Gringai roamed the southern valleys, the plains to the west were regarded as Worimi country and the Biripi held the country to the north.

Their peaceful existence had been shattered in the 1820s when men came bearing land grants written and stamped by European bureaucrats who had unilaterally claimed ownership of the land. All because James Cook had planted a British flag in the sands of Botany Bay.

It had taken the best part of four decades for the white men to make their way inland from Sydney Cove, but once they arrived the impact was unyielding and permanent. The settlers cut and cleared, then fenced and planted, carved their roads and built their timber and stone homes with iron roofs.

The crops grew quickly and were bountiful in the silty loam soil; a strange mix of tobacco, citrus fruit, turnips, wheat and corn was trundled by wagon down to the town of Paterson, where it was loaded onto river steamboats bound for Newcastle and beyond to Sydney.

Settlements turned into villages and then towns, mostly with names from the old country chosen by the first to arrive. Gresford and East Gresford, linked by a one-kilometre track, were among them, named after the Welsh town where the area's first landowners had lived. First there were rough homes, then shops and churches, schools, hotels, town halls and court houses to hold the community to account. It was, according to a letter to the editor in the *Sydney Morning Herald*, 'an orderly, sober, well-conducted community'.

In 1841, a young man named Henry John Lindeman came to town to open a medical practice. East Gresford was beginning to flourish, with a new Catholic church being built and consecrated by the then Bishop of Australia, John Bede Polding—'a measure of importance to the populous neighbourhood', the local Maitland newspaper noted.

Henry was a doctor, as was his father before him. He had graduated from St Bartholomew's Hospital and the Royal College of Surgeons in London and set up a practice in Southampton but, despite its prestige and security, the profession appeared to be a means to an end—a way to please his father perhaps—rather than his desired path in life.

Henry was a man with a wanderlust, having already travelled through France, Germany, India and China before deciding that England offered few prospects compared to the excitement of beginning a new life on the other side of the world. In February 1840 he married Eliza Bramhall, the eighteen-year-old ward of a local businessman, and a month later he and his new wife boarded the barque *Theresa*, where he had signed on as ship's surgeon to pay for their passage as they sailed for Australia.

Either Sydney was a disappointment or, more likely, Henry was looking for something more than simply transplanting his medical practice from one side of the world to the other, because the couple did not stay long in the main colony, then a bustling town of 35,000 people. Opportunities lay inland.

Within a year of arriving in East Gresford, Henry's purpose had become clear. Not only had he established his surgery but he had also bought six parcels of land outside the town, on the banks of the Paterson River. He called his 800-acre property 'Cawarra', an Anglicised version of the Aboriginal word describing running water.

He and Eliza also now had a daughter, Harriet, who would be the first of ten children. Henry built a slab cottage on the land and set about experimenting with crops, including tobacco and sugar, and running cattle. Then, inspired by his travels through Europe and a belief that the soil and climate here could produce table wine of quality, he decided to create a vineyard.

Wine had been produced in the colonies since vine cuttings were brought out by Governor Arthur Phillip on the First Fleet in 1788, but with mixed success. John Macarthur, the pioneer of the wool industry, was the first to establish a commercial winery and Gregory Blaxland, known mostly for being a member of the expedition, with William Wentworth and William Lawson, who crossed the Blue Mountains, was the first to export wine. Although arriving two decades later, Henry Lindeman would help bring a new, quality phase to the industry; he intended to allow his wine to mature and improve before sale.

His initial efforts were dismissed as vinegary but by 1850 Lindeman was able to present two samples—a red hermitage, 'sound, of good flavour', and a white hermitage, 'delicate of pleasant flavour'—to the local vineyard association. As the *Sydney Morning Herald* reported: 'In answer to inquiries, Dr Lindeman said the vines were young, the present samples being made from the first year's produce.'

In another report he talked of growing vines in a mixture of river soil and vegetable mould, and fermenting the wine in open vats before it was casked. The results were promising but Henry wanted to let it mature, so he imported oak barrels from France in which to let it rest. In September 1851, as he prepared to bottle 4000 gallons, an arsonist burned down his winemaking building and destroyed the cellar he'd built beneath and its contents. Despite a reward, the identity of the 'ruffian' was never discovered. Just as he was about to produce his first full vintage, Henry Lindeman had been all but wiped out.

When his fifth child, Sidney Alfred, was born two weeks after the arsonist's torch, Henry had little choice than to return to his medical practice and begin rebuilding his fortune, although there was another, more tantalising lure. Gold had just been discovered near the New South Wales town of Orange, followed soon after at Ballarat, Bendigo and Castlemaine in Victoria. The Australian goldrush had begun and the madness would spread like fire.

According to family lore, Henry packed his bags and headed to Victoria, hoping to cash in on the hysteria and population explosion, both as a medic but also try to strike it rich. Two years later, so the story goes, he headed home with his pockets full of gold, ready to restore and rebuild the vineyard.

Among the family tales is the story of the night Henry became lost in the bush on the way home, only to find wandering cattle bearing the Lindeman brand that led him back to Cawarra.

More often than not, family dynasties are created by forebears with vision and determination, whose struggles and passions, combined with a measure of luck, are instrumental in the family's success. But in the retelling, sometimes fact and fiction become merged, and details are mangled or innocently embellished in the enthusiasm of the tale.

Such was the case with Henry Lindeman. Delightful as the family story is, these events have been romanticised. Author Dr Philip Norrie, in his 1993 book on the Lindeman family history, found no evidence of Henry holding a miner's licence or being at any of the Victorian diggings. It is also unlikely, Dr Norrie concluded, that he spent so long away from home, given his wife fell pregnant again in 1853. Instead, Henry sold two hundred cattle—'first-rate cows, bullocks, heifers and steers', according to newspaper advertisements, to raise the funds he needed to rebuild the cellar.

There is, however, evidence that he did do some prospecting, and was successful—not in Victoria but around the town of Mudgee, about 250 kilometres to the west of East Gresford. In its issue of 10 November 1852, the *Maitland Mercury and Hunter Valley General Advertiser* published a report of activity in what it called the western goldfields, including activity around Louisa Creek, a tributary of the Meroo River near Mudgee where thousands of hopeful prospectors had flocked after the discovery of two large nuggets.

Among them was Henry Lindeman, who bought two claims around a nearby waterhole. In October, he struck it lucky, according to a report in the *Empire* newspaper on 6 November:

> A waterhole was drained here by Dr Lindeman with some success. In three weeks, he took eighty ounces of gold, among which there were two nuggets weighing twenty and fifteen ounces respectively. The other day he sold one part of the claim for £15 and the other for one fourth of the proceeds. There will be very few persons at this creek in a short time, unless the weather becomes settled, so as to allow the bed being thoroughly worked. The country in the immediate vicinity is, however, almost untouched, and so far from there being any reason to think that it is not rich in deposits of the precious metal, there is every reason to believe the contrary.

The price for gold at the time was £3 per ounce, which meant that Henry had made around £240 and then sold his claim, presumably to head back to East Gresford. In relative income terms, it meant he was taking home around $300,000.

Lillian, the youngest of the Lindeman children, recalled her mother saying that they had been ruined financially by the fire and her father had agreed to go into a gold mine near Mudgee to work as a doctor because there had been so many accidents.

'After he had made a good deal of money he started the wine, fixed up the cellars and began all over again.'

So, the story, in essence at least, was true. Perhaps even the wandering cattle.

Whatever his means, Henry Lindeman was determined to succeed. The vines were still intact and, after rebuilding his cellar, this time in stone, he started the maturing process again. By 1854 the business was back on track and his first vintages were receiving widespread praise around the colony. He had also built a new two-storey home and welcomed his sixth child, Charles Frederick, into the world.

In 1858, Lindeman's exported its first wine and by the 1860s the company was winning medals in London and Paris. Henry bought smaller vineyards near the town of Corowa on the Murray River and at Rutherglen, across the border in Victoria, where he diversified into heavy sweet wines such as port, muscat and sherry, and also distilled brandy.

His main interest, however, was in producing light wines suitable for drinking with a meal. In 1860, one journalist wrote of a 'pale, clear and light wine possessing bouquet and a very delicate flavour', concluding: 'It must be Dr Lindeman's wine.'

By 1870 Henry had moved his winemaking operation to Sydney, establishing new headquarters there, including a winery, cellars and a bottling complex at a building in Pitt Street. He became a loud voice in the political battle between winemakers and the more powerful lobby of rum producers. When the NSW Parliament passed laws unfavourable to wine, he thundered: 'It clearly shows that the rum bottle interest is all-paramount, and the majority of the House are its abject slaves.'

By the time he died in 1881, Henry Lindeman had helped put Australia on the world stage in terms of wine and was regarded as one of the industry's pioneers. He was a wealthy man, yet had always remained living in the house he built at Cawarra. His grave is among those in the cemetery at St Anne's, the tiny church at the southern border of East Gresford, where his headstone notes only that he had lived for sixty-nine years and eight months.

2

AN INDEPENDENT SPIRIT

Henry Lindeman introduced his sons to the business several years before his death, although only three would remain involved with its operations. Arthur, the eldest son, would be the winemaker and Herbert, the youngest boy, was trained as the taster, his father insisting that the human palate was the only true test of a wine. Overall management for the business would fall to Charles, the middle son born in 1854 as his father rebuilt the winery business after the cellar fire.

The brothers traded under the name H.J. Lindeman and Company after their father's death and continued the company's success internationally with medals at Paris and Bordeaux, among other exhibitions. They also became a dominant force in domestic competitions as their father's dreams of a flourishing wine industry came to pass and the state's infatuation with rum faded.

If Henry had been the visionary, then Charles—tall and square-jawed, with piercing eyes and a mop of rust-coloured hair—was the champion of Lindeman's quality, as the company became the country's biggest producer and its most successful exporter. Faced with accusations by jealous competitors that they used additives to produce extra flavour, Charles lobbied the NSW Premier Sir Henry Parkes, offering to donate £1000 to charity if government inspectors could find 'any colouring matter, added spirit or flavouring, in fact anything that is not absolutely grape juice'. None was found.

What had begun as an experiment by their father had become an empire as the operation was moved from Pitt Street to the Queen Victoria Building, in George Street, where the company transformed the basement into a giant cellar. The plaudits flowed, such as from the *Sydney Mail* in August 1893: 'Science and skill have been brought to bear on the vineyard's yield . . . and the business grew and prospered and is now in full bloom, promising to go on like some of the old wine houses of France, the reputation of which is ever before the world. Since 1881 Mr Charles F. Lindeman has taken charge of the business which, under his care, has increased to very large proportions. Prizes innumerable have been won in France and Australia and, as stated in one of the papers, Mr Burgoyne, the British wine merchant, before leaving Australia recently, spoke of Lindeman wines as the best in Australia.'

While the vineyard at East Gresford continued to expand and others were acquired, the heart of the operation was now Sydney, where Charles would set up a home with his wife,

Florence. Following the trend of large families, they would have seven children.

First would come four sons, neatly spaced two years apart—Frederick the eldest in 1884, followed by Grant (1886), Rupert (1888) and Roy in 1890. At this time Charles was busily expanding his business empire by buying into hotels which, of course, would carry Lindeman wines in their cellars.

On 8 January 1892, as the new house was being completed, Florence gave birth to their fifth child—a daughter they named Enid Maud.

Literature would in time play a frequent and significant role in the life of Enid Lindeman. This was often because of the people with whom she surrounded herself, those she admired and whose advice she sought.

As a child she had two favourite books, both written by Australian women. The children's classic *Dot and the Kangaroo*, the story of a young girl who becomes lost in the bush and is befriended by a kangaroo that gives her magic berries and guides her home to safety, was published in 1899 when Enid was aged seven, sparking the imagination of a child who already adored her own pet kangaroo, which followed her around like a dog.

Drawing on the lost child trope and fantasy of works like *Alice in Wonderland* and *Hansel and Gretel*, *Dot and the Kangaroo* was an early story of conservation; its author, Ethel Pedley, entreated her young readers to appreciate and respect the fragile beauty of the Australian bush and its animals.

It was a lesson that would stay with Enid. Her love of animals would continue through her life as would her fascination with the natural landscape of her homeland, and she spent as much time exploring the wilds of northern and central Australia as the ballrooms and racetracks of Sydney and Melbourne.

Her teenage years were influenced by another novel, *Seven Little Australians*, which seemed to mirror so many aspects of her own life, from the matching number of children in the fictional Woolcot family to their home, Misrule, in Parramatta not far from the Lindeman home, Bramhall, in Strathfield, and even a country property where they spent holidays, as the Lindemans did at Cawarra.

Enid could identify with the adventures of the mischief-making Judy and her older brother, Pip. The author, Ethel Turner, lauded the 'lurking sparkle of joyousness and rebellion' that set Australian children apart from their English and American counterparts who were, in Turner's mind, boring paragons of virtue.

This conclusion matched many of Enid's own experiences of a childhood in which she was closer in age to her four older brothers than to the two sisters who would come after her—Nita, five years younger, and Marjorie, a full decade behind. Circumstances forced her to compete against the boys and hold her own by learning to ride, hunt, shoot and fish as adeptly as they did—skills that helped create an independent spirit that drove much of her adult decision-making in a man's world.

The seven Lindeman children grew up in the southwest suburb of Strathfield, an area initially created as a series of agricultural holdings, roughly at the halfway point between the main colony and Parramatta, but eventually subdivided to provide housing as Sydney's population continued to grow and push outwards.

It seems a strange area for a wealthy man like Charles Lindeman to build a home, which he named Bramhall after his mother's family, 15 kilometres outside the city centre where he travelled almost every day to oversee the cellar at the Queen Victoria Building, when he could easily have bought in one of the inner suburbs that stretched along the southern shore of Sydney Harbour.

Perhaps that was his chief reason. By the beginning of the twentieth century, Sydney's population had reached almost 500,000, crowding its inner suburbs, whereas Strathfield had space—*freedom* as Enid would describe it to her own children, reflecting on a childhood of open spaces, picnics on secluded beaches to the booming sound of crashing surf and the camaraderie of harvest time among the vineyards of Cawarra.

These were powerful influences, as her eldest son, Rory, would later reflect about his mother in his 1950 book *My Travel's History*: 'A beautiful woman, and much spoiled by those who loved her, she would sometimes come to my nursery in a shimmer of beads, her hair closely cropped to her head. If she had time before going down to dinner, she would sit on the end of my bed and tell me stories, or read me snatches out of the books she had enjoyed as a child. I retain vivid memories of stories she told me of her tomboy youth spent with her brothers and the fun they had while the grapes were being gathered.'

At almost 6 feet tall, with the jawline of her father and the blue-green eyes of her mother, Enid always attracted attention, even as a teenager attending Ascham School, then in Darling Point, Sydney, for girls of well-to-do families, where she won prizes for music, painting and elocution and appeared in school plays, as noted by the school magazine *Charivari,* which detailed the school's day-to-day affairs.

Enid was best known for her sporting prowess. Rangy and athletic, she quickly won the nickname Diana when she arrived at the school aged fifteen, a reference to the Roman goddess of the hunt and indicative of her influence on the sporting field. The students were encouraged by Principal Herbert J. Carter, who believed in the benefits of sports for *young ladies*, and was supported by his wife, Antoinette, whose photographic albums make up a large proportion of the school's extensive archives.

One photo of the school's Basket-Ball side (an early field version of netball) shows Enid towering, giraffe-like, over class-mates. She also played tennis for the school as well as the ball game rounders, helping to coach other students.

But it was the introduction to games such as croquet and golf and learning to ride a horse that would become the more important social skills in her adult life, as would a talent for art, sewing fine tapestries, watercolour painting and even creating murals that would adorn walls of her homes.

Enid was a weekday boarder, living from Monday to Friday in a grand colonial house, 'Mount Adelaide', that stood on Darling Point Road with views across the deep waters of Sydney Harbour to the distant shoreline of Mosman, long before the Opera House and Harbour Bridge were conceived. It was a vista she would remember decades later when she bought a home on the other side of the world that commanded an equally imposing vista.

Enid attended the Ascham School for only two years, in 1907 and 1908, and left just before her seventeenth birthday with no plans to attend university—a seemingly aimless education that, according to the school's archivist Marguerite Gillezeau, was all too common for young women of well-to-do families: 'I would say Enid came to Ascham specifically to complete her last two years of school. She was in sixth form, the top class, although I doubt she matriculated. It was very rare in that era for girls to matriculate from Ascham, not because it wasn't a good school academically, but because the majority of the parents weren't on board with the idea of their daughters going to university. The staff were constantly trying to promote the idea of tertiary education, but it wasn't until after World War I that it was taken more seriously by the parents when the social reality of the post-war era became apparent.'

Instead, Enid Lindeman left school with one goal in life—to marry well. It was not necessarily a shortcoming on her part, a lack of imagination or laziness, but merely the expectation for women in the first years of the twentieth century. Tradition stated that brothers divided the spoils of family assets—the eldest usually taking the lion's share—while their sisters cleared the path and avoided becoming financial burdens by finding husbands. Love was a secondary consideration to the practicalities of lineage.

That was certainly the case in the Lindeman family. Henry Lindeman's five sons—Arthur, Sidney, Charles, Herbert and Henry—took control of the fortune and business while sisters Harriet, Mary and Matilda dutifully married a doctor, a politician and a lawyer. Louisa and Lillian went even further, wedding the sons of rival vineyard owners, which not only fulfilled their obligations but built new financial bridges for the Lindeman empire.

The rare exception to this rule was if a woman could not find a husband; in that case she would remain in the protective bosom of the family. Not that marriage necessarily provided financial security for women, given what the *Weekly Chronicle* in South Australia described in 1894 as 'the practically unlimited powers' a man had to organise and control family finances.

But the beautiful Enid Lindeman was never going to be a spinster.

3

LETTER FROM AMERICA

In the autumn of 1912, a wealthy middle-aged American businessman named Roderick Cameron arrived in Sydney to oversee the expansion of his shipping company. It was his second trip to Australia, and the month-long journey from his home in New York—first across the continent by train to San Francisco and then by steamship across the Pacific—was reason enough to stay for several months before returning.

Cameron was named after his father, the New York shipping magnate Sir Roderick Cameron, who had nurtured the business from its beginnings in 1852 when, as a lowly clerk in a Canadian export company, he had seen an opportunity, chartered a steamship and had begun taking passengers and supplies from North America to Australia to join the goldrush that was rapidly expanding across the continent.

The venture was an immediate success as thousands of hopeful men made the journey on what he called the Pioneer Line. The business continued to grow in the years after the goldrush faded, as Cameron expanded into transporting farm machinery, as well as general produce, to Australia, New Zealand and later to Europe.

By the 1880s Sir Roderick had shifted to New York and became one of that city's most prominent businessmen. He had also established a commercial presence in Sydney, where he mingled with its political elite, including the Premier Sir Henry Parkes, who would visit the US to cement economic ties. He had got to know business leaders such as Charles Lindeman, with whom he worked on several trade delegations, including representing New South Wales in the World's Trade Fair held in Philadelphia in 1876.

When Sir Roderick died in 1900 at the age of seventy-five, his second son and namesake took over the business, and continued to foster the relationships in Australia. Roderick Jnr had visited in 1908; when he returned to cast his eye over the operation in 1912, he based himself in an office in Pitt Street.

He was a serious and studious man with soft features and anxious eyes, who in photographs grimaced rather than smiled and looked older than his forty-five years. He was also single, highly unusual for a man of his wealth, and understood how important it was to have sons to whom he could pass on the family name and fortune.

There had previously been some talk of a marriage to the daughter of a society family but he had pulled out of the engagement. Now it seemed he had put aside any notions of a wife and family and was content to concentrate on the business empire he managed on behalf of his siblings.

But that would all change a few months after he arrived in Sydney, when Roderick was introduced to twenty-year-old Enid Lindeman at a charity ball held at the Town Hall. He was immediately smitten by the tall, graceful woman and decided that it was time to roll the marriage dice. Enid's feelings about a man old enough to be her father were never recorded, although, given the speed of their engagement it seems likely that she was attracted by his quiet smile and sureness as an older, successful man. After all, men around the ages of her brothers had always been regarded as competition rather than romantic partners.

Enid's mother was against the union at first, concerned at the significant age difference, but when the businessman made it plain that he was prepared to stay in Sydney and win her approval, Florence Lindeman eventually changed her mind. She gave the couple her blessing when her eldest daughter turned twenty-one on 8 January 1913.

It was a time of change for women. The suffrage movement in Britain was at its loudest, forcing debate not only about political emancipation and equality for women but also about changing the marriage vows and, among other things, removing the expectation that wives had to 'honour and obey' their husbands.

But society would move slowly, stymied by antiquated attitudes and expectations: 'A new danger has arisen on the horizon of woman,' a December 1913 report in the *Daily*

Telegraph warned about a study of female university students. 'If she is clever and is educated she has less chance of being married than if she remains just a simple young person of attractive appearance and manners. In fact, the more educated she becomes, the less chance she seems to have of marriage.'

Enid Lindeman fell somewhere in between, having been home-schooled before her final two years of secondary education. Whether she had ambition or not was irrelevant and, despite their age difference, Roderick Cameron was a marital catch.

Their wedding on 12 February 1913 was described by *The Bulletin* as 'a festive affair'. The morning ceremony at St Paul's, Burwood, was conducted by her great uncle, the Rev Septimus Hungerford, before a reception for two hundred or so guests back at the family home.

The unplanned nature of the union was highlighted by the fact that no one from the Cameron family had made the long journey from New York. Instead, Roderick's best man was a Sydney businessman named Colin Caird, whose only connection was through his business relations with Charles Lindeman and a shared Scottish heritage.

Yellow in all its subtle shades was the season's fashionable colour and a description of the wedding party's outfits dominated newspaper coverage, including *The Bulletin*, which noted a few days later that the bride was 'gowned in cream duchess satin with a tulle veil and small coronet of orange blossom'. Her six bridesmaids wore lemon chiffon and, after the ceremony, Enid changed into a grey crêpe de Chine coat and skirt and a black velvet hat, set with ostrich plumes, before the couple left to drive down to Bowral for the honeymoon.

The media coverage was very different back in the United States where the *Washington Post*, among others, made subtle hints about the age difference and haste of the ceremony.

> Friends of Mr Roderick MacLeod Cameron were greatly interested as well as surprised to learn that he and the daughter of a prominent merchant of Sydney, Australia, were married yesterday in that distant city. Only members of his family and business associates were informed that his long stay in Australia was to culminate in his marriage. The bride of Mr Cameron is Miss Enid Lindeman, whose father went to Australia many years ago and established a large export trade. The transportation business of Mr Cameron, and expansion of that established by his father, the late Sir Roderick Cameron, brought him into commercial relations with Mr Lindeman long before he went to Australia, about a year ago, when he first met Miss Lindeman.

16 May 1913

My darling mother,

We seem to have done nothing but travel the last week. The last day I wrote to you was on the 7th and we have been on the go ever since. I'm just longing to hear from you or Dad, it seems such ages since I last heard from anyone and we would not get any letters till about the 1st June as we don't get to New York till then.

The newlyweds had sailed from Sydney in early April aboard the steamship *Ventura*, among the two hundred and fifty passengers who settled in for the three-week voyage across the Pacific to San Francisco via Samoa and Honolulu. After arrival, it would normally take another five days to make the journey across the vast continent by train to New York, but Roderick Cameron was in no rush.

Instead, he wanted to show his bride the wonders of her new home and set off inland by train toward the Yosemite National Park, arriving at the hamlet of El Portal. Here, they stepped back in time and onto a stagecoach that would take them through treacherous, unsealed roads to the centre of America's wilderness gem.

Enid was spellbound by the scenery during the four-hour drive, leaning out of the coach as far as she dared on a trail that clung precariously to the snow-capped mountainsides above the Merced River that boiled and bubbled like a raging sea while alpine forests stretched, uninterrupted by humans, as far as the eye could see. That evening, she sat on the verandah of the Sentinel Hotel, beneath the towering granite peak after which it was named, and watched in wonder the Yosemite Falls in the distance, the thin line of water plunging hundreds of metres into a seemingly bottomless chasm: 'Try and imagine that height . . .' she wrote in admiration.

It was a world far from her usual city life of fine clothes and social parades, and yet strangely comforting given the Lindeman family's connection to the land. But these were not the gentle slopes of the Hunter Valley, as Enid discovered the next day when she eagerly volunteered to hike several miles of trails and climb the side of a cliff. She wanted to get a closer look at one of the nearby falls, the Vernal, and sit by the side of the Emerald Pool, where the waters gathered before being swept over the edge and crashing like thunder on the boulders below.

And it seemed that, despite Florence Lindeman's initial concerns, Rory, as Enid now called Roderick, was an attentive husband. She wrote: 'Rory was very anxious for me to see them and was afraid it was too far to walk, so rather than I should miss them he got a large rope and tied it around my waist then around him. It is a two mile trail up the side of a mountain. I quite enjoyed the walk and Rory didn't seem to be any the worse for it.'

The journey continued two days later. The roads were even rougher as the stagecoach took them deeper into the park, where ancient sequoia trees grew in giant stands and deer roamed without fear of humans. Guns were banned year-round and the park was about to be handed to a civilian team of rangers to manage the delicate balance between conservation and tourism. Enid was thrilled at the sanctuary as she fed squirrels by hand.

The journey east continued, first by stagecoach and then by an overnight train into Arizona, where Enid sat down to write a letter after watching the sun set over the Grand Canyon.

Despite its natural glories, the trip was beginning to wear her down physically.

> *It made me as ill as if I was sea sick, so rough I wonder I have any inside left. That drive took us seven hours and we changed horses nine times. All that jolting was hell but then we had to catch the train . . . and spent all that night and all the next day and the next night in the train. Ah! Ye Gods, I can't tell how sick I was. Poor old Rory did all he could in the way of making me comfortable. He got a drawing room car that has twin beds and a couch, and all to ourselves so I could lie down all day as well. We arrived here at the Grand Canyon at 8.30 so I went straight to bed and didn't get up till lunch time, then in the afternoon I wrote the first part of this letter to you and at 6.30 we drove out nine miles to see the sunset on the Grand Canyon. It's quite the most wonderful sight in all the world. I'll enclose a post card and let you have an idea what it's like. The colours are marvellous, and they seem to change every hour or so.*

Her mood had improved the next day when they visited a nearby Native American reservation and watched women making baskets and weaving rugs. But it wasn't the craft work that grabbed Enid's attention: 'One woman had the sweetest baby you ever saw. Only nine weeks old and slipped into a basket alongside her. It looked as if it couldn't move a finger and yet it was as good as gold. I sat there for quite a while nursing it and the mother was pleased as punch, laughing and talking away in her own tongue.'

It was also clear that whatever Enid and Roderick's initial reasons for marriage, their relationship had blossomed. The couple were very much in love, their evenings spent together playing cards as Rory taught his wife the basics of gambling: 'I've won £4 from Rory—$20,' she wrote proudly. 'He will be starting to feel sorry he taught me the game.'

She was also becoming playful with her husband: 'This climate is the devil for one's skin. Mine feels like parchment and any bit of metal you touch gives you an electric shock. If I think Rory looks too peaceful, I run my feet along the carpet and then touch the end of his nose with my fingers and get a spark. It makes him jump out of his seat.'

In all the news and travelogue, there was one thing Enid was not telling her mother. The travel illness was not the result of a bumpy ride and Rory had good reason to be concerned about her ability and safety to climb mountain trails. The clue lay in her clucky delight in nursing the Native American woman's baby: Enid was three months pregnant.

4

A BIRTH AND A DEATH

One of most prestigious residential addresses in New York at the turn of the twentieth century was Murray Hill, a neighbourhood bounded to the north and south by East 42nd and East 34th streets, and to the west and east from Madison Avenue through to the East River.

Future president Franklin Roosevelt lived on 36th Street, as did the influential financier John Pierpont Morgan, who built a library next to his home. The fabulously wealthy Vanderbilt family kept a townhouse nearby, surrounded by many of the merchants and industrialists who had made their fortunes during the so-called Gilded Age of the nineteenth century.

Sir Roderick and Anne Cameron had owned a large house at the southernmost tip of Murray Hill, the corner of East 34th Street and Madison Avenue, where they raised their seven children—five daughters and two sons. By all accounts,

Sir Roderick was a fearsome man, at times overbearing and particularly proud of being the only man in New York with an English title, bestowed on him by his native Canadian government for his contribution to business.

He also owned a large property on Staten Island, a ferry ride past the Statue of Liberty to the south of the city, where he established Clifton Berley, one of the country's best-known horse studs. He was considered one of the fathers of US thoroughbred racing: 'I have clung tenaciously to my farm and shall hold it for my children,' he once declared, confident the island would one day become a city. 'What grounds have I for such hope? Well simply this: We are within an hour of Wall Street, the great civilizer and founder of cities.'

A century later Staten Island *is* one of the city's five boroughs, the grandeur of Clifton Berley swallowed up by the suburbia that Roderick Cameron accurately predicted. A lake that was once on his property and the local recreation club both bear his name.

But for all their wealth and prominence, the Cameron family would not be immune from tragedy. Anne Cameron had died of fever in 1879, three days after delivering their seventh child, a girl named Isabelle. A year later, nineteen-year-old daughter Alice would succumb to tuberculosis and in 1906, Isabelle, who had established a career as an artist and writer, would also die suddenly after being mauled by a dog.

Roderick Jnr, the youngest son and middle child, had taken over the management of the empire when his father died in 1900. His brother Duncan, two years older, was the natural heir but had been disgraced earlier when he became embroiled in a divorce case in which he was accused of taking money from his wife and being violent in a two-year marriage that ended with his wife 'kidnapping' their daughter.

It had been a messy affair, publicly as well as privately, and was only compounded when Duncan, penniless after wasting an inheritance from his mother, fled to London in the late 1880s, where he ran up debts to a jeweller for expensive gifts he bought for several girls, including 'an actress'. Sir Roderick had travelled to London to front court on behalf of his son, only to leave fuming and embarrassed by events.

And so the mantle of successor had fallen to Roderick Jnr, steadfast, principled and anointed by his surviving sisters who, unusually, had been given equal shares in the multimillion-dollar inheritance left by their father.

For all his quiet ways, Roderick Jnr would prove a steely businessman, pursuing not only the family's shipping interests but taking a lead in New York life—as a member of the exclusive Knickerbocker and Union clubs, a property developer and a proponent of change. His energy was perhaps best illustrated by what another man in his position might have considered a minor matter and not worth his time—his decision to fight and overturn what he believed to be an unfair tax on owners of pet dogs. He won.

There was precious little room for sentiment in his life. In 1910, he and his older sister, Margaret, decided to demolish the family home in Madison Avenue as well as the house next door. They did not want to rebuild a grander home to show off their wealth, but to construct a sixteen-storey office building.

It proved a canny, if controversial development. The commercial centre of New York, a city hemmed in by water on three sides, was creeping ever northwards and the Cameron Building, as it would be named, would be among the first to be built in an established residential area, much to the annoyance of wealthy bankers and industrialists, whose mansions and brownstone townhouses lined the genteel cobblestone streets.

But Cameron stood firm, even refusing an offer of $600,000, triple what they had paid to purchase the land, to abandon the project and then winning a lawsuit brought by some of their wealthy neighbours who argued that, if allowed, the project would set a dangerous precedent.

The neighbours were right. Roderick Cameron's audacious victory would spark a commercial property boom that would alter the face of the city. The Cameron Building still stands more than a century later, no longer on the edge of the city proper but in Midtown, the heart of the city and home to many of the city's iconic buildings, including the Empire State Building, just a few blocks to the east, and the Macy's flagship Herald Square department store, which inspired the movie *Miracle on 34th Street.*

❧

Enid Lindeman was born in a colonial city built at the edge of the world and raised on its suburban fringes. She had lived in a neighbourhood bound by picket fences, large yards and unsealed roads, a place of space and freedom and silence interrupted occasionally by the lonely whistle of a train pulling into Burwood Station. The city centre, 15 kilometres east, was a place of mostly four-storey buildings where horses and carts and lumbering trams still dominated the streetscape; its glorious natural harbour was tucked away at the northern end—an entry and exit to the world beyond.

The young bride and mother-to-be was now living in the middle of a city ten times the size of her childhood home, an island metropolis where silence was impossible as cars milled in chugging, tooting masses, and ships steamed and hooted on their way up and down the East and Hudson rivers on either side. The city rose like a forest, topped by the 57-storey Woolworth Building, then the world's tallest skyscraper, which had opened a few weeks before Enid and Roderick finally arrived in early June after their overland adventures.

Enid's only comfort was that both the Lindeman and Cameron families had retained and cherished a slice of nature—the homestead in the Hunter Valley where, as children, Enid and her sisters had spent their summer holidays; and the estate on Staten Island.

Enid knew her world had changed forever the morning she walked outside the Cameron Building, where her husband maintained a penthouse apartment, to find people stopped in the street to watch her pass by. Years later one of Roderick's sisters would tell the *New York Times* of being with Enid that day. Although now heavily pregnant, she was tall and graceful; cars slowed down 'to get a better view of this vision of perfection', according to the sister. It seemed far-fetched, but it was clear that the young mother-to-be had stepped into the social spotlight of one of the world's major cities.

The Lindemans might have been a prominent family in Sydney, but the Camerons were in another league. They were among *The Four Hundred*, a list of New York's most fashionable citizens, drawn up by a prominent lawyer and social arbiter named Ward McAllister, and supposedly based on the number of guests who would fit into the ballroom of the Astor family's summer residence at Newport, Rhode Island.

McAllister regarded those on the list as the beau monde of New York society; he explained that it was used to compile the guest list for the three most exclusive dinner dances of the season. 'If you go outside that number, you strike people who are either not at ease in a ballroom or else make other people not at ease,' he warned.

While Roderick ran the family business, it was his sisters whose social lives were prominent. Margaret, the eldest, who had been presented to the British Court, flitted between New York and Washington. The previous year, a younger sister, Catherine, had married Judah Sears, whose family owned the iconic department store chain; he was a member of the Colony Club, Richmond Country Club and Turf and Field Club. The youngest sister, Anne, had married Belmont Tiffany, heir to the jewellery fortune, who regarded the fabulously wealthy Vanderbilt family as nouveau riche.

Although the sudden marriage of their brother to such a young woman came as a surprise, the sisters gathered around their new sister-in-law and her name was swiftly added to society lists.

But for all the wealth and social access, Enid was isolated in this new, strange and huge city. In Sydney she had lived with her parents and two younger sisters and had four older brothers close by, but in New York she was surrounded by mother figures rather than sisters. At forty-one, Anne was almost twice Enid's age, while Catherine was forty-three and Margaret forty-nine. The two married sisters were busy with their own families and Margaret spent most of her time in Washington while Rory was busy running the shipping business.

Years later, Enid's family would discover a cache of photographs among her most precious private papers. They were mostly carefully lit studio portraits; among them was a handful that had been taken when she first arrived in New York and which showed an innocent, still-blossoming beauty with shining eyes. Her features and hair were yet to be refined and coloured by age and the life experiences that lay ahead but there was a touch of sadness in her smile—a young woman surrounded by luxury, but yearning for the company of the family she had left behind.

The letter she had written to her mother a few months before, as she explored America's wilderness with her new husband, was also among the papers. It was one of hundreds she must have written over the years and yet one of the few that she'd kept. Was there something special about its contents or had she never posted the twenty-page missive written from the frontier wilds of America? Otherwise, how would she still have it in her possession?

The Camerons spent the summer of 1913 among the lakes of the Adirondacks, a mountain range north of New York, where many of the city's social elite had built luxury campsites long before the Hamptons was turned from a region of potato farms into a summer playground for the rich.

Rory and Enid joined Catherine, Anne and their husbands at Spitfire Lake, the grandest of the St Regis Lakes, and attended one of the events of the season at Pine Tree Point, the 'Japanese-themed' camp of oil magnate Herbert Lee Pratt. Here, the lawns were so expansive that guests played golf in the afternoon before dinner, as the gossip columns gleefully reported: 'Extra butlers were brought from New York for the occasion and an orchestra of coloured musicians provided music for dancing. Coloured singers and entertainers were also in attendance.'

When the couple returned to the city, Rory made an appointment with his solicitor. Until now he had not bothered writing a will, but all that had changed. Not only had he married, but Enid was now seven months pregnant, and his wife and child-to-be needed to be recognised in the event of his death.

A few months later a son was born in the Staten Island house and named after his paternal grandfather—Roderick William Cameron. If Enid had felt the need for the Lindemans to be recognised, perhaps by giving her son the middle name of Charles after her father, she didn't push the issue, which only emphasised that she was alone, away from the Lindeman family.

The birth was announced in the *Sydney Morning Herald* almost a month later. It read, simply: 'CAMERON—November 13 at New York, the wife of Roderick M Cameron—a son.'

But the joy would be short-lived as tragedy struck the Cameron family yet again. Rory was diagnosed with cancer and would be dead before his newborn son had celebrated his first birthday. He spent the last month of his life in the German Hospital, a private facility in central New York, whose doctors had no chance of arresting a disease that was still decades away from effective treatment.

The obituaries that followed would shy away from a cause of death, instead focusing on his business activities and his club memberships—an 'active businessman' whose company was 'known throughout the world'. Back in Australia, the focus of the awful news was on his wife, as the *Sydney Morning Herald* noted: 'The beautiful girl of twenty-three who married a millionaire of forty-five, is now widowed.'

Enid should have been celebrating her second wedding anniversary on 12 February 1915. Instead, she was on a train with her young son, rattling across the vast continent of North America on her way from New York to San Francisco and a steamship journey to Sydney. This time there was no time for sight-seeing, just heartache and the desire to be back in the bosom of the Lindeman family.

Clifton Berley had become a prison of despair, the city of New York suddenly alien and forbidding. In the years to come there would be suggestions that she had not been accepted by the Cameron sisters, but she would always maintain contact with, and visit, Anne, who would become an important, almost grandmotherly figure, in the lives of her children.

Three weeks later, *The Australasian* newspaper noted Enid's return to Australia: 'Mrs Roderick Cameron, who was Miss Enid Lindeman has arrived from New York on a visit to Sydney. She is now a widow.' Other newspapers such as the *Sydney Morning Herald* would soon latch onto the story, not for its tragedy as much as the money the young widow might have inherited and the terms of the will: 'The beautiful Mrs Cameron . . . must wear widow's weeds for two years and she must live in America and her son must be educated there,' the paper reported. The *Mirror* concurred, adding erroneously that Rory Cameron had died when he was knocked down by a car and that Enid would forfeit her fortune if she dared to remarry.

Both statements were incorrect.

Rory Cameron's will made no such demands, instead bequeathing 'my dearly beloved wife' all his personal effects, which included furniture, cars, carriages and horses, as well as seven-tenths of his share in the family estate, Clifton Berley, and the income from his business activities, which he believed would produce an annual income of at least $10,000.

Enid was a rich woman, a multimillionaire even if she did remarry. The will addressed this eventuality, stating she could still keep half the income stream but the remainder would be put into trust 'for all my children'. Clearly, at the time he made the will, Rory was not aware he was ill and was hoping to have more children. Neither did he distinguish between male and female children, insisting that any residuals be held in trust to 'share and share alike'.

There was an additional reason that Enid had fled New York—another man.

Bernard Baruch was a 45-year-old New York business and political enigma, a brilliant financier, the original lone wolf of Wall Street, who eschewed joining an established brokerage and in later years would become an adviser to three US presidents. He was also in love with Enid.

In early 1915, as she struggled to come to terms with Rory Cameron's death, Enid and Baruch struck up a friendship, probably meeting at one of the high society events to which they both would have been invited. At first glance, they had little in common but, in spite of their differences, or because of them, there was an immediate frisson and the friendship quickly, and unexpectedly, turned into something more.

It seemed that Enid enjoyed the company, protection and counsel of older men and Baruch, a tall and wiry man who would become famous as a park bench statesman, often sitting and chatting with people in Central Park to gauge the public mood, fell into that category.

Baruch's attraction to her was equally complex given that he was, supposedly at least, a devoted husband and family man with three young children. He was clearly taken with Enid's presence and entrancing looks but he was also intrigued by her vulnerability and need to be protected.

Although their affair would be brief, Enid would always consider him a mentor and protector, and many years later would despair when he could not come to her aid because World War II made travel almost impossible.

Although they tried to conceal it, their friendship would not only be revealed but sullied by rumour and innuendo. By some accounts, Baruch had seduced Enid when she was just sixteen years old and it was Baruch who had introduced her to Rory Cameron. Other rumours suggested that Enid had lived with him in New York and then taken off to Hollywood, where she had a brief but successful stint as a scenery painter.

None of it was true but the stories provided delicious newspaper copy and, as Enid settled back into Sydney life, it was inevitable that she would attract media attention. *The Mirror* dubbed her the 'Merry Widow', quipping that she would 'leave a trail of admirers' when she decided in early 1916 to leave Australia again.

5

EUROPE BOUND

It is easy to see why Enid wanted to return to Australia so quickly after Roderick Cameron's sudden death, encouraged no doubt by Florence Lindeman, who would have missed her eldest daughter and wanted to meet her new grandson. But what drove the young mother to leave again barely a year later and travel, with such a young child, halfway around the world towards a war zone?

Was it the gossip that surrounded her return to Sydney, or had the familial comfort she so desperately sought now become claustrophobic? Perhaps she was rebelling against society's expectation that a young widow should simply disappear into the folds of her family and one day find a new husband who was prepared to take on someone else's child. Or was Sydney simply too provincial for a young woman who had seen some of what the world had to offer and was excited at what else she might discover?

Even though Enid was keen to leave in the autumn of 1916, there was a lot she loved about Australia, especially the outdoor lifestyle. For all the carefully staged photographs that would be taken of her in the years to come, Enid's private album would also contain a handful of unguarded moments, most noticeably during an apparently carefree summer of 1915–16, during which she sunbaked with friends on a harbour beach lined with rickety changing shacks.

Most powerful among them is an image taken as she emerges from the water, hair salty and eyes bright and challenging, her cotton bathing suit hugging her lithe, tanned figure, nipples erect and obvious. In an era of cowed modesty and feminine subservience, Enid looked like a modern woman, aware and unafraid of her physical presence. It was a photograph she would always cherish, given its place in her private papers.

By chance, it would also be celebrated four decades later when notorious gossip columnist Andrea Jenner recalled witnessing a beach appearance by Enid, apparently in a bathing suit given to her by Annette Kellerman, the famous swimmer turned film star: 'As we walked along that yellow sand I followed well behind her, the men would almost swoon. This is no exaggeration.'

Andrea was herself swooning. Dorothy Jenner (her real name) had met Enid in 1915, on Enid's return from America as a young widow. Dorothy had her eyes set on an acting career in Hollywood, which she would pursue; this was probably why she found Enid so alluring, describing her entry into Sydney society as 'volcanic'.

'I'll never forget the first time I saw her,' Andrea would write for the Sydney *Sun* in 1954, after her acting career had ended and she had become a journalist. 'She was dressed as American widows did—very pictorially—and when she walked, crowds used to gape. I was one of them. Her beauty was quite peerless. She set the style for her admiring pals and introduced the bobbed head to Australia. She was nice and fun and generous. In all that she did, I copied her slavishly . . . cut my hair . . . walked with the same swinging gait and did a dash on Manly Beach in the same, daring bathing togs . . . as she brought from America . . . Annette Kellerman's.'

It seemed that, a year after her husband's death, Enid had shed not only her widow's weeds but the wedding ring that adorned her left hand. The money from Roderick's will gave her the freedom to travel and there was the lure of the bigger world that lay beyond the heads of Sydney Harbour. After all, she'd had a tantalising taste of New York and its opportunities; despite the tragedy of her husband's death, that experience must have excited a young woman whose desire was to explore rather than hunker down in mediocrity. Should being a single mother have precluded her from that opportunity? Of course not.

The war may have also been a factor—the desire to 'do her bit'. Seventeen male members of the Lindeman family were in Europe fighting in some capacity; some of them would die with heroic acknowledgement and others would simply die. It was a sacrifice emphasised by Enid's father, Charles, who had offered to help returning soldiers begin new lives in agriculture and who publicly railed against the British government when it decided to restrict its non-essential imports, including Australian wine.

Lindeman Wines, under the Cawarra label, had been investing heavily in new vineyards and was making significant inroads into the British market, so it was galling to be cut out of a lucrative market at a time when members of the Lindeman family were dying in the trenches for the Mother Country, particularly when wine from California, Spain and South America—'countries that do not fight with us'—were still exporting to London.

Enid, her mother and sisters, Nita and Marjorie, had been heavily involved in fundraising across the city, frequently listed in polite newspaper accounts of events supporting a seemingly never-ending rollcall of appeals—the war chest, battalion comforts, widows and children relief, repatriation fund, patriotic appeal and the Australia Day fund that buoyed spirits and made participants feel as if they were contributing to what was described as 'The War Effort'.

Most events were small—front-room afternoon teas, backyard garden parties, street stalls and school room fetes—but others were on a grander scale, such as the charity musical at Manly in February 1916, in which Enid donned a rose-red bathing dress and black silk hosiery to play Cora Curl-Curl in a 'surfing ballet'.

But to Enid these events must have only confirmed the small-town nature of Sydney, and its distance from the rest of the world. She had outgrown the picket fences and quiet railway station of Burwood. With Europe beckoning, she applied for a US passport, courtesy of her brief marriage, for herself and her son who, like his father, would always be known as Rory. They could travel to London, a hazardous journey even though Germany was wary of attacking passenger vessels, fearing it would spark US entry into the war.

The passport application to the American consul in Sydney stated that she intended to return to New York within a year, although she seemed to be in no hurry. Her relationship with Roderick's sisters was friendly enough, if distant in age and interests, and, although she had given them a commitment that their nephew would be educated in the US, that day seemed a long way off. Instead, she was keen to live 'temporarily' in England.

She must have left a positive impression because the American Consul-General, Mr Joseph Britain, not only approved and stamped a temporary travel document—Passport No. 65—but also enclosed a personal introduction to his UK colleague.

A few weeks later, in March 1916, Enid hosted a farewell afternoon tea party for friends at the Australia Hotel in Castlereagh Street, one of the city's grandest establishments, and then boarded a steamship to London. Enid Lindeman was on her own, free of family shackles and expectations, and off to explore the world. She would not return for almost a decade.

If Enid was looking for excitement and adventure in London, then she was to be disappointed. The city was drab and subdued. Even the usually bright spring window boxes remained bare, unplanted by citizens guilty about living with colour while the battle raged across the Channel. More than a million men would die in the second half of 1916 at the Battle of the Somme.

Sydney was largely sheltered from the visual reminders of the conflict: the death toll was simply a typed list of names in the daily newspapers. But in London, there were daily reminders of the human toll, not just the dead but the displaced: the streets were dotted with canvas 'rest huts' for soldiers on leave. Many of these men were dirty, lonely and homeless; they could barely pay sixpence for a rough sleeping berth and threepence for a much-needed bath.

Placards exhorted women to wear old clothes, to stop wearing expensive furs and to put away their jewellery, as an example to others. The sale of ball gowns had collapsed, not only because households had less money to spend on entertainment but because there were fewer dances. No one had reason to celebrate. Pearl grey had become an exotic shade in a fashion world of largely black, where colour was only added as an afterthought in touches of embroidery and stitching.

'The season'—the summer months when the aristocracy closed their grand country mansions and came to London to celebrate being wealthy—was virtually non-existent, with functions and ceremonies dramatically reduced in the face of the mass deaths in Europe. Even the traditional presentation of young women debutantes to Buckingham Palace was abandoned. King George V and his wife, Mary, were concerned with the royal family's public image and desperate to downplay its links to the German aristocracy, eventually adopting the surname Windsor to replace Saxe-Coburg-Gotha, the family name that had descended to them from Queen Victoria's beloved husband, Albert.

In November 1916, as autumn turned to early winter, Enid lodged an application for a permanent US passport. The document she filled out revealed her intention to travel to Paris. It seemed a strange, risky decision given that she would be moving closer to the war. The city itself was deemed safe, filled with British command officers, and, unlike London where she was alone, Enid planned to stay with relatives who could help with taking care of Rory.

Unlike the photographs taken at the Sydney beach the previous summer, the dark, grainy image attached to the application did little to flatter her; she was dressed in a dark woollen suit and large hat. The hand-written notation alongside it perhaps offered a better description: 'Aged twenty-four years old, five feet eleven inches tall, high forehead, brown hair, blue eyes, fair complexion, short nose and an oval face.'

The Paris winter of 1916–17 had been colder than usual. Coal was expensive and in short supply, and frozen canals made delivery difficult. Likewise, a scarcity of grain had forced officials to insist that bakers use a new, rustic recipe instead of making the city's famed fine-white loaf bread.

Confectionery-makers were ordered to close their doors on Tuesdays and Wednesdays to quell the consumption of cakes, tarts and candies. Theatres and music halls were closed for one day a week as the city sought to cut back on power.

This was a city of compromise. Its young men were drafted into the war, to die in the clag of the Somme, replaced at home by female workers, creating a new lexicon to describe this feminised workforce: among them a *fatrice* who delivered mail, a *conductrice* who sold tickets on the Métro and *munitionettes* who worked on factory assembly lines building ammunitions.

There was a business school for women, the École de Haut Enseignement Commercial pour les Jeunes Filles, where the daughters of 'academic families' could learn a range of practical skills in politics, law and economics, while Parisian fashion houses were designing new ranges of daywear, with shorter skirts and looser corsets to suit working women.

Despite the frequent appearance overhead of lumbering zeppelins, there was an overwhelming sense of optimism among citizens, and a belief that the restrictions and shortages were a short-term pain because an end to the conflict was in sight and it was just a matter of time before Germany was defeated. As one newspaper correspondent noted: 'As long as it is necessary to deflect the energy of Paris, which was expended once in the shape of light and gaiety, to the sterner purpose of national defence, Parisians will not grumble, and the day will come when the lights of the city will shine as they have never shone before.'

Equally, the city's fashion houses refused to be cowed. As the magazine *Paris Mode* noted about the coming summer:

> It would be a great mistake to suppose that this terrible time of war had paralyzed the creations of French fashions. In a time of women taking the place of the men in the factories, it still appears that a desire to be womanly has seized upon ladies. Though women did appear to the world as women before the catastrophe, they now wish to re-enter into the spirit of feminine intelligence and devotion to beauty. A lady exhausted . . . in daily duty in hospitals and munitions factories will show her state of mind in simple, daringly short muslin dress. In these small details, we are seeing the new women after the war who will emerge.

Despite its challenges, or perhaps because of them, Enid quickly settled into the rhythm of a city that, unlike its cousin metropolis across the Channel, refused to abandon its sense of self. She took an apartment on rue Mirabeau in the 16th arrondissement, one of French society's favourite addresses, in a block one street back from the Seine. From her windows, she had a view of the Eiffel Tower.

She was here to explore the city and to play her part in the war effort, spending her days dressed in the grey and white uniform of the volunteer nurse, one of the 'helpful ladies', largely untrained, who flocked in their hundreds from England to tend to the wounded in makeshift private hospitals.

A lone photograph, clipped as if it had been squeezed at some stage into an ill-fitting frame, shows Enid among colleagues. Their starched and neatly pressed uniforms cannot conceal their exhausted and haunted faces, which betray the physical and psychological hardship of their day-to-day task. Enid, as usual much taller than her colleagues, is gazing past the photographer, as if in deep thought.

She would never speak at any great length about what she witnessed, other than to remark once that morphine was the only relief she could administer to the poor wretches brought in with shattered limbs. The experience would leave its mark.

A few months after arriving in Paris, Enid decided that she needed more involvement in the conflict than offered in overcrowded hospital wards. Whether frustrated by the limits of her nursing knowledge or excited by the opportunity to push the boundaries for women, she purchased and outfitted her own ambulance—probably a refitted car—and began bringing back wounded soldiers, travelling the perilous roads between the city and the battlefronts, some of them less than 50 miles from the city centre, often as shelling continued.

In doing so, she followed the lead of a band of brave women who challenged social expectations and began taking greater and more dangerous roles as the war progressed. These women were led by a group of aristocratic daughters who, like Enid, used their own money to outfit their own ambulances, many driving under the auspices of an all-female charity called the First Aid Nursing Yeomanry.

Some women kept diaries which gave an insight into their courage. Lady Dorothie Feilding, a British heiress who was awarded a Croix de Guerre for bravery, described a night in early 1917 when she was involved in the rescue of badly wounded soldiers. The ambulances were being stopped several kilometres from the front lines, forcing them to switch to smaller cars to make the rest of the journey:

> A sentry told us where some of the wounded men were lying up in the trenches close to the river, so we left the car and carried our stretchers to go and look for them . . . There was an officer and a Tommy very bad. It was five kilometres to walk each way carrying stretchers and taking cover and walking over slippery banks the last bit. Also, it was 8.30 by the time we got them to the ambulance. And we lost our way in the dark and the ambulance couldn't light up on account of Germans . . . The Tommy had his foot blown away by a shell and a bullet in his back as well. He was amputated as we got back, and I hope will live but it is still touch and go. The officer was shot through the right leg. Both were soaked and nearly dead already from exposure but pathetically grateful to us for getting them out.

Enid had found the adventure she seemed to be craving, about as far from Strathfield as was possible.

6

THE TRANSFORMATION

Paris would change Enid. She was no longer the gawky schoolgirl towering over her contemporaries in team photographs or the shy young wife of a New York businessman who missed her parents and fled home to hide from the world when things went awry.

The attention of men like Roderick Cameron and Bernie Baruch had made her aware of her power as a woman, particularly in a city like Paris where she now found herself single and available in the socially unmoored environment of war.

Gone were the modest, corseted dresses of an Edwardian mother and widow, replaced with loose, elegant silks and satins of French designers. Tall, slim Enid was the perfect clothes horse, her schoolgirl French forgiven by men in her thrall.

Rory would recall what he called 'my mother's transformation' as she returned to the apartment at night and changed from her nurse's uniform into a spectacular evening outfit before going to dinner. His favourite was a beaded and fringed dress from the fashionable House of Worth (the term haute couture was first used to refer to the work of Englishman Charles Frederick Worth in the mid-nineteenth century), in which she would be photographed by Baron Adolph de Meyer, *Vogue* magazine's first staff fashion photographer. Rory never questioned 'the comings and goings'—where his mother went or with whom.

Likewise, Enid's hair, once kept long and worn pinned, had been cut short and free. She was a woman of the future and it would be no surprise that she would meet and become close friends with Gabrielle 'Coco' Chanel, already successful as a designer, who had opened her first Paris boutique—a hat shop—just before the war.

It was a time of stricture and change. Rationing had been severe in Paris, but the chic restaurants still thrived, among them Larue's at 27 rue Royale, where the menu boasted blinis with caviar and cream and sole poached in champagne, and Café Voisin at the corner of rue Cambon and rue Saint-Honoré, where dishes like wolf in deer sauce, stuffed head of donkey and elephant consommé were served. Then there was the chandeliered opulence of Ciro's, on the ground floor of the Hotel Daunou, and the Café des Ambassadeurs, at the Place de la Concorde end of the Champs-Élysées, where concerts and revues were staged.

When city officials decided to slap a war tax on those wealthy enough to eat out, the clientele of these restaurants didn't blink. Further attempts to rein in people's eating by insisting that restaurants limit customers to just two rather than three courses also failed. Instead, diners were billed in two sittings which, if anything, prolonged their enjoyable experience.

At these restaurants, British officers—in office jobs because they were well-connected or injured or too old—frequently entertained beautiful women. Enid was among the most beautiful—an enigma who seemed almost childlike and yet was a widow and a mother. She was an exotic, heady mix of youth and mystery: an American, at least technically, who looked British and sounded Australian, with a slight lilt that would take many years to evolve into an amalgamation of the accent of all three countries. It was here that the mystique surrounding Enid Lindeman was born; it would create a society icon but, equally, almost destroy her.

Among her favourite photographs of the time was a snapshot taken after a game of tennis, almost certainly in the European summer of 1917. In it, she is sandwiched between two senior uniformed British Army officers, both wearing white tennis shoes and holding racquets. One of them is grinning and smoking a cigar. The men, both smug, seem to regard Enid as a trophy but she appears to be no meek participant or victim; rather her arms are clasped around their waists in ownership. They are part of her personal harem of suitors.

Within a few months of her arrival in Paris, word got back to the London War Office that the statuesque Australian was causing havoc among officers competing for her attention. One unnamed aide had already threatened suicide because she wouldn't accept his advances. Whether this 'threat' was part of the mythology that would grow up around Enid is uncertain, but he would not be the only soldier left broken-hearted and contemplating taking his life after meeting Enid.

Among her admirers was Walter Carandini Wilson, the grandson of an exiled Italian nobleman who had fled to Brisbane, Queensland, where Walter and his two brothers were born before the family moved back to Britain. Walter not only had the dark, smouldering good looks of his Italian heritage but played rugby before the war for England, where he would be mentioned in dispatches five times and be awarded, among a swathe of medals, the Distinguished Service Order for gallantry. Wounded twice on the Western Front, he was now serving on the General Staff of the British Army in Paris.

While 'impressed with his commitment', as she later told friends, Enid spurned Walter's desire for marriage, although they would remain close. Wilson vowed never to marry and, true to his word, was still a bachelor when he died in 1968, leaving his estate to Enid and her children.

There were others, like a soldier named Jack Coats, who tried to leave his fortune to Enid only for her to refuse when she discovered he had a wife and child. Jack's cousin, the gardener and writer Peter Coats, made reference to the affair in his memoir, *Of Generals and Gardens*, in which he wrote: 'Enid had many close and infatuated friends, among them a cousin of mine, the rich and glamorous (and slightly second-rate) Jack Coats who, wife and child notwithstanding, left her his fortune, which Enid told me, and I am sure it was true, that she refused.'

There would be a phone call to Enid's house many years later from a Mrs Erskine, whose husband, an ageing retired general, was dying. 'Where is Enid going to be buried when she dies?' the woman asked.

Surprised by the strange question, the servant who answered the phone replied that she didn't know.

'Well, go and ask her,' Mrs Erskine demanded. 'My husband has always loved her and as he was not able to be beside her in life, he wants to be beside her in death. Tell Enid that she must make up her mind as I don't intend to keep digging him up.'

Among the men she met was Valentine Browne, a captain in the Irish Guards, whose friends knew him simply as Castlerosse, a shortened version of the title he held as the eldest son of the Earl of Kenmare, an aristocrat whose lands included the Lakes of Killarney in the west of Ireland.

Just before the war began, in the summer of 1914, Valentine had spent an idyllic few months on the continent, the most memorable of which had been in Holland as a guest of Alice Keppel, the ageing mistress of King Edward VII. She had filled her chateau with a heady mix of aristocrats, lords and earls and dukes, along with a 'glittering flock of English beauties and their swains'.

Here, attended by footmen and butlers in tails and white gloves and surrounded by scented Japanese gardens and canals, the 24-year-old Valentine, witty, slim and handsome, spent his days at the races, his evenings with one girl or another and his nights gambling away money as if it had no consequence. It only confirmed to him that inherited privilege was a way of life.

The sun shone brightly until late July, when the mood inside the gilded mansion darkened as news of the impending conflict began arriving via telegram, first in rumours and snippets, then hints and increasingly dire predictions. When the British Prime Minister Herbert Asquith called his daughter Elizabeth home, the household scattered. A despondent Valentine would recall catching 'one last look at peaceful, affluent, complacent Europe' from the back of a motorboat as he sped back to London.

A week later, dragged from the golf course by an urgent telegram from his father, Valentine stood in front of the Earl in evening dress. 'There you are, old boy. I saw George Morris today. He will take you over with the first lot. It is comfortable to know that you will be in a good regiment. In an hour we shall be at war.'

Lieutenant-Colonel George Morris was the commander of the Irish Guards. A few days later, dressed in a hurriedly bought uniform and holstering a borrowed revolver, Second Lieutenant Viscount Castlerosse was thrust into the brutal reality of conflict. Life had changed in a blur, his bed now a dusty carpet at Wellington Barracks in central London awaiting deployment.

The first few weeks in France passed without incident. In the absence of action, Castlerosse established a reputation for being an entertaining buffoon; on one occasion he escaped a charge of 'Creating a Nuisance in a Wood' by declaring that he was 'a martyr to constipation' and, on another, he charged off blindly with his sword drawn, only to lose his way and his kit in the darkness.

But the humour would not last. Although he couldn't have known it, Castlerosse had arrived in France at a pivotal moment in the war, even at this early stage. In its first major battle, the British Expeditionary Force of 80,000 men under Field Marshal John French had been defeated defending a strategic canal near the Belgian city of Mons and was pulling back into northern France as the German First Army, three times its size and armed with 600 guns, advanced under the command of General Alexander von Kluck with orders from Kaiser Wilhelm to 'walk over General French's contemptible little army'.

The First Irish Guards had reached the town of La Longueville, in the direct path of the enemy and their ultimate goal of Paris, when Castlerosse heard the thunder of guns for the first time. He would later quip that he was about to eat an omelette when the alarm sounded; he regretfully abandoned his meal as his platoon positioned itself on top of a ridge with orders to engage. Then suddenly they were told to pull back, in what would become known as the Great Retreat.

A week later, and almost 100 kilometres closer to the capital, the First Irish Guards and the Second Coldstream Guards were chosen to make a sacrificial stand: a few thousand men trying to slow the Germans and allow the rest of the army to get to relative safety and form a solid defence of Paris. George Morris told the troops, including Castlerosse: 'I don't expect to see any of you alive again.'

On 1 September, just six weeks after leaving Alice Keppel's Dutch mansion, Castlerosse prepared himself to die. He and his second in command, another aristocratic scion named Harold

Alexander, sat in a damp field as they watched the last of the British Army make its way south. A thin rain had begun to fall as the rumble of the soldiers disappeared behind them. The silence was broken by Alexander, who began talking about the ordeal ahead—not his fears, but rather the privilege of sacrifice. Castlerosse listened, first in shock and then in admiration of a man whose valour would see him later rise to the rank of Field Marshal Earl Alexander of Tunis.

The ensuing confrontation would become Irish Guard lore as they fought in the gloomy beech forests of Villers-Cotterêts against a force that came at them from all sides. A slow withdrawal would be regarded as victory as Colonel Morris, mounted on his horse and smoking cigarettes in a long white cardboard holder, rode from one fighting point to another, cajoling his men. When one group dived for cover under machine-gun fire he called out, still astride his horse: 'They are doing that to frighten you.' To which an officer replied: 'They succeeded with me hours ago.'

Morris, beloved by his men, would be killed a few minutes later.

Second Lieutenant Castlerosse, with the words of Alexander ringing in his ears, had initially encouraged his platoon to hold its ground and open fire on members of an advance German unit who appeared behind almost every tree. He watched with glee as the grey helmets retreated—a small victory in an otherwise hopeless situation. A few minutes later an officer appeared and ordered him to withdraw, just as the Germans regrouped and advanced again, this time with a cover of machine-gun fire.

Castlerosse drew his men together to retreat. As they reached a road where they would make the next stand, Castlerosse raised his arm to ward off a pesky wasp and was struck by bullets which shattered his elbow and forearm. He collapsed and fainted, waking in a pool of blood 'the shape of the lower lake of Killarney' as the Germans marched past. His platoon was safe, at least for the moment, but he had been captured and was in great pain, his arm bent behind him at an odd angle.

A German battalion fell out to rest next to him. One soldier, eyeing the distressed enemy officer lying nearby, began to prod Castlerosse with his bayonet, exploring the wound. It was torture at its most base; the man had lost any sense of humanity as he tickled and teased to cause pain for the sake of pain. Castlerosse obliged, screaming not only in agony but in fury at the savagery of the soldier, who merely grinned and pressed again, exploring the ragged tissue. Castlerosse screamed again, unable to contain his anger and drowning the pain with a howl that, in hindsight, probably saved his life.

A German officer, annoyed by the noise, strode up and demanded to know what was happening. Having admonished the soldier, the officer turned to the stricken prisoner, who was still cursing his assailant. 'Castlerosse!' the officer exclaimed. Valentine looked up and recognised a man he would later identify simply as 'Von Cramm'; a few weeks earlier, he had been playing cards with him in a casino.

Von Cramm ordered the soldier to apologise to Castlerosse and then arranged for the Red Cross to treat his wounds. He left the young aristocrat with a note, which he would always keep.

It read: 'If ever a German should fall into your hands be kind to him as I have been to you.'

His wounds bandaged, Castlerosse was loaded onto a cart alongside two corpses and taken to a church in the town of Vivières, where he joined several hundred injured men from the battalion. Ninety of them would die overnight, including one soldier who lay across Castlerosse's legs on the crowded floor 'writhing like a sackful of snakes', and another who lay next to him, 'cursing God fluently and terribly'.

It was, he would write in an unpublished memoir, the most romantic night of his life. He may have meant that it was a night of the highest possible emotion, given its beautiful but wretched sadness.

'The weather was fine, and the little chapel was lit by the stars and the moon. The man next to me had his thigh shattered and wounds in his body. He lay groaning for a while, and then, as the moon came out, his eyes fell on the pictures of the Stations of the Cross. He started to recite the Stations, and the wounded and dying responded, excepting my other neighbour, who cursed God through his teeth. Seldom, I imagine, has there been a more poignant service. At the last Station of the Cross my comrade's voice faltered; he croaked like a raven, then fell dead.'

Castlerosse felt certain he would die too, but a few days later, with the arrival of a French cavalry unit, he was rescued. He was taken to an Allied hospital base and stabilised before being sent back to London, his war over in a few months—at least in a fighting sense—but his life forever changed by the experience.

7

CAVIAR CAVENDISH

While convalescing in London, Valentine Castlerosse became reacquainted with a captivating French woman named Jacqueline Forzane, a model, sometime actress and self-described *cocotte* (courtesan), whom he had met at a Deauville casino in the carefree days before the war. At that time, he had been drowning his sorrows at the bar, having lost a considerable sum of money, when she took pity on him and bought a bottle of champagne, which they shared before parting ways on the promise of meeting again.

He would recall being amazed that such an exotic woman could be interested in him. So, when she reappeared in his life (he believed by chance), Castlerosse was not about to let her go again. Within days he had proposed marriage which, with one eye clearly on his title and the other on his fortune, Jacqueline Forzane readily accepted, although insisting that he first gain the approval of his parents to formalise the arrangement, in case there were recriminations later on.

It was at this point that things went awry. The Earl and his wife were enraged; they regarded Mademoiselle Forzane, the daughter of a modestly successful painter, as little more than a well-dressed gold digger. Instead of agreeing to meet her and approve the union, Lord and Lady Kenmare sent an emissary to buy her off and end the affair. Forzane retreated to Paris only to have a lovelorn Castlerosse follow her, setting off a chain of family interventions to force him back to London.

Castlerosse's mother, Lady Elizabeth, was already distraught that her favoured son, the second-born Gerald, had been killed in battle, while Valentine, the least favourite of her five children, had survived. These feelings she had made clear to him. She complained about Castlerosse's behaviour to her brother, the banker Lord Revelstoke, who agreed that his nephew was an embarrassment to the family. He, in turn, contacted his friend, the Earl of Derby, who happened to be the Secretary of War and stationed in Paris, and asked if he would intervene. By the time Castlerosse stepped onto the platform at Gare du Nord, Lord Derby had issued a personal command for him to report back to London for new orders.

That might have been the end of it except that, a few months later, Castlerosse managed to convince his father that the infatuation with Forzane was finally over. He was allowed to return to Paris, where a staff job had been created for him. He booked into the Ritz, ate lunch at Les Ambassadeurs and spent his evenings at the Traveller's Club. Such were the disparities of war.

Castlerosse had hoped, of course, that the spark in the Forzane relationship could be reignited. They spent evenings walking hand-in-hand by the Seine and he moved into her apartment but, in the end, it fizzled, the moment over, and she went off to marry a Norwegian naval commander while a disconsolate Valentine moved back into the Ritz.

But in a strange turn that life often conjures up, the end of one relationship would mark the beginning of another or, in Valentine Castlerosse's case, meeting two people who would have a profound effect on his life. The first was Max Aitken, the Canadian-born businessman who would later become Lord Beaverbrook, the most important newspaper proprietor of his day. Under Aitken's sponsorship, Castlerosse would become his most famous columnist as well as his close friend and a frequent recipient of his financial rescue.

They would both later recall the lunch at Les Ambassadeurs, where it all began—not the specifics of the conversation so much as their impressions of each other. Castlerosse would describe Beaverbrook, an honorary colonel in the Canadian Army, as 'a man who laughed with you and encouraged extravagance of statement' while Beaverbrook regarded the man he mistakenly noted down as Lord Rosscastle as 'a gallant and forthright young man, full of amusing quips and shrewd observations'.

Both assessments would prove accurate and important in their lifelong friendship, as Castlerosse would later write: 'The luncheon was riotous good fun but little did I realise the effect that meeting was going to have on my life. Maybe it was that I was always coming to him with my troubles, and troubles were as plentiful as thorns on a rose bush. But before long Max Aitken and I were friends, and he was my never-ending lord of appeal.'

The other person Castlerosse met around this time was Enid Cameron, whose looks and free-wheeling confidence must have reminded him of Jacqueline Forzane. The two women emanated the same sort of beauty—*incandescent* was how noted English photographer and socialite Cecil Beaton described it—both of them examples of a new kind of woman, with attitudes that were dangerous and attractive. Enid was everything Castlerosse wanted in a woman: not only tall and beautiful, but capable and independently wealthy, as well as being a keen golfer, which was his great passion.

Despite his private shyness, Castlerosse presented as a man of confidence, intelligence and wit. He was handsome and near Enid's own age, which made a pleasant change from the officers from the British Embassy who had clamoured for her attention. The pair hit it off immediately, as the journalist Leonard Mosley would note in his 1956 biography of Castlerosse, describing the romance with Enid as having 'defied conventions together in Paris during the war': 'Enid was then a wild and beautiful young Australian who had been widowed after only a few months of marriage and was finding the fevered life of a nurse in France an effective anodyne for the pain of bereavement.'

Years later she would refer to their romance as 'fun', too short-lived to become serious as word got back to Lord Revelstoke that his nephew was, once again, causing havoc. Lord Derby agreed to intervene.

It defies belief that, in the midst of planning for a battle as important and devastating as Passchendaele in mid-1917, the British Secretary of War would become side-tracked by concern over the behaviour of one of his officers. And yet it seems that Lord Derby did, indeed, dip his toe into the muddy waters in an attempt to find a solution to the behaviour of Valentine Browne, the nephew of his friend and colleague Lord Revelstoke.

Derby, while travelling back and forth between London and Paris, apparently took time out from his duties to confront Castlerosse—who had steadily risen through the ranks, as the sons of aristocrats tended to do, and was now a captain—and to warn him off women like Jacqueline Forzane and Enid Cameron.

Enough was enough, he declared, ordering Castlerosse to return to England and report to Warley Barracks at Brentwood, a summer camp for the Essex Regiment, for 'light duties'. And there he would stay. In a post-war photograph of the officers of the Irish Guards, he is a gloomy figure, standing with his injured right arm still held across his body as if it was a sling.

Lord Derby then turned his attention to Enid Cameron who, he thought, was causing too much anxiety among his men. The solution, he decided, was to find her a husband. And he had in mind just the man.

On 11 September 1898, when he turned twenty-one years old, Second Lieutenant Frederick William Sheppard Hart Cavendish was serving with his cavalry regiment, the 9th Lancers, in

Muttra, India. In the months before his birthday, he had written to his family's solicitor back in London to check the details of the financial windfall due the day he 'came of age'.

Colonel Benjamin Greene Lake, from the firm Lake & Lake, confirmed that there was a small fortune of £15,000, which was some compensation for having lost both parents. His father, a soldier named Thomas Cavendish, had died when he was just two years old and his mother, Cecelia, just a few months before his coming of age. This was even more reason that the money left to him and his older brother, Henry, should be carefully salted away and drawn only as a fillip to his modest military salary.

Cavendish was hoping for a 5 per cent yield on his money, he told Colonel Lake, who confirmed that he could get at least 4 per cent, which would give him income of about £50 a month. It was important, Lake advised soberly, that Cavendish did his best to live from the income alone, rather than touch the capital, particularly if he hoped to marry and retire from the military.

The young officer was content with what he believed to be 'honourable and proper' advice from a former senior army officer and reassured by the £50 that appeared in his bank account each month. After all, Lake & Lake was a reputable firm with a bustling business employing thirty clerks and operating from New Square, Lincoln Inn, for more than a century. And Colonel Lake was the chairman of the disciplinary committee of the Incorporated Law Society. What could go wrong?

It was two years before he realised something was seriously amiss. He was in South Africa fighting the Boer War when he received a cable telling him that his investments had turned sour and there was almost nothing left of his capital. Lake & Lake had taken not only his money, but the funds of several clients, and invested heavily in a coal mine in Kent which had failed.

Cavendish had been duped into believing that his regular income was an investment return when, in truth, Benjamin Lake and his cousin George were simply paying it from the dwindling capital, which they siphoned off by opening a series of bank accounts that appeared, on the surface, to have been sanctioned by Cavendish.

And now it was all gone. Cavendish returned home in January 1900 to appear at the Old Bailey and give evidence against Lake, who had been caught and was on trial for several frauds. The case was a sensation because of Lake's position at a time when the legal profession was under pressure to improve the behaviour of its members, who seemed all too willing to misuse their clients' money.

Like the good soldier he was, Cavendish gave firm but unemotional testimony, told by his lawyer to speak matter-of-factly about the series of letters he had been sent that set up the ruse. He had never given permission for his money to be invested in speculative ventures, quite the opposite, in fact, due to the importance of the money to his future.

There were infrequent letters over the years, in which Cavendish would, typically, thank his solicitor 'for doing so well with my money and for being so kind as you always have been'. To which Colonel Lake would reply, saying: 'I am very glad to have been able to do so well with your money, and hope this considerable addition to your income will enable you to live in comfort'.

The evidence was clear cut, the witnesses providing a succession of unchallenged accounts of serious fraud. But Benjamin Lake remained defiant, blaming the fraud on his cousin, who had mysteriously died in Berlin. Justice Wills said he had no doubt that the initial crimes had been committed by George Lake, but that Benjamin had been aware of the continued behaviour: 'What misery, disaster and family ruin you have spread abroad by your defalcations I cannot estimate,' he said before jailing Lake for twelve years.

It was cold comfort for those investors such as Frederick Cavendish who had lost their life savings. There was no hope of recovering their money, let alone compensation, because Lake & Lake had gone under with its investment strategy.

Cavendish returned to South Africa, his course in life now set and his options limited. A few weeks after returning, he was wounded in action at Koodoosberg Drift. The clasps to the Queen's Medal he later received would include campaigns at Belmont, Modder River, Paardeberg, Diamond Hill, Wittenberg and the Relief of Kimberley.

Army life suited him, a series of staff jobs ensuring that the dangers of the conflicts in South Africa were minimised and his rise through the ranks inevitable, particularly after he joined the Freemasons. As for a wife, he had no use for permanent female companionship and no desire for children that would interrupt an otherwise carefree lifestyle in which he earned himself a reputation not only as a top-flight polo player but a man who knew how to enjoy himself, hence his nickname of 'Caviar Cavendish'.

He was awarded both the Queen's and King's medals for service in the Boer War, after which he went back to India, where he served as aide-de-camp to the Lieutenant-General of India before being recalled to the War Office in London, where he served under Field Marshal Douglas Haig, the man who would lead Britain's armies in the Great War.

When hostilities erupted in September 1914, Haig posted Cavendish, now a major, to army headquarters in Paris, where he would be mentioned four times in dispatches for his bravery as a commanding officer along the front line at Ypres. By mid-1917 he had been promoted to colonel.

Haig also used Cavendish in diplomatic roles off the battlefield and must have considered him a reliable figure, because he is referred to several times in Haig's personal diaries. Haig frequently used him as his ear to the ground in liaising with the French military commanders and once in escorting the French Prime Minister Aristide Briand.

Lord Derby also knew and respected Cavendish, having met him in South Africa during the Boer War when Cavendish was the chief press censor, a role for which he was mentioned twice in dispatches for his 'tact and discretion' and his 'thorough knowledge of men and affairs'. Those skills were again to the fore when Derby approached Cavendish and suggested he might be willing to solve another 'problem'—Enid Cameron.

Pat Cavendish knew only the barest details about how her parents met: 'My father and mother's marriage was arranged,' she insisted in an interview for this book. Aged ninety-four, she was long past any concerns that she and her brother, Caryll, were the products of a pragmatic rather than loving marriage.

'At the time, it was considered best to get rich, young widows safely married and then let them get on with whatever they wanted to do,' she would write in her memoir, *A Lion in the Bedroom*. 'Lord Derby cleverly produced my father. Contrary to all the gossip since, he was far from rich, only having his army pay to recommend him, but he already had a formidable reputation for bravery and a penchant for lovely ladies. Lord Derby thought that my mother and Cavendish would make an ideal couple. He told her: "This can't go on; I have found a husband for you." At least, that is what my mother told me.'

On Monday, 18 June 1917 at the British Embassy in Paris, 25-year-old Enid Lindeman married a man fifteen years older than her, whom she had known, at best, for a few months. Lord Derby, perhaps ensuring that the couple turned up on the day, was there to give the bride away.

There was no grand celebration or honeymoon, according to Pat: 'Daddy went back to the Front and Mummy went back to driving ambulances.' The only formal acknowledgement was a notice in the *Sydney Morning Herald*, which caught the attention of other newspapers and magazines. The Sydney *Punch* reported it with glee: 'Handsome Mrs Roderick Cameron, who was one of the beauties of Sydney society as Enid Lindeman (before marrying the wealthy American who was old enough to be her father) has taken unto herself another spouse. She was married this month to Lieutenant Colonel Frederick Cavendish of the 9th Lancers, now on duty with the general staff in France. She has a decided weakness evidently for picturesque names.'

The gossip writer for the Sydney *Mirror* followed suit, suggesting that, although Enid might now forfeit the money she received from the Cameron estate it mattered little because she was marrying into the 'ducal class' of British aristocracy: 'Various tales were afloat as to whether Mrs Cameron would lose her fortune if she married again. It was generally understood that there was a time limit of a few years (probably now expired). Mrs Cameron left all her Sydney admirers lamenting over a year ago, and word now comes that she is married to a relative of an English Duke. Australian girls have captured members of the British aristocracy but have never entered the ducal class before. Her husband is Colonel Cavendish, the family name of the Duke of Devonshire.'

Both assumptions were wrong. Enid's fortune from Rory Cameron was safe and she was was not marrying a rich aristocrat but a professional soldier with little more than a good family name and a steady income.

The newlyweds moved into Cavendish's digs, an apartment behind the Arc de Triomphe from where they could hear the dull boom of the German siege gun Parisians called Big Bertha. It was fired most nights from 120 kilometres away to bombard the city, more as a psychological weapon to attack the morale of the citizens.

The horror was always close. One morning, they walked past a block of flats that had been hit the night before. One of the rooms had been cut in half, leaving some of the furniture intact, a bed and a chair and a picture hanging on the wall. The bed was still occupied by the tenant, a woman, who had died in her dressing-gown.

Enid decided to send Rory, about to turn three, and his governess to the town of Dieppe, a fishing port on the Normandy coast, where they would be safe from the guns while she stayed with her new husband to see out the war most believed would soon be over.

8

THE COMPANY OF MEN

The end of the war in November 1918 brought relief and a surge of naïve optimism that humanity could never again fall into such self-destructive horror. The world seemed bright and full of opportunity and, while it was not uncommon for wartime romances to fall apart once the smoke had cleared, Enid's marriage seemed firmly fastened by its unconventional convenience rather than any sense of romance. She had security and freedom in equal measure.

Frederick Cavendish had always been married to the army and that's where his loyalties remained. He was a highly decorated officer, a lieutenant-colonel with a chest full of medals, having been made a Companion of the Order of St Michael and St George as well as receiving a Distinguished Service Order.

There were also medals from France, including the Croix de Chevalier Legion d'honneur and the military Croix de Guerre (with palm); and from Belgium, which awarded him its highest civilian honour, the Order of Leopold (Commander), and its own Croix de Guerre. It came as no surprise when, in March 1920, he was promoted to command the 9th Lancers, the regiment he had served with distinction for more than two decades.

But the gloss of the appointment quickly wore off when he spent the first year of his command in Ireland as the country descended into civil war. The regiment's official history described the task: 'The whole regiment was vigorously engaged in the wearisome and thankless task of maintaining or restoring order in a district alive with nocturnal foes and secret malcontents who could be relied on only to help rebellion and impede loyalism whenever safe opportunity offered. In this bitterly hostile Ireland, more distressful than ever before, even in her own chequered history, by reason of the plague of civil war that was now rending her in twain, the Ninth spent an unhappy year.'

Enid was content to stay in London with Rory, travelling back and forth to Paris, where she had bought an apartment at No.1 rue Mirabeau that her children and grandchildren would come to know as the 'pink building'. It was here that she really belonged, in the midst of the post-war celebrations, where she quickly became something of a celebrity.

'She was, quite rightly, considered to be amongst the great beauties of her period,' wrote Rory in his 1975 book *The Golden Riviera*. 'I remember one day standing in the hall of the Hotel de Paris with my governess, watching her walking down the central stairs. She moved beautifully and held herself very erect and had this extraordinary aura about her that made people stare. They would get up to watch her as she passed. On this particular occasion she was lunching at the palace. A tricorne hat dipped saucily to one side of her head, and she was dressed all in grey chiffon with a bunch of parma violets at her slim waist. I can even remember her shoes; black and shiny with grey steel buckles. Reaching the hall, she stopped to talk to some friends, at the same time easing on her gloves. Seeing me, she blew me a kiss and waved goodbye as she stepped into the waiting car. Naturally there followed the usual remarks, and I remember feeling immeasurably proud.'

But when Cavendish and his sodden men returned to England in the summer of 1921 life changed once more. The respite lasted barely a month as the regiment was reassigned, this time to Egypt. On 15 September, twenty officers and 423 soldiers sailed for Cairo from Southampton aboard the wartime hospital ship *Braemar Castle*, along with twenty women and children, including Enid and Rory.

The Cairo position offered social status and adventure in the unstable political environment of the Middle East immediately after the war. Dozens of Britons—civilian and military—had been killed during the uprisings of March 1919 and the city would remain volatile, with frequent outbreaks of violence and killings of civilians as Egypt moved toward an unsteady independence.

Cairo was two cities in one. 'Old Cairo' was a zigzagging labyrinth of narrow streets suitable only for horse-drawn carts and pedestrians, still largely pre-industrial in its structure and daily life with the hubbub of tiny stalls and waif-like boys selling water from earthen jars. 'New Cairo' boasted wide, paved streets marked with tramlines and crisscrossed by electricity lines, manicured gardens, sporting clubs and gilded hotels fed by water steam-pumped from the Nile.

Britain's four decades of occupying Egypt may have been drawing to an end, but day-to-day life remained one of colonial privilege, centred around private clubs like Gezira's, and the Jockeys, and the opulence of hotels like Shepheard's, with its granite pillars that mimicked the ancient temples being unearthed at dig sites around the city, and the weekly balls at the Savoy and the Mena House with its garden parties beneath the Great Pyramids.

Enid had exchanged the refined style of Paris for the exotic mystery of the Middle East, and she thrived. She recalled it later as one of the most memorable times of her life, with picnics beside the Pyramids and languid journeys drifting down the Nile on feluccas; with grand balls in sandstone mansions set among glades of palms like architectural oases and moonlit horse races into the Sahara.

By day she played golf at Gezira's and helped with her husband's polo ponies, proud of her ability 'to ride as well as any man'. Frederick Cavendish had been a member of cup-winning teams during his time in South Africa after the Boer War and the success of a cavalry regiment's polo team created particular prestige at a time when the relevance of horseback soldiers in motorised warfare was being questioned. Even at the age of forty-five, he was the star player in a team that lost only once during his tenure—in a match that he missed.

There was one other loss, although it could be put down to diplomacy rather than performance. It was when Edward, Prince of Wales, visited the city in 1922 and played an exhibition match for the Sultan's team against the 9th Lancers. The diminutive but magnetic prince played well, according to newspaper reports at the time, as did Frederick Cavendish, while Enid watched from the stands. She and the future king would cross paths on many more occasions over the years, their lives entwined by circumstance—and partners.

Enid was a woman who preferred the company of men to women, not only for their adoration but also their earthy, irreverent camaraderie. Her favourite story was about a trooper who was brought before a military court for having sex with an ostrich. When questioned about the offence, the trooper retorted: 'Sir, if I'd known there was going to be all this fuss I would have married the fucking bird.'

She sometimes dressed as a man to sneak into the officers' mess of the barracks at Abbassia, on the outskirts of the city, where she played the piano or the slide whistle, much to the delight of the men, thrilled at the outrageous behaviour of their commanding officer's wife. But it also, perhaps inevitably, led to stories of infidelity, some of them true but others fed by her own sense of mischief, including rumours that she had slept with every officer in her husband's regiment.

'My mother was the most incorrigible flirt,' Pat would write in her memoir. 'She told me years later that somebody had dared her to sleep with the officers and she couldn't resist. Whether she actually did manage to sleep with every officer, one wouldn't know . . . she loved a good story . . . and what my father thought of all this, history does not relate. I often wondered if Mummy was ever really in love with any man. She loved their company and her whole life was centred on pleasing men, but she did not remain faithful to any of them.'

On 4 November 1922 the British archaeologist Howard Carter uncovered the tomb of the Egyptian boy-king Tutankhamun. Carter and his financial sponsor, the redoubtable Earl of Carnarvon, had almost given up on an eight-year search that had been interrupted by war and disappointment when, by accident, the top of a staircase was uncovered, leading the way to the spectacular discovery.

When he realised its importance, Carter sealed the entrance and sent for the Earl, who was in London. The cable read: 'At last we have made wonderful discovery in the valley. A magnificent tomb with seals intact. Recovered same for your arrival. Congratulations.'

Carnarvon took almost three weeks to reach Cairo, and on 26 November the two men tentatively entered the chamber, Carter capturing the moment in his diary: 'Lord Carnarvon said to me: "Can you see anything?" I replied: "Yes, it is wonderful." I then, with precaution, made the hole sufficiently large for both of us to see. With the light of an electric torch as well as an additional candle we looked in. Our sensations and astonishment are difficult to describe as the better light revealed to us the marvellous collection of treasure.'

What emerged from the darkness resembled what he would describe as 'the property room of an opera of a vanquished civilisation'. As he peered into the chamber, Carter could see an overturned chariot glinting with gold, a shrine with a gilded monster snake, carved chairs and translucent alabaster vases, a gold inlaid throne, ebony effigies of a king, lion and Hathor-headed statues. 'Our sensations were bewildering and full of strange emotion. We questioned one another as to the meaning of it all. Was it a tomb or merely a cache? A sealed doorway between the two sentinel statues proved there was more beyond, and with the numerous cartouches bearing the name of Tut-ankh-Amen.'

News spread quickly, and Cairo's hotels were soon filled with journalists from around the world. Carter kept them at bay for weeks as he and Lord Carnarvon explored the tomb, near the city of Luxor, then more than a day's drive from Cairo, and began removing artefacts.

A select few were permitted to visit the site, among them Enid Cavendish who had met and entranced the 55-year-old earl when he booked into the Continental-Savoy in Cairo. Not only did Enid become one of the first people to enter Tutankhamun's tomb, but she also took her young son.

Rory would retell the story on several occasions in later years, the memories still fresh in 1985 when he was interviewed by the US magazine *Architectural Designs*: 'I remember vividly the footprint of a sandal in the dust, left there, Mr Carter told me, by a high priest who had stepped forward to print a seal on a plaster wall behind which lay the sarcophagus. The visit would have a profound effect on my life, igniting a passion for beautiful objects. After that, my idea of pleasure was to go every afternoon to the museum, accompanied by my mother or the nanny.'

In his 1950 memoir *My Travel's History* he wrote:

> I was eight years old at the time of the opening of Tut-ankh-Amon's tomb, and I remember one day Lord Carnarvon taking me down to see it. You can imagine what an impression that would make on a child—the dimly glittering gold and foot-prints in the dust made by mourners or priests dead for over 2,000 years.
>
> It is more than just memories of a happy youth. Does one believe in reincarnation? I really don't know. But I have the most extraordinary feeling about Egypt; so, has everybody, I suppose. The past lives here as it does nowhere else, such as the distant past and yet at the same time so strangely near and intimate.

9

A FATHER AND A SECRET

On the afternoon of 23 June 1924, a dozen or so military men and two women gathered in one of the smaller dining rooms at Buckingham Place, in London, for a special luncheon with the King, George V, his wife Mary and their son Henry, Duke of Gloucester.

This was a formal occasion, a gathering of some of Britain's most senior army officers in their finest dress uniforms, including the head of the Royal Military College, Sandhurst, where, earlier in the day, the King had inspected the 'gentleman cadets' on parade as well as the commandants of the 1st Royal Dragoons, Royal Pavilion Guard and the 13th/18th Royal Hussars.

Also on the guest list was Colonel Frederick Cavendish, the newly minted commander of the 1st Cavalry Brigade who, unlike his fellow officers, had brought along to the lunch his young wife. Almost eight years after leaving Sydney as a widow with her infant son to seek an adventure on the other side of the world, Enid Lindeman of Strathfield was having lunch with the King and Queen of England.

A handful of non-military guests were also in attendance, including several leading politicians, among them the banker John Baring, the Baron of Revelstoke and uncle of Valentine Castlerosse, whose intervention in his nephew's amorous activities in Paris had begun the chain of events that had led to the arranged marriage of Frederick and Enid. No doubt a coincidence.

The matters discussed that afternoon would remain in-house but the event itself, news of which unusually found its way into local newspapers, announced the arrival back in England of the Cavendishes. They had returned from Cairo in March, at the end of Frederick's three-year stint in Egypt which had passed with little in the way of military skirmishes beyond the occasional peace-keeping role. But the lack of military engagement did nothing to harm Frederick's continued rise and he would retire four years later with the rank of brigadier-general.

The 1st Cavalry Brigade was stationed in the town of Aldershot, the 'home of the British Army' in Hampshire, and Frederick and Enid had been given a comfortable house in the nearby village of Cove, Farnborough. Keeping with the colour theme of their various homes, the family called this the White House. For all her apparent wayward tendencies, Enid, at the age of thirty-two, seemed content to settle back into the life of an officer's wife.

Not that she was alone in her marital transgressions, whatever the truth of their extent. Freddy Cavendish, now in his late forties but still handsome and ramrod straight, had a reputation of his own that suggested he also enjoyed something of an open marriage. As a friend would note later: 'His outstanding quality was a robust and active joie de vivre, which no mischance could quell. With a nature as generous as his he could not help radiating this, with the result that a meeting with "Caviar" always left one with the sense of a touch of colour added to the gaiety of life.'

Since his return to England, Freddy had begun an affair with a young French woman named Françoise Lascelles. It was clearly a fling rather than a serious relationship because, when she fell pregnant, he resorted to solving this potentially embarrassing problem by adopting the same tactic that resulted in his own marriage—finding a replacement husband and father.

Remarkably, Cavendish managed to convince a fellow officer, a lieutenant-colonel named William Kay, to agree to marry the young woman and to raise the child as his own. Philip Kay was born in early December 1924 and, as arranged, was given the surname of his stepfather. The young man would follow both his 'fathers' into the military where his record, for some strange reason, quietly noted that he was the 'illegitimate son' of Brigadier-General Frederick Cavendish.

During World War II, he was mentioned in dispatches for bravery and was awarded a Croix de Guerre. He was captured behind enemy lines during a covert operation and spent the last year or so of the conflict in a prison camp.

Returning to England after the war, Philip joined Frederick Cavendish's old regiment and served time in Egypt before leaving the British Army and taking a commission with the French Foreign Legion, where he again saw action and was awarded two more Croix de Guerre for acts of heroism.

Still restless, and with a failed marriage behind him, Philip emigrated to Canada in 1953, where he carved out a new military career, this time as a renowned paratrooper. Awarded the Canadian Order of Military Merit after parachuting into North Vietnam at the age of forty-nine, he would reach the rank of major before retiring when he was crippled in a traffic accident.

After he died in 1992, his fellow officers would remember a man who insisted on leadership qualities and standards: 'Major Kay was always the first to jump from an aircraft, particularly when the winds were high or the drop zone dangerous. Even though he approached retirement age, Major Kay never once relaxed the exceedingly high standards that characterized his military service.'

It seems likely that Enid knew of her husband's affair and the imminent birth of Philip Kay but it would have been hypocritical for her to have judged him harshly, given her own transgressions. One of the tenets of her moral code was: 'Never be afraid, never be ill (or don't talk about it) and, above all, never be jealous.' Even so, her displeasure seemed clear when she suddenly decided to go home for Christmas—a 'flying visit', as she would describe her first journey back to Australia for eight years—because it meant three months of sea travel, there and back, just to spend a few weeks in Sydney. Frederick, always on duty, watched her go.

Enid's arrival in mid-December 1924 brought immediate attention in the social pages of papers such as *The Bulletin*, whose women's columnist noted, somewhat cattily: 'Mrs Cavendish, who will be remembered here as the beautiful Miss Enid Lindeman who married the wealthy Roderick Cameron. Her second marriage has brought her a Brigadier-General and a social tone.'

A social tone? The naïve pettiness of the comment only confirmed to Enid that she had made the right decision to leave Australia. Little seemed to have changed since her departure; this kind of chip-on-the-shoulder attitude she regarded as an ugly wart on a society that supposedly stood for values more profound. It smacked of envy.

No one would have batted an eyelid if a man had lost his wife, cavorted with the opposite sex and then remarried, so why should she have had her life choices critiqued in this way? It was true that she was wealthy and privileged but that was hardly her fault and money alone provided little surety in an unsteady world.

Enid had risked safety and comfort to travel overseas with her young son, played her part in softening the impact of World War I by working as a nurse and driving an ambulance, and had raised Rory to open his eyes to the world, ultimately leading him into a successful career in architecture and interior design. And she had married a penniless war hero, not a ticket to a society ball. Yet her contribution was being reduced to the erroneous accusation that she was a social climber.

Other newspapers preferred to follow Enid's whirlwind of social engagements and her sense of European fashion. The 1920s was all about the elongated body: tall and thin was in, and Enid had the perfect figure for styles like the black satin 'tube dress' she wore to the New Year race meeting at Randwick. Her choice was mentioned glowingly by four papers.

Photographic portraits were commissioned—one of them by Bernice Agar, who had shot to fame as Australia's most successful female photographer—but there was one thing the journalists missed as they eagerly followed Enid's visit, right up to the day she boarded the *Osterley* to return to England: she was pregnant.

Whatever her feelings about Frederick's infidelity, they were now irrelevant as she began her long journey back to Europe. By the time she gave birth to a daughter, Patricia Enid, in a private London clinic on 30 June 1925, all would be forgiven. Or, at least it would be tucked away as a forgiven, but not forgotten, hiccup.

Unsurprisingly, Pat (as she would always be known) was never told about her 'illegitimate' half-brother. However, she responded with little surprise when she learned of it in later life; she was under no illusion about the pragmatic nature of her parents' relationship, although she sensed that Frederick had stronger feelings for Enid than Enid did for him.

Pat once sat with her father on a railway station platform, waiting for Enid to arrive from a trip to the city. When she didn't show up as expected, her father didn't go home but stayed forlornly on the platform, not knowing if his wife had missed the train or had changed her mind and wasn't coming.

To Pat, this event was indicative of her father's desperate desire to win Enid's heart. 'He must have waited for hours,' she noted sadly in her 2004 autobiography, *A Lion in the Bedroom*, adding: 'My mother was a very rich woman and the soul of generosity, so my father was able to indulge in strings of polo ponies, hunters and everything his heart desired, except possibly the love of my mother.'

Romantic love may have been absent, but Enid was clearly content in the relationship. If Pat's birth was in retaliation to Frederick's straying from the marital bed, then the arrival fifteen months later of her brother, Caryll, was very much a deliberate decision to secure the marriage, in spite of its weak foundations.

The next few years would pass in relative domestic harmony. Pat later recalled her and Caryll's daily routine: they were assigned to nannies dressed in striped uniforms, starched white aprons and ruffled caps, 'like one of my stuffed straw dolls'. As with many people, her childhood memories are sparse and mostly associated with getting into trouble, such as eating discarded match heads and munching gravel from the front driveway of the house.

Frederick Cavendish, free of the tiresome practicalities of raising children, took delight in teaching his daughter to ride a horse, at first on his back around the house, then on a pony strapped with a wicker basket, like a baby saddle, through which her tiny legs would be fastened, because she couldn't reach the stirrups. When she was just five years old, he entered her in a gymkhana.

Pat recalled that day with clarity. He ordered her to grip the reins and hold tight the martingale before playfully slapping the flank of her horse to send her on her way: 'The jumps looked huge to a tiny child, but I can still feel the excitement of sailing through the air,' she would later write. 'I felt like a fairy princess. I was given a prize and my father was so proud of me. I remember him saying: "You would have been a great addition to my regiment."'

Summers were spent in France, mostly in the northern beachfront resort town of Le Touquet, made famous because of its casinos and its golf course, frequented by the Prince of Wales and his upper-class entourage. The Le Touquet holidays, which usually lasted two months, would become one of the most enduring memories of Pat's early childhood.

There was no shortage of money, thanks to the late Roderick Cameron whose estate regularly replenished the family coffers with a steady income from the US operations of the family empire. However, although she would develop a flamboyant, laissez-faire approach to the roulette tables of Le Touquet, Enid also continued to invest in real estate.

She built a house she called The Berries adjacent to the eighteenth green of the local golf course, large enough to accommodate Australian family members, who had begun to visit regularly. She also bought an open-top Buick painted with black and white squares, which she proudly drove around the town, aware that few women ever got behind the wheel.

She delighted in piling half-a-dozen dogs into the car with the children and driving to the nearest beach for a picnic. It brought back memories of her own childhood and the booming surf on the deserted coastline of the mid north coast of New South Wales where a relative had kept a holiday home. 'Sandy sandwich days', Pat and Caryll called them as they competed with gusting winds and hungry dogs on beaches that were otherwise near-empty, the English tourists shunning the cold waters of the Channel and preferring the more refined comforts of the resort town.

Yet Australia still beckoned and in 1929 she returned, this time taking Frederick and the children, ostensibly to attend the wedding of her younger sister Marjorie, but also to introduce her husband of now twelve years and their two young children to the Lindeman family.

The media reception this time was generous. The gossip columnists, having retracted their barbs, instead showered her with praise while following her spectacular fashion trail. The *Western Mail* was taken by her 'strikingly cut magpie frock with a tail of deep pink tiger lilies that set off admirably her clear complexion'. 'Graceful and distinctly vogue,' assessed the *Telegraph* about her race-day outfit of an ecru lace frock and pony-skin coat with sable collars and cuff, while *The Sun* was in raptures about 'a gown of pink marocain with glittering embroideries of rhinestones at the shoulder, completed with leaf-shaped chiffon panels and a wrap of black velvet, lined with white satin and trimmed with ermine.'

'Her beauty is quite outstanding,' gushed *The Home*'s correspondent. 'At the races during Easter week she easily carried off the palm as being the loveliest woman present.'

After almost five months, the Cavendishes headed home, not to the White House at Cove but to Paris.

Frederick Cavendish had retired from the army. He was fifty-two years old and looked, in photographs, more like his children's grandfather than their father. Slightly dishevelled in his civilian suit, his hair speckled grey, the burdens of a lifetime of war were etched on his face and the wreathed star of the Legion of Honour was forever on his coat lapel.

Enid, by contrast, was becoming more alluring. Her own hair had turned silver by her thirty-sixth birthday, supposedly the effect of a serious bout of pneumonia but more likely her genetics at play. For many women, such premature greying would have been calamitous, but it only added to her mystique—a lustrous shade that seemed to shine when coupled with eyes that appeared to flash anything from green or blue to grey and hazel, depending on her mood and outfit, which had gone decidedly French—Chanel suits and short-pleated skirts showing 'plenty of leg', as Pat would recall.

Cavendish had been allowed to retain the use of the White House at Cove, but the lure of Paris was irresistible, and they would spend most of their time between the city apartment on rue Mirabeau and The Berries.

Frederick was in Paris, alone, on the night of 8 December 1931, while Enid was with the children in Le Touquet. Pat was six years old and in her memoir recalled her mother standing her on a table to speak directly to her at eye level.

'She told me she had terrible news; that my father had died, and she had to leave us and go to Paris. I remember knowing that something dreadful had happened to Daddy, as my mother was hugging me and crying but I wasn't exactly sure what death meant.'

Frederick had been discovered by his valet collapsed in the sitting room of the apartment. He'd had a cerebral haemorrhage and was barely alive. A doctor was called, but he could do nothing to save him.

Enid had been widowed for a second time. The marriage had endured despite its cynical beginning fourteen years before, held together by children, friendship and a tacit understanding they both had a certain amount of personal freedom that a more traditional union might not have allowed.

The reality of Frederick Cavendish's financial position became evident several months later when his will, penned on his return from the Australian trip, was read and probate declared: 'I desire to be cremated and my ashes cast to the winds,' he had declared without specifying a place. 'I direct that my wife shall enjoy the use of all my silver, cups and furniture until my children become entitled.'

The rest of his assets should be sold and his debts paid.

The residual was to be held for his son, Caryll, for when he turned twenty-one, just as Frederick had been left a sum by his father. His daughter, Pat, would get nothing. Not that it mattered as the net value of his estate was only a little over £286.

10

MARMADUKE

Marmaduke Furness was born to wealth. Not the kind that is handed down through the privilege of the idle, landed aristocracy but money earned from instinct, capacity and work ethic.

His father, Christopher, came from near enough to nothing. The youngest son of a Durham grocer, he left school to join a coal company as a buyer. Quick, willing and audacious, he was soon travelling through Europe on behalf of the company with a free rein to use his wits. In 1870 nineteen-year-old Christopher was in Sweden on a business trip when he recognised an opportunity that would be the launching pad for a career that would make him one of the titans of Victorian Britain's industry.

It was the beginning of the Franco-Prussian War and the French had blockaded the Elbe River, which was strategic because of its importance to trade through central and northern Europe, from the Czech Republic, through Germany to the North Sea.

Young Furness bought up cheaply all the flour and other produce that was lying idle in Swedish and Danish ports and then shipped it to England, using steamers that could find no other work because of the blockade. His gamble paid off and he was able to pour the resulting profits from selling flour into establishing his own shipping line.

Fortune favoured the brave and within five years his company was building steamships and trading between Britain, North America and Canada. After he bought out a rival firm, Withy, he became one of Britain's biggest employers and richest men. At its peak, Furness Withy would have 215 ships, its vessels identified by their black funnels with a blue stripe in which the letter F was emblazoned.

Furness's immense wealth allowed him pleasures and luxuries, including construction of the first steam-turbine private yacht, on which he crossed the Atlantic several times. He also had a reputation for philanthropy, including the establishment of a pension scheme for retired seamen and an innovative agreement that allowed his employees to set aside part of their wages to buy a share of the business in return for industrial peace.

He implored the young to follow his lead, once writing: 'No power can prevent the young, educated man from achieving some kind of success, although persistent work and effort are essential. The young must learn and the middle-aged and old must encourage and help them and have as well, open minds, receptive to new ideas and the spirit of the age—progress.'

It was a career that was not dissimilar in its vision and persistence to Henry Lindeman's. It even more closely matched the success of Roderick Cameron Snr, especially when Furness, like Cameron, was knighted by Queen Victoria in 1895 before entering Parliament as the Liberal MP for the north-east city of Hartlepool, and was ultimately bestowed with a peerage, becoming the Baron of Grantley in Yorkshire.

But, just as his empire reached new heights, Furness was cut down by what was described as 'ill-health' and most likely cancer. When he died in 1912, aged just sixty, *The Times* published a glowing tribute which read, in part:

> Nobody could be closely associated with Lord Furness, either in business or public life, without being impressed by the restless energy and insatiable desire for thoroughness which he carried into every task to which he set his hand. A new invention or a new process of manufacture always found him on the look-out, and plant and machinery, however recent in installation, were unhesitatingly scrapped the moment they appeared out of date or inferior to those at the disposal of business competitors. His presence at the head of an undertaking usually made itself felt in a series of drastic changes and improvements, and if the way to financial success was sometimes long and arduous, at any rate the fault never lay in a lack of initiative and enterprise.

If there was one, significant, failing in Christopher Furness's life, it was his relationship with his only child, Marmaduke. He regarded his son as being spoiled and indulged by a mother who allowed her son to leave Eton simply because he thought it too difficult and irrelevant.

Despite his disapproval, which was keenly felt by the young man, Furness had no hesitation in bequeathing Marmaduke his titles and businesses, which included a shipping, coal and iron manufacturing fortune, and lands totalling almost 30,000 acres.

But he had no faith in the young man's ability to run anything but a fox hunt. Life had been handed to Marmaduke on a plate, and he had demonstrated a playboy attitude that a self-made man like Sir Christopher loathed. As he warned his son: 'Keeping millions is sometimes harder than making them.' Instead, Furness insisted that the day-to-day management of the businesses be handled by an older cousin who, as fate would have it, died within two years of Sir Christopher's own death.

In 1914, Marmaduke, aged thirty, now had full control, and good luck would shine on the now 2nd Baron Furness of Grantley as World War I provided a boon for the ship-building industry. Furness-Withy factories were bursting to fill government contracts to build or supply ships for the conflict which meant, of course, that he was excused from any social disgrace for not volunteering. Instead, he saw out the war in the clubs of London and by its end, as a further reward for his business services, he had been given the title of Viscount, the next rung up the peerage ladder.

More strategically, Marmaduke then promptly sold off most of the family business in a deal worth a staggering £9 million, reputedly negotiated on the back of a menu in a London restaurant. He became one of the world's richest men, thanks to the industriousness of his father and the dubious fortunes of war.

Marmaduke had one redeeming feature—his wife. He had married Ada 'Daisy' Hogg, daughter of a marine insurance agent, when he was twenty-one and she was twenty-three; by the time he inherited the Furness fortune, the couple had two children. His daughter, Averill, was born in 1908 and his son Christopher in 1912, named after the grandfather who had died a few months before the boy was born.

Unlike her husband, Daisy took an active role during the war. Using the title Lady Hogg, she worked as a volunteer at the Royal Academy in Piccadilly, where the Red Cross had established a central workroom in the academy's galleries to make swabs, bandages and dressings to be sent to the front. When supplies of wool ran low, the women used dog hair to spin and knit the items.

Marmaduke adored Daisy, a petite woman with copper hair and a steely stare, of whom he once said: 'If I should lose my fortune, I know of many places where I should soon build up another, but if I should lose Daisy I would not know where to look for another like her.'

Of his many luxuries, Marmaduke Furness was perhaps proudest of his yacht, *Sapphire*. He hadn't built it; instead, he had bought it at a bargain price after the eleventh Duke of Bedford grew weary of this particular bauble. Bedford, a selfish and forbidding man according to his own grandson, had originally commissioned the yacht to be built as the best in Britain and had taken delivery of it in 1913, but he only enjoyed one summer as its owner before war forced him to hand it over to the British Admiralty for use during the conflict as a patrol vessel along the Strait of Gibraltar. When he got her back in 1919, the Duke decided to sell and Furness, flush with cash from the recent sale of the family company, was eager to buy.

At almost 40 metres long, the *Sapphire* was the largest steam yacht that had been built in Britain up to that time and was among the largest private vessels in the world. She was a triumph of engineering for the period, built to be 'as unsinkable as possible' with a double hull and watertight bulkheads. She boasted four lifeboats and two motor launches, one of them solely used to carry luggage to and from the boat.

The yacht had six teak-lined staterooms, each with their own bathroom, along with dining, smoking and drawing rooms. It was more like an Edwardian country house than a yacht: the upstairs–downstairs class divide was enforced by housing the crew, servants and attendants below decks.

Immediately after his acquisition, Furness wasted little time before setting out in March 1920 with his wife and friends on a four-month odyssey. They travelled across the Mediterranean and down the Suez Canal before steaming across the Indian Ocean, through Southeast Asia and as far as Japan. By the time they returned, after a journey of almost 50,000 kilometres, it was time to head to the calm waters of the Mediterranean for a summer of cruising.

In the aftermath of the Great War, there seemed little that could disrupt a life of pure indulgence but wealth and privilege does not buy health and, after their return to England in the autumn, Daisy fell ill.

When she underwent surgery in December 1920, her condition post-operatively was described as critical. It would be mid-February before she was released from hospital, only to be sent south to Brighton for further rest.

In the meantime, Furness had taken his mother and Averill and Christopher to Cannes aboard the *Sapphire* and then returned, hoping his wife would be well enough to travel and join them. She had made steady improvement and, by the time the boat reached Britain, her doctor declared her well enough to travel, provided she had a medical team beside her at all times.

After fetching Daisy, the *Sapphire* left Southampton and steamed down the English Channel at a satisfying clip of fourteen miles an hour. On the second day, she entered the Bay of Biscay, the gulf that extends along almost half the French coastline and the top of Spain, still on course for Cannes.

It was here that the benign weather changed for the worse. The gulf is notorious for its fierce winter storms, fed by westerly winds from the US that roll waves across the Atlantic, increasing in size and power to rise steeply when they reached the shallower waters of the bay. As the vessel continued down the French coast, the winds rose and the smooth ride quickly turned into a heaving nightmare, even for a large ship like the *Sapphire*, which began to founder as she reached the latitude of Bordeaux.

Nauseous from the constant rolling and pitching of the boat, Daisy's condition deteriorated quickly. The medical staff, ill themselves, could do little to stem the constant stream of vomiting, although they even resorted to a strange combination of ice and champagne in a vain bid to quell her nausea. It did the opposite in fact: her retching becoming so violent that she burst the stitches of her surgical wounds. Daisy was now in a critical condition, haemorrhaging from the re-opened fissure.

Furness and the crew were unsure whether to turn back to London, seek the nearest port or continue to head south and hope the storms would abate. They chose the latter, unintentionally sealing Daisy Hogg's fate. That night she died, on white linen sheets and silk that could not ease her agony, just as the winds abated and the *Sapphire* reached the coast off the Portuguese city of Oporto.

The drama had now turned from an emergency, of keeping Lady Furness alive, into honouring her death. Her stateroom had become a makeshift morgue. The crew discussed heading to Oporto, where she could have been embalmed before being taken back to England for burial at the family manor at Grantley. Furness vetoed this suggestion, insisting that her remains should be placed in the safe hands of an English undertaker.

That would mean pushing on toward Gibraltar, a further 500 miles away; the ship's captain believed this was possible but risky, given that temperatures would inevitably rise the closer they got to the African coastline. But Plymouth was a further 600 miles behind them and the winds were rising again, so the decision was made.

They could feel the heat two days later as the ship rounded Cape St Vincent, the southernmost tip of Portugal. It was mid-afternoon and the ship's refrigeration was designed for food and entertainment, not to chill a corpse. It was clear that the situation could not last more than a few hours before decomposition became a problem.

The Spanish city Cadiz lay to port, perhaps two or three hours away, and Gibraltar was at least a further five hours ahead. Another decision had to be made and, yet again, Furness chose to head where a British undertaker could be found.

It was another miscalculation. Two hours later, with the ice that had been hastily stacked around her body rapidly melting away, Furness brought the *Sapphire* to a halt. They had run out of time and his beloved wife would have to be buried at sea. Daisy's body was wrapped in canvas and the ship's blue ensign, the naval reserve flag it carried. At sunset, the engines were stopped and the crew stood solemnly while the captain read a prayer for those who die at sea. Nearby, Furness paced the deck, unable to watch as her body was lowered into the now calm sea.

The *Sapphire* didn't dock at Gibraltar, but steamed past toward Cannes. The British consul was notified of this by wireless, yet another decision that would raise questions about Daisy Hogg's death over the next two decades.

Marmaduke Furness would spend five years searching for a replacement wife. He thought he'd never find one but then, in the late summer of 1925, he was introduced to a sparkling brunette named Thelma Morgan, a recently divorced 21-year-old New

York socialite whose identical twin sister, Gloria, was married to the magnate Reginald Claypoole Vanderbilt.

They met at a dinner party in Paris after which Duke—as Furness now called himself with a nod to his recently acquired title and justified as an innocent shortening of Marmaduke—took her dancing. They made the rounds of the Parisian nightclubs until dawn, 'when the sun was turning pink over the Montmartre', and stopped to buy flowers on their way back to the Ritz. Romance followed, and they married ten months later.

At first, the union seemed solid. Thelma, bedazzled by the splendour of Duke's life, was surrounded by luxury in private and public, where restaurant waiters would bow low and call him 'Milord': 'I'm afraid I was somewhat smug and pleased when women would look up with what I thought was a little envy as we entered a restaurant,' she would later write in her memoir *Double Exposure*, co-authored with her twin sister. 'Travelling with him was almost like travelling with royalty. We would be met by top-hatted station masters and escorted to our compartments; we would be followed by secretaries and two valets. I once asked him if one valet valeted the other: "You know dear," he answered. "I think you're nearly bloody well right at that."'

In 1929 there was a child—a boy they named Anthony—but soon afterwards cracks began to appear in the relationship. Despite his wife's youth, it seemed that more children were not part of Duke's plans. The child was an obstacle to be ignored and he could barely tolerate 'that boy' as he grew older.

Duke also appeared to be growing bored with Thelma. At first there were seemingly innocent social flirtations with other women, but things escalated when whispered rumours suggested that the dalliances were not so innocent, particularly when he went alone to Monte Carlo one weekend. He had told Thelma he was staying at the Hotel de Paris but instead he stayed at a villa being rented by a former Ziegfeld Follies dancer named Peggy Hopkins Joyce, one of the women with whom he had been flirting.

The marriage seemed to be in trouble, although Thelma was advised by friends who knew Duke that his affairs were part of the reality of such a marriage and it would be best to ignore his antics and, if need be, to find her own fun. She took the advice seriously, and began a fling with Edward, the Prince of Wales.

The pair had met a few years before, but now they began a fully fledged affair. Remarkably, or perhaps understandably because of the prince's position as the next in line to the throne, Furness accepted the relationship and even appeared with them in public—'Duke took our friendship in his stride—in the sophisticated Englishman's stride,' she would write.

But jealousy ultimately reared its ugly head and Furness angrily suggested that Anthony was a love child of the prince rather than his own, and demanded that the boy and his mother leave Burrough Court, his main country house in Leicestershire, and live in a London house.

It was clear that their marriage was doomed. It was just a matter of time. Besides, he had met someone new. Her name was Enid.

11

'HE LAID THE WORLD AT MY FEET'

Marmaduke Furness was holding a winning poker hand when he first spotted Enid Cavendish at the Le Touquet casino in the late summer of 1932. He immediately lost interest in the cards as he followed her progress through the room: 'I have seen many beautiful women but, from the moment Enid entered the room, my heart stopped,' he later told friends.

Afraid that she might leave the casino and disappear, Furness threw in his hand, left the table and hurried after the receding figure so as to introduce himself. Over the next week, he showered Enid, who was staying at The Berries with the children, with gifts. He sent her jewels and flowers and put his chauffeur-driven Rolls-Royce at her disposal. She sent everything back.

Undeterred, and even encouraged by her reticence, Furness upped the ante. When he discovered that she was booked to travel back to London on the *Golden Arrow*, the luxury train that had revolutionised travel by reducing the journey between London and Paris to less than seven hours, he convinced her to cancel the ticket and fly back with him on his private plane.

This time she accepted, the notion of air travel too exciting to ignore. When they arrived back in London, he took Enid to dinner at the Savoy, where he presented her with the title deeds to the apartment she was renting in Chelsea. In fact, he gave her the title deeds to the entire building, having negotiated this purchase within days and apparently without concern for the cost. Duke was not trying to impress a prospective girlfriend; he was wooing a new wife. And Enid was hooked.

Her first two marriages had been instigated by much older men to satisfy their needs—a middle-aged businessman who needed a wife for respectability; and a military officer who wanted to please his superiors. She had been, essentially, a chattel to convenience. Until now.

This relationship felt different. Here was a man aged forty, with two marriages behind him and three children, who had placed her on a pedestal to be worshipped. She had no real need for money, thanks to Roderick Cameron's estate, which continued to pay a healthy income, but how could she resist. 'There was nothing in the world that Duke was not prepared to give me,' she told friends many years later. 'Of all the men who loved me, and some were as rich as Duke, only he laid the world at my feet.'

A venal response perhaps, but there were also the children to consider. Rory was now in his late teens, with money behind him and ready to take on the world, but Pat and Caryll were aged seven and six respectively, and the sudden death the year before of their father remained fresh. Perhaps Duke could be a father figure to them.

Furness was still married to Thelma, although they had been living apart for months. Besides, she was still spending most of her time with the Prince of Wales. Duke therefore needed a divorce if he was going to marry Enid Cavendish. Although both he and Thelma were guilty of adultery, it was clear that the prince could not be dragged into the centre of marital proceedings. The blame would have to be placed solely on Duke's shoulders. He readily agreed, and Thelma launched legal proceedings, accusing Duke of having an affair with a French woman named Helen Grislain. When Duke did not defend the concocted accusation—hardly a scratch on his character—the case sailed through the courts in a few months. The way was clear.

It was a pointless exercise in terms of shielding the Prince of Wales, as the newspaper coverage confirmed. When the divorce was granted, giving Thelma custody of Anthony and a generous annual income with which to raise him, the Associated Press reported: 'Viscountess Furness, twin sister of Mrs Reginald C Vanderbilt of New York, obtained a divorce today from her husband, Viscount Furness, chairman of the Furness Shipbuilding Co Ltd. She was given custody of her son and costs against the viscount. She brought the action last month, charging misconduct. Viscountess Furness . . . was married to the shipping magnate in 1926. Since then she has been a prominent figure in British society, frequently seen in the company of the Prince of Wales at social events.'

The reference wasn't even subtle, and it was typical of the reports that found their way into a plethora of British and American newspapers, ever eager for scandal among the aristocracy.

❦

Thelma celebrated her divorce in the arms of the Prince of Wales, although she knew there was ultimately no future in the relationship. As she would later write: 'The king [George V] was still alive, but I knew the day would come when the prince would have to take his place on the throne and all of the responsibilities that went with it.'

Although she didn't state it, Thelma was alluding to her assumption that an English monarch would not be allowed to marry a commoner, let alone a divorcee. She was right in one respect—that their relationship would soon be over—but it would not be because of Edward's ascension to the throne, rather because of the Machiavellian moves of a trusted friend: Mrs Wallis Simpson.

Thelma had introduced Wallis to the prince several years before, at a party she'd hosted at Burrough Court while Duke was away overseas. It was an uneventful affair that night, she would recall while dismissing various versions of the meeting that suggested there was an immediate electricity between Wallis and Edward.

Instead, Thelma would insist that she made the mistake of

asking Wallis to 'look after him' while she was in the United States for six weeks visiting her sister. They were having lunch at the Ritz when the famous exchange took place.

'I told her of my plans, and my exuberance, and offered myself for all the usual yeoman's services. Was there anything I could do for her in America? Were there any messages I could deliver? Did she want me to bring anything back for her?

'She thanked me and said suddenly: "Oh Thelma, the little man is going to be so lonely."

'"Well dear," I answered. "You look after him for me while I'm away. See that he does not get into any mischief."

'It was later evident that Wallis took my advice all too literally. Whether or not she kept him out of mischief is a question whose answer hinges on the fine points of semantics.'

Thelma did not help her own cause when, aboard the ship on the way back from New York, she openly flirted with the Aga Khan, Imam of the Nizari Ismaili Muslims, one of the world's richest men. Aly, as he was known by his friends, showered her with attention and a room full of roses. Word got back to the prince, who fell silent when she asked if he was jealous. Two weeks later, at a weekend at Edward's country residence, Fort Belvedere, she realised her mistake when she watched Wallis and Edward sharing private jokes at dinner: 'Wallis looked straight at me, and then and there I knew. It was Wallis—of all people.'

Thelma confronted Edward that night. 'Darling, is it Wallis?' she asked bluntly.

Edward froze. 'Don't be silly,' he said crisply before leaving the room and closing the door quietly.

London's city streets were almost empty on the morning of 3 August 1933 as Marmaduke Furness and Enid Cavendish made their way to the Westminster registry office. It seemed that one of the country's richest men wanted to avoid the spotlight as he wed Enid, 'the beautiful Australian' as she would be referred to in newspaper reports, who invariably drew attention when she ventured onto London streets.

But the attempt to keep it low-key was in vain. The couple arrived thirty minutes before the registry doors were opened and they were forced to wait with the milling reporters and photographers, who had been aware of the impending nuptials since late May, when the *Daily Express* announced it on its front page. A week after the revelation, the couple had appeared together at Epsom for the running of the English Derby: Furness buoyant and grinning in top hat and tails alongside his taller, elegant bride-to-be who also seemed happy, if more reservedly, to be photographed.

But if the reporters were expecting a fanfare wedding then they would be disappointed. The ceremony was conducted 'in a barely furnished room with no flowers', according to one scribe astonished at the sparseness of such an event. It had almost been delayed because the court had dragged its heels finalising the decree nisi for Furness's divorce from Thelma Morgan and the document had only arrived three days beforehand.

Duke had brought along his pilot, Tom Campbell Black, as best man and Enid was accompanied by her younger sister, Nita, and two close friends. The formalities were over in barely twenty minutes; the only sign of wealth was the large diamond engagement ring and platinum wedding band on Enid's third finger. She was dressed elegantly in ice blue, with a spray of orchids.

Even the mid-morning reception at the Dorchester Hotel was frugal, with a handful of guests enjoying a few glasses of champagne before the happy couple was whisked away to Stag Lane Aerodrome in Edgware, north London, where Duke's latest aircraft lay waiting to take them on their honeymoon—first to India and then a safari in Africa.

The aircraft's interior had been stripped and fitted out to provide sleeping quarters and a dressing-room, with four armchairs and its thick carpeted floors making it resemble a reception room more than the inside of an aircraft. There was even space for a butler and a maid.

The 'aerial honeymoon', as it was dubbed, captured the attention of the US and Australian media. The concept of private air travel was an almost unheard-of luxury; there were photographs published of the newlyweds stepping aboard their silver aircraft, flown by Campbell Black.

The Australian newspapers seemed to have forgotten their earlier critique of Enid's marital adventures. The Sydney *Sun*'s correspondent revealed a recent meeting and sang her praises as a down-to-earth woman:

> I renewed acquaintance with that divine creature, Viscountess Furness, who you will remember as Enid Lindeman, of Sydney. She was gowned to perfection in oxidised lamé and silver fox, while her faultless throat was hung with pearls and not the Woolworth variety either, darling. And here's something for you to dwell on. She's a darling. She greeted me as if I were a human being and not the bunyip in the family cupboard like so many other peeresses of Australian origin do to their old and erstwhile dear friends. Such small mindedness, I think, and such bad publicity, for nothing except perhaps fire travels as fast as the news of a snub, and after all there are peeresses and peeresses these days. Unhappily, many of the darlings have cheapened themselves so glaringly that you can buy them, shop-soiled and tarnished, two a penny in the catacombs of Mr Selfridge.

But there were hints of darkness ahead. One media report revealed that Furness had ordered a 'nursery wing' to be added to Enid's house at Le Touquet, where the Cavendish children would be housed when the family stayed in France. Duke appeared to be separating Enid from her children.

12

CHAMPAGNY LORDY

Pat and Caryll only became aware of their mother's new husband after Enid had returned from the honeymoon. Pat later wrote of the day she met her new 'father', when the children were brought by staff from their London house on a long train journey north to Burrough Court.

Enid came down to the nursery 'wing' to greet her children with the surprising and unsettling news: 'Darlings, I do not know what you are going to call him, but I suggest that when I take you to meet him, you call him Daddy and do not forget to kiss him on the cheek and do a little curtsey and bow.'

Duke was waiting in an upstairs library, sitting in an armchair with a drink in one hand and a cigarette in the other, a jumble of paperwork on a side table. He made no move nor smiled as the children approached, no doubt dreading the moment as much as them. Pat recalled: 'He was a dapper little man, impeccably dressed and with reddish, sandy hair that had been brilliantined flat, not a single strand out of place. In all the time I knew him, I never saw him less than immaculate. Caryll remembered him as *peppery* but to me, he was always too cold, too icy to be described like that.'

Pat performed as her mother suggested—a curtsey followed by a peck on the cheek, which he accepted without a response. But when she called him 'Daddy', he stopped her sharply: 'I am not your father and do not address me as such.'

The little girl had been asked to manufacture a relationship for the benefit of an adult, but had been rejected. She was crestfallen: 'I realised then that he did not like me. For the entire time of Mummy's marriage, he was never actively nasty but he kept us at a distance and preferred us to be out of his view.'

Marmaduke Furness may have married Enid Cavendish, but he had no intention of taking responsibility for, or forming supportive relationships with, her children. He had also insisted that his new wife hand over the Cameron fortune as part of the marriage agreement.

Rory's share would be set aside and handed over to him in just over a year, when he turned twenty-one, while Enid would live in luxury and never have any financial concerns, provided that the money was controlled by him. Even ownership of the block of Chelsea apartments he had bought her on a lustful whim would revert to his name.

Years later Pat remained confused by her mother's acceptance of the financial agreement, which seemed at odds with her character. Was she trying to ensure that Rory's fortune was safe or was it simply a self-protective measure adopted by a woman who was taught, to her ultimate detriment, to trust that men were the ones who should run money and households?

Pat's cynicism was well-founded. Enid's decision to trade her cherished independence for a promise of comfort, however luxurious, would prove a significant mistake and one she would regret.

'My mother seemed to spend her life at lawyers reversing the outcome of wills,' Pat wrote in her autobiography. 'Her generosity and sense of fair play were truly remarkable. She was totally unconscious about the value of money and was the most completely generous being. This quality of innocence transcended the beautiful façade and was the essence of her charm and the attribute that drew everyone to her.'

As for her relationships with men, Pat described her mother as a chameleon: 'She devoted herself totally to whichever man was in her life at the time. With every new lover she would become his ideal woman and his interests would become hers. It always amazed me that my mother, who was brought up with four brothers to become a brilliant shot and horse rider who insisted on doing everything as well as her siblings, could so transform herself into the quintessence of femininity for her husbands and lovers. Looking back, I can imagine that one of the reasons men were so passionate about her was that she could excel at all the masculine sports. The contrast between that and her femininity must have been irresistible.'

Indeed, it was a bewitching combination. Duke had not only been entranced by Enid's long, lean beauty, which was straight out of the fashion pages of the 1930s, but also by her competence in a hunt—she was a skilful horsewoman, who could ride with the hounds after foxes and shoot pheasant, deer and grouse as well as any man. For a man whose social life existed around the hunting season and the famous Quorn Hunt, which stretched between Nottingham, Leicester and Melton Mowbray, this made Enid the perfect woman.

But for Pat, her mother's love for Marmaduke Furness was another matter. She had plenty of money and his title made no particular difference to her life, given that she held no great desire to mix with the aristocracy: 'I don't know what she saw in him,' said Pat. 'He was horrid, and she was wonderful. Maybe he was good in bed or, more likely, she was trying to save him.'

When Pat questioned her mother many years later about suspicions over the death of Furness's first wife, Daisy Hogg, and whether Duke may have killed her, Enid was insistent that it wasn't true. 'Darling, don't be ridiculous. He might have been a dreadful stepfather and an even worse father, but he was a man of honour.'

Any interaction Pat and Caryll had with Duke was by chance, and invariably brief. If they travelled with him by train, the children would not join him in his private carriage; they would enter and leave the train before and after Duke boarded and alighted—neither seen nor heard.

At home they were kept out of sight, housed in a separate wing of the house with their own staircase and staff. They were restricted to spending an hour or so in the morning with their mother on those days when she ate breakfast alone in her bedroom while her husband was out riding.

Those occasions were magical for a child, their mother sitting in bed surrounded by her art and needlework as well as a variety of animals—dogs, a parrot, a mongoose and even a pair of foxes. Invariably it would end up with a mad, noisy romp around the room as the children pretended to be on a hunt.

Family movies, mostly shot by Enid, give a glimpse of these tender moments, beginning in the early 1930s when Pat and Caryll are shown wading for shellfish during summer holidays at Le Touquet and their father, Frederick Cavendish, is filmed giving piggybacks to his children, unaware that he will be dead within a few months.

On another reel, shot a few years later after she had married Marmaduke Furness and labelled, tongue-in-cheek, as 'The terrible children', Enid had filmed the children playing dress-up games in the ivy-covered grounds of Burrough Court. Although there is no sound, it is clear that Enid is directing the action from behind the camera as she enlists the help of her butlers and maids, dragged from their domestic duties to play supporting roles as they turn the driveway into a racetrack. The children, squealing with delight, speed around on bicycles chased by an excited pack of poodles and staff.

The hijinks continue at a staged afternoon tea party in the courtyard, which erupts into a food fight. There is a later scene, in which the children hurl pillows at one another and drop cushions onto the heads of unsuspecting 'guests' from upper-storey windows. Enid only makes an occasional appearance in front of the camera, a serene and doting mother attempting to compensate for her third husband's callous demands that she lead a separate life from her children. Instead, and possibly in secret, she traced their lives from toddlers to teenagers for posterity.

Their older brother, Rory, rarely visited and preferred to stay in Germany, where he was studying architecture. He was completing an education that had begun in a wartime Paris kindergarten and included an Arab school in Cairo, a private school in England, a college in Switzerland and now a university in Munich. When he did venture back to see his mother and siblings, Rory preferred to meet in London rather than having to face his new stepfather, who would become increasingly angry at the influence the young man had over Enid.

Duke's language matched his ire; he was prone to outbursts of swearing and fits of pique that belied his neat, composed appearance. He was a wealthy but unhappy man, riven by his own father's rejection of him which manifested itself in bouts of jealousy and rage.

To a small girl like Pat, Burrough Court seemed like a castle, with its endless rooms and corridors. In reality, it was a grand hunting lodge built in 1905 that could accommodate up to twenty guests in the kind of luxury that only the very wealthy might expect.

Furness had two valets and Enid four lady's maids. There were six cooks in the huge kitchens and a retinue of butlers and

The Lindeman brothers took over the reins of their father Henry's business empire, principally run by Charles, Enid's father, who is in the centre.
Enid Lindeman private albums

A girl among men: young Enid's attitude to life is evinced in this circa 1896 photograph of her standing in the midst of the male-dominated Lindeman family.
Enid Lindeman private albums

An early portrait of Enid (centre) with her mother, Florence, and younger sister Nita. *Enid Lindeman private albums*

Roderick Cameron was a wealthy 45-year-old New York bachelor when he arrived in Sydney in 1912 and met 20-year-old Enid Lindeman. *Enid Lindeman private albums*

Enid on the day of her wedding to Roderick Cameron in 1913. *Enid Lindeman private albums*

The young widow with baby Rory in New York in 1914. She would return to Sydney soon afterwards. *Enid Lindeman private albums*

Enid cuts an amazing figure emerging from the water at Manly in 1915 wearing a swimming costume once owned by swimming legend Annette Kellerman. *Enid Lindeman private albums*

TOP LEFT: Enid always stood out in a crowd, this time as a World War I nurse in Paris where she also drove a private ambulance.
Enid Lindeman private albums

TOP RIGHT: Paris 1917: Enid was popular with British Army officers stationed in the French capital. Eventually, she would be married off to an officer to quell the fuss.
Enid Lindeman private albums

LEFT: Enid and her second husband, Frederick 'Caviar' Cavendish. It was an arranged marriage that lasted fourteen years until he died of a brain haemorrhage.
Enid Lindeman private albums

Three years after World War I ended, Frederick (mounted, second left) was stationed in Egypt. In 1922, thanks to her friendship with Lord Carnarvon, Enid (centre) and son Rory were two of the first people to enter Tutankhamun's tomb. *Cavendish family collection*

Enid and her younger sister Marjorie. The Lindeman girls were much-photographed beauties, this taken in 1925 when Enid was pregnant with daughter Pat. *Photo by Bernice Agar*

Enid was a devoted mother, pictured here with Caryll and Pat, her children with Frederick Cavendish. *Cavendish family collection*

Marmaduke Furness, Enid's third husband, called himself Duke and expected to be treated like one, a tyrant who demanded freshly ironed shoelaces each day. *Author's collection*

Burrough Court: the grand hunting lodge kept by Marmaduke Furness boasted a private airstrip and a zoo. *Author's collection*

Pat and Enid at Burrough Court in the late 1930s. Both loved horses and would join forces in later life to train and race thoroughbreds. *Cavendish family collection*

maids who escorted the food in a grand procession into the dining hall whenever the table was laid for sumptuous dinners, which were frequent.

Outside, there was a long avenue leading up to the entrance of the main house, where the white-pebbled courtyards were raked and any stained pebbles removed. This replenishment occurred twice a day, to eliminate marks from wheels and horses' hooves so as to present a perfect, pristine surface for Duke when he left the house or returned from an outing.

Guests were greeted by two footmen dressed in yellow shirts and plum-coloured trousers and jackets. In the evening they would change into a more formal attire of knee-length plum breeches and cutaway jackets with gold stockings and waistcoats.

The manicured grounds were tended by dozens of workers, who clipped and reclipped topiaries of peacocks and pyramids and columns topped with perfectly round balls. Hedges bordered a maze of beds, one of roses, another herbs and vegetables. There were ponds filled with fish and elaborate fountains.

Marmaduke Furness was not only an icy man with an eye for beautiful women and a love of fox hunting but, in modern parlance, he almost certainly harboured an obsessive-compulsive disorder. His demand for neatness began each morning with boot boys, who were given the thankless task of polishing his boots and shoes and threading new, freshly ironed laces. The assigned boy would sit in a small room off the butler's pantry, Pat watching in awe as he scrubbed and polished feverishly before presenting them to 'his lordship' for approval. They were often returned, Furness dissatisfied.

At the back of the house stood the stables, with black-and-white gables in a mock-Tudor style and boxes for a hundred horses, which were walked out each day through an archway beneath a clock tower. The tack room smelled of saddle soap and lavender wood polish; one of its walls was lined with glass display cabinets filled with silver cups and trophies, and the other three with shelves and hooks. Here the bridles and saddles were hung after having been washed, and sheets and blankets were stacked after being neatly folded.

Each horse had two blankets in the Furness colours of plum and gold; the edges of the straw bedding in their boxes were trimmed and plaited so there were no strands hanging untidily. The stable doors were refreshed with paint every evening to cover scuff marks from horses' hooves.

Likewise, the dairy farm that adjoined the main property was kept pristine. The jersey cows were groomed by six o'clock each morning, their tails brushed in case Furness visited on his regular morning ride. The separate stables for the giant Percheron draught horses were kept in similar order, as were the kennels. He owned a mix of hunting dogs, beagles and hounds, as well as house dogs, mainly poodles favoured by Enid. The breeds were kept apart, tended by kennel boys dressed in white coats; his dogs were paraded at various shows, where their successes filled yet more cabinets with trophies.

To top it all off, there was a zoo at the end of the garden. Duke had long been in love with Africa, not just as a hunting ground but as a source of living animals for his personal entertainment. He owned several species of monkeys and parrots among a variety of birds, plus porcupines and a rabbit-like mammal called a hyrax, which Enid kept as a pet. Furness had even built a giraffe house, topped with a giant glass dome, but he was never able to get one of them back to England.

Furness liked to travel in style. His Rolls-Royce was staffed by a driver and a footman; it was painted maroon, with a silver bonnet emblazoned with the Furness crest and solid silver doorknobs. When he journeyed by train to London, Duke used a private carriage, readied as the scheduled train service approached the station and hitched to the rear, out of sight of the regular, fare-paying passengers.

One story told around the Burrough Court kitchens centred on the day that Furness found himself in his carriage toilet, complete with gold chain and ivory handle, but lacking toilet paper. Without anyone to come to his aid, Duke was forced to use several £5 notes the size of a handkerchief that he carried in a gold money clip. Each wipe cost £300 in today's money, prompting one servant to quip: 'For £5, I'd have wiped the shit up myself if I'd known.'

Duke had an airstrip and hangar built at Burrough Court, from where he and Enid would travel regularly to play in the casinos of Le Touquet, Biarritz and Deauville, or attend race meetings at the famed Iffezheim racecourse near the German town of Baden-Baden.

They could also fly further afield to America, India or Africa, where Duke had now bought a safari lodge in Nairobi. He spent several months there each year, usually from April to June, between the end of the English hunting season and the beginning of the European summer.

In Kenya there was a fleet of Rolls-Royce limousines waiting, fitted out to be driven off-road for safaris, and a champagne bar. There were two chauffeurs for each vehicle, one dressed in a black cockaded cap and black uniform, and the other in white. At the property on the outskirts of the city, the staff were dressed in the Furness colours—yellow cotton robes called *kanzus* and wide, plum-coloured cummerbunds and fezzes.

Duke's lodge backed onto the famed Muthaiga Country Club, where Duke and Enid mingled with the likes of Lady Idina Sackville and Alice de Janzé, both part of what would become known as the Happy Valley set. Enid would later recall spending the night at one of Idina's house parties, during which she got up in the night and had to step over a group of naked bodies writhing on the sitting room floor. Enid didn't blink; she got her drink of water and went back to bed. She loved sex but was not one for orgies.

Kenya was where Duke had met Tom Campbell Black, who not only flew his planes but influenced his increasingly larger purchases. His first was a single-engine Puss Moth, which was used to fly crates of champagne supplies from Nairobi into Duke's safari camps. The hillsides would be littered with empty Dom Pérignon bottles after 'Champagny Lordy' decamped. On one occasion, so it was said, he sent Black to Scotland for grouse and salmon.

Black was an accomplished pilot who would become famous for several flying race victories, including the 1934 London–Melbourne race, during which he and his co-pilot took just seventy-one hours to make the journey. He was also famed for his selfless rescue of two German airmen whose plane had crashed while flying across the Sudan in 1931. When told they were missing, he flew off in search of them; he landed in treacherous desert to save the men, who were sheltering beneath the damaged wing of their plane, having been without water for two days. One of the Germans was Ernst Udet, a revered German flying ace who would later write that he had felt his brain dehydrating before Black arrived with water.

But Black was not without flaws, and was wont to drink with his boss while flying, a free-wheeling attitude which almost ended in tragedy one evening as Duke and Enid returned home from a trip across the Channel. As the aircraft skimmed low to touch down on the end of the runway, Black misjudged the height and the wheels clipped a hedge and sent the plane skimming out of control.

Black managed to put it down but the aircraft ended up on its nose, tail in the air, its wing crumpled and its wooden fuselage smashed beyond repair. Even so, the local press downplayed the severity of the accident, stating that Furness and Enid were both thrown clear of the plane and injured slightly. Furness sustained cuts and bruises, and Enid an elbow injury; while Black, who would die a few years later in a bizarre accident when his plane was hit by an RAF bomber as he taxied toward the runway, was badly shaken.

Also aboard was one of the maids, acting as a stewardess. She escaped injury and later recounted the chaotic scene to the staff in the Burrough Court kitchens. Furness had been drinking heavily during the flight and had encouraged Black to imbibe several glasses of champagne which, she thought, affected his judgement and caused the accident.

It had been near sunset and darkening quickly as they came in to land. Duke was smoking a cigar and drinking a glass of whisky, unaware that the plane was rocking slightly while Black searched for the end of the strip in the fading light and steadied for a landing. Enid, who never drank anything stronger than Coca-Cola, was sitting beside her husband and seemed to sense that something was amiss. The maid had watched as Enid reached across, just as the plane dipped to land, and grabbed the lit cigar from Duke's mouth, announcing: 'Darling, I am going to put this out or the plane might catch fire.'

The crash gave Duke the opportunity to upgrade once more. This time he acquired a Lockheed Electra, similar to the plane flown by tragic American heroine Amelia Earhart. The plane was a forty-fifth birthday present for Enid. As the local newspaper reported:

> There are gifts and gifts and I have just heard of one presented to Lady Furness, who was formerly Miss Enid Lindeman of Sydney, which makes diamond bracelets pale into insignificance. Keeping in mind the air-mindedness of the times, Lord Furness made a nice little offering to his wife in the shape of a £15,000 Lockheed six-seater aeroplane, fitted with wireless.

> But all the seats have been removed to accommodate four armchairs, well upholstered, and adjustable to any angle, and a small cocktail bar has also been installed. It is a nice little bus in which to tour the Continent, complete with pilot, valet and lady's maid.

Enid was clearly pleased with her gift, patiently posing for photographers on the tarmac like a modern-day red-carpet celebrity.

13

A JUNGLE ROMANCE

Averill Furness took after her mother, physically and in personality. She certainly looked like Daisy Hogg, with the same chestnut hair, the square jawline and the resolute, challenging gaze that was evident in photographs taken of them at similar ages.

Averill was striking in an athletic way—more comfortable in jodhpurs and boots than in an evening gown and heels. She was a confident rider and a crack shot who, it was proudly boasted by her father, had shot her first deer at the age of twelve and brought down four stags with successive shots at sixteen. It was an unusual observation about a young woman whose contemporaries would have pursued indoor activities and followed the latest fashions of London.

Given her father's position in society, she might have been photographed glamorously by the society magazine *Tatler*, but instead she chose the lesser-known Fleet Street tabloid *Bystander*, in which she posed alongside a family hunting dog, dressed elegantly but plainly and staring at the camera with what appears to be mild amusement—a woman unafraid to stake her claim in a man's world and who did not suffer fools gladly.

It should have been no surprise then that Averill would fall in love, not with one of the flim-flam boys who rode alongside her on fox hunts with the Quorn, Cottesmore and Belvoir packs but with an older, robust and independent outdoors man.

Such a man arrived at Burrough Court one day in July 1931, not stepping from a Bentley chauffeured to the front door but from a truck delivered to the rear of the main house.

His name was Andrew Rattray, a Scotsman from a good family and with a decent education, but he was not from the Furness family, nor anywhere near in terms of wealth, privilege or social position. Rather, he was employed as Lord Furness's designated 'white hunter'; he organised and led hunting safaris when Duke and his then wife Thelma Morgan made their annual pilgrimage to Africa to escape the British winter.

Rattray had made the journey to Britain—his first time home in thirty years—to deliver animals to add to the Viscount's zoo. The load included several types of monkeys and two Grévy's zebras, which Furness hoped could be domesticated, something that had been previously attempted with little success.

Furness was unsure how to treat Rattray on arrival. He was an employee and probably belonged in the servants' quarters but he was also a human curio of sorts. Thelma would recall her husband saying: 'He is an interesting man, and he will probably have much to say that could be interesting to our friends. So, let's have him eat with us.'

Duke had no way of knowing that this decision would change the course of his family's life, mostly because of his own shortcomings. The dinner was an entertaining affair; the hunter held the guests enthralled with his tales of the African plains, including the day he fought a leopard with his bare hands and survived by shoving one hand down the beast's throat to suffocate it. His hand was badly mauled but he survived.

The stories were thrilling and Rattray looked the part, with a deep tan and thick Scottish burr, and tall and lean from an active life that hid the fact he was almost fifty, two years older than his employer.

Averill, aged twenty-three, was mesmerised by the stories and the man in front of her. She cared little about his age and much less about his social status. It was his life and adventure that she found attractive. She had been incensed five years before when her father, aged forty-three, had announced he was marrying 21-year-old Thelma Morgan but he had persuaded her that all that mattered was love. Surely the same rules applied to her.

The next day, Rattray coaxed her into riding one of the zebras that he specialised in taming. The animal at first consented but then it bit Averill and soon the wound became infected. The local doctors struggled to contain the poison but when Rattray stepped in and used his own jungle salve on it, her wound healed. Instead of being angry at him, Averill was smitten, and pined for him when he left a few days later.

Averill held her feelings secret for several months. But in December, a few days before she was due to leave for Africa with her family, she decided to share her feelings with Thelma, hoping that a woman just four years older, and more like a sister in age than a stepmother, might understand.

Thelma, in *Double Exposure*, recounted her recollection of the conversation, in which Averill gushed that she was in love with 'Andy' and wanted to spend the rest of her life with him in Africa. Thelma tried to dissuade her, insisting that Rattray lived in primitive conditions.

'I don't care how he lives,' Averill responded. 'I love Andy. Promise me you won't breathe a word of this to father.'

Thelma was not convinced: 'This speech had a strange sound coming from a girl who had always lived in the centre of extraordinary luxury, with personal maids and two or more cars at her disposal. What was she thinking?'

Thelma pondered after the conversation with Averill, and decided that Duke should be told. But when confronted, he became angry and accused her of lying. 'What the bloody hell do you mean?' he thundered. 'What are you trying to do, Thelma? I don't believe you. I don't believe a word of it.' With that he left, slamming the door behind him.

The next day Thelma left Burrough Court, but not for Africa with the others. The argument with Duke over Averill's relationship with Rattray had proved to be the final straw in her own fragile relationship. The marriage was past the point of saving; she was leaving Marmaduke Furness for the Prince of Wales.

❧

True to his word, and exhibiting a blindness and hypocrisy he would live to regret, Furness ignored the warnings of his now estranged wife. She was being a troublemaker, he decided. The very idea that Averill would fall in love with a servant, and an older man at that, seemed preposterous.

The safari went ahead, but Furness did not directly confront his daughter or the man she purportedly loved. It was clear that the relationship between father and daughter was strained, and would become worse after they left Nairobi to travel several hundred kilometres south to Maasai land, near the border with Tanzania.

Averill would later report back to Thelma that there had been several escalating rows as she tried to reason with Furness about her feelings. Eventually she demanded to be allowed to return to Nairobi and take the next ship back to the UK.

Furness agreed and sacked Rattray on the spot, his final duty being for him to escort Averill back to the inland capital. It was 24 anuary 1932 and the couple left camp the next day for the five-day ride back to the city, where she booked passage on the steamship *Francesco Crispi*, which was due to leave Mombasa, Kenya's principal coastal city, on 1 February. She would travel through the Suez Canal to Port Said, across the Mediterranean, around Spain and Portugal and up the coast of France to Southampton—a journey that normally took almost three weeks.

The night before she was due to leave for Mombasa, Averill had dinner at a Nairobi hotel with Rattray. Rather than a farewell, the meal ended with a marriage proposal; instead of taking the train the next morning, the pair scurried to the office of the district commissioner, who held the authority to conduct weddings. The commissioner was absent, but his deputy agreed to perform the ceremony with Averill's maid, a Miss Marjorie Kirsopp, and a stenographer from the office staff as witnesses. The formalities were over in a few minutes.

The next morning, Averill hired a pilot to take the news to her father. A later newspaper account described the scene:

> The glad news was sent by an aviator who succeeded in landing near Lord Furness's camp. The bride had explained that she was following her father's advice and in fact treading in his footsteps as a dutiful daughter should and knew he would rejoice in her great happiness. His Lordship read the first sentence and started as if a lion had roared in his ear. Then his face slowly assumed a purplish tint as he finished and stalked away from his tent without comment. After an hour's wait the aviator asked how soon the answer would be ready: 'There is no answer' said Lord Furness, from which the newlyweds deduced that there was an exception to Lord Furness's rule of love.

Furness abandoned the safari and rushed back to Nairobi, but it was too late. The couple, who had initially stayed with friends, had moved from the city and into Rattray's modest house on the outskirts of Isiolo, an isolated town 280 kilometres north of Nairobi. Averill had traded the luxury of Burrough Court for a timber bush shack that was little more than a single room with basic furniture, the walls hung with half-cured pelts.

Bubbling with fury, Furness took out an advertisement in the *East African Standard*, which read: 'From after January 24 Mr A. Rattray ceased to be my white hunter to safari, and from that date he has no authority to order anything on my account.'

As innocuous as it appeared, the advertisement piqued media interest. Andrew Rattray was well known and respected in the area. What could Furness's grievance be to sack such a successful hunter?

The secret was out, and the newlyweds were tracked to their shack by an intrepid Reuters reporter. Both of them gave interviews. They were in love, despite their age and class differences, Rattray said; their decision to marry had been made on the spur of the moment. It was simply the 'natural course of events', Averill insisted, adding that she had no regrets: 'We are married, and that's that.'

The jungle romance made headlines around the world: 'Peer's underling wins daughter, loses job' screamed the *Daily News* in New York; like many US papers, it adored British social scandal. *Time* magazine described Lord Furness's 'wrathful roar resounding through the veldt'.

Back in London the press coverage was less sensationalised, but it observed that Viscount Furness had 'temporarily disowned and disinherited his daughter'. He was attempting to have the marriage annulled. 'You will regret this as much as I do,' he told her.

Thelma took a different view. Despite her initial doubts, she cabled Averill with her best wishes when the news broke in London. Perhaps she understood the hypocrisy of her husband's stance.

Averill replied immediately, happy to have the support of one member of the family. She told Thelma that her father's sacking of Andy had been a blessing in disguise and, despite the continued insults, they felt free to pursue their new life. 'I had no idea how the papers at home would get hold of this. Of course, there is a devil of a lot of talk here, but things are quieting down now, I think. If I come home to Burrough it is only to pick up my things. Honestly Thelma, it is absolutely impossible to exist anywhere near him and keep one's reason. Anyway, all that is past now, thank God, and for the first time in my life I am really happy.'

She predicted that her nineteen-year-old brother, Christopher, who was known in the family and by friends as Dick, would follow suit, unable to maintain a relationship with their father: 'Poor old Dick will be the next one to go, I suspect. He is never allowed out shooting on this safari but has to remain in camp washing lorries and building grass banyas.'

Despite her new, rustic abode, Averill had no intention of returning to Burrough Court: 'After the delights of the wide-open spaces of Kenya, I can never go back to the humdrum social life in England.'

In November 1933, just a few months after Furness and Enid's marriage, Andrew Rattray was reported to be dead. News had filtered out from Kenya that the hunter had fallen ill with a fever and had had to be nursed in the wilderness by Averill for several days until a plane could be arranged to fly him back to Nairobi for emergency treatment. He had a heart attack soon afterwards and died with his wife at his bedside.

The tributes that flowed revealed Rattray was more than just a hunter for hire. He had been a war hero in the Second Boer War, a captain in the famed Thorneycroft's Mounted Infantry and later mentioned in dispatches. After the war he remained in Africa and became a respected farmer; he grew coffee and sisal on an experimental farm, on land that had been granted to him by the Tanganyika Government so he could train zebras, which lacked the stamina of horses but had a natural resistance to the tsetse fly.

Marmaduke Furness had not spoken to his daughter since her marriage almost two years before. The Viscount now reached out to try to reclaim their relationship. All had been forgiven and she had been reinstated as an heir: 'Come back to my heart,' he implored in a cable.

In a grand gesture acknowledging his poor judgement, Furness sent a wreath clearly marked with his name to be laid on Rattray's grave in the cemetery at Nairobi. But it would be to no avail; Averill was in no mood to forgive or forget. When Rattray had visited the UK earlier, Duke had rebuffed attempts by his former 'white hunter' to broker peace, sending 'the bloody tradesman' away from the house without even seeing him. Duke's belligerence had now caused Averill to shun his own pleas for forgiveness. Thelma later wrote in her memoir about the young woman's brief visit to London a few months later, to finally retrieve the possessions she'd left behind two years before.

> Averill came straight to me the moment she arrived. Although never pretty in a feminine way, she was always meticulously groomed. Her lovely red hair always gleamed from daily brushing, her skin had a well-scrubbed, wholesome look, her nails were beautifully manicured and her clothes were carefully brushed and pressed. But now she was dishevelled, unkempt. Yet lack of grooming was not the only cause of the appalling change in her appearance. She had not only coarsened, but she had suddenly matured—in a thick, ugly way. There was now no longer any resemblance to the slight girl who had been the Honourable Averill Furness. Yet in her trouble she had turned to me, and I wanted to help her.

Thelma's catty judgement just highlighted the fact that, while she had sacrificed love to marry for wealth and position, her step-daughter had sacrificed wealth and position to marry for love.

Averill left London and returned to Kenya without seeing her father or his new wife, Enid. Duke continued his appeals for a reconciliation, even instructing his East Africa representative to provide her with funds, but she rejected his offers, despite the fact that she was forced to give up the farm and now lived in poverty in a tiny community at the edge of the Mount Kenya National Park.

14

CRASHING THE GILDED HALLS

By the mid-1930s there was a handful of Australian women who had married into the upper echelons of London society—'crashing the gilded halls of Mayfair', as one proud Australian publication put it.

The loves and occasional scandals of these women had given the social columnists plenty to write about. Women like Florence Morphy, the daughter of a Victorian magistrate who had married Ivo Bligh, captain of the England cricket team and become Lady Darnley; or Sheila Chisholm, the Goulburn sheep farmer's daughter who had married the son of the Earl of Rosslyn and had had an affair with Albert, who would later become King George VI.

There was also the former Miss Nell Stead of Melbourne, who, as the Duchess of Manchester, led a wild life through the gambling clubs of Soho. To a lesser extent, there was Patricia

Richards of Cootamundra, whose divorce from the Earl of Jersey created a media sensation; Lady Portarlington, who had grown up in Melbourne as Winnafreda Yuill; Baroness Doverdale, who was once Miss Audrey Pointing of Sydney; and Lady Bective, the former Elise Tucker of Randwick in Sydney.

And now there was Enid Lindeman, the new wife of one of Britain's richest men, who glided into London society as if she'd been there all her life, 'a quiet figure in society happy in her new surroundings', according to the London correspondent for *Smith's Weekly*.

Although she was now aged well into her forties, Enid was drawing more attention than ever, whether at the card tables of Europe's casinos, where she was said to have won enough one evening to buy a townhouse in Mayfair, or flitting off for a weekend visit on the continent in her silver private plane, or riding and shooting on the hunt as if she had been born in a saddle.

But there was another side to Enid, who was known to order her chauffeur to stop the car while she spoke to homeless men on the streets of London. Many of them were former soldiers; she would often give them money or arrange accommodation for them.

She would occasionally drive herself. One night she was caught speeding in Mayfair and hauled before the magistrate's court, where the arresting police constable told of the encounter: 'It is a brand-new car,' she had told him. 'Also a high-powered one and difficult to estimate one's speed.' The case was dismissed.

Enid kept a pet cheetah with a diamond collar. She had rescued it during her honeymoon trip to Africa and brought it back to London: she often took it with her as she drove around the city in the Bentley and would send Pat with her governess, a surly Austrian woman named Miss Unger, to walk it in Hyde Park, a few hundred metres from their London house. Pat recalled other strollers staring and hurriedly walking away.

Enid's favourite pet was the hyrax which often sat on her shoulder like a parrot. Her friend Coco Chanel even designed a dress with a high collar in which the hyrax, a notoriously shy animal, could hide.

She was a woman with her own style and quickly became a favourite of portrait photographers, as much for her looks as for her title and money. She was 'the only woman who could look through a camera as if it wasn't there', according to Gregory Harlip, one of London's best-known celebrity photographers of the 1930s, who exhibited Enid's portrait alongside the likes of Vivien Leigh, George Bernard Shaw and Prince Frederick of Prussia.

Enid was popular in oils, too. In 1935 she sat for the famed painter Sir John Lavery, a senior academician at the Royal Academy. Titled simply *The Viscountess Furness*, the finished portrait was hung for the academy's prestigious summer exhibition. As one Australian veteran newspaper correspondent reported:

> The private view of the Royal Academy! The London season set in swing and the usual masses of people pouring into the

> courtyard of Burlington House. Maybe it's because of the extra influx of Jubilee crowds, but I don't quite remember having to fight my way in QUITE so hard as this time. Across the seething seas of England's blue blood, I glimpsed a singularly sweet face smiling out from a canvas. On closer examination I found it to be none other than our newest Australian peeress, Lady Furness. Sir John Lavery has painted her in a frock of clinging brown chiffon, with a dark fur cape thrown across her shoulders, a lovely string of pearls and several magnificent diamonds. This is one of the really outstanding portraits of the year.

In 1936 iconic British fashion designer Norman Hartnell, dressmaker to the Royal Family, declared Enid to be among the world's ten best-dressed women. 'Despite her middle age, her glorious white hair and svelte figure lend themselves to the proper exhibition of clothes,' he said. 'She is also tall, which is a distinct asset. Wisely, she wears dark colours, chiefly blue and black. Perhaps it is her personality as much as anything else that makes her so individual.'

The next year, a poll of London fashion houses also placed her high on the list of the Empire's best-dressed women, sandwiched between the Duchess of Leeds and the actress Gertrude Lawrence. Of Enid, the judges remarked: 'Tall and elegant, with finely chiselled features and deep blue expressive eyes, Lady Furness is one of the most admired women of London society. It was for regal loveliness in the evenings and trim, graceful appearance in well-cut tweeds and yachting slacks that she was placed fifth among the Empire's smart women. Lady Furness thoroughly understands the art of dressing, has such great personal charm, and is so completely unconscious of her loveliness that she is always the complete and perfect picture. For evening wear, Lady Furness likes long, clinging lines which admirably set off her sylph-like figure.'

Enid's beauty was not just physical but the alluring combination of classical, statuesque looks and an attitude that bordered on indifference, an undefinable beauty identified by the novelist Elinor Glyn in 1927 who wrote: 'To have "It", the fortunate possessor must have that strange magnetism which attracts both sexes. He or she must be entirely unselfconscious and full of self-confidence, indifferent to the effect he or she is producing, and uninfluenced by others.'

Enid also embodied this description by Cecil Beaton, when he implored women: 'Be daring, be different, be impractical, be anything that will assert integrity of purpose and imaginative vision against the play-it-safers, the creatures of the commonplace, the slaves of the ordinary.'

The intrigue about Enid Furness and her lifestyle was only heightened by the frequent appearance in London of Thelma, the former Lady Furness, who insisted on continuing to use her married title. Enid and Thelma were rivals in a sense, at least for legitimacy, but they always seemed to keep their distance socially, moving in different circles and appearing in different publications.

Thelma's role in the Wallis Simpson affair had caused a sensation, and she was not shy when it came to publicity. If she was not commenting on the affair openly, then she was at least feeding behind-the-scenes titbits about the relationship and its genesis, first when Edward ascended the throne at the death of his father, George V, in 1936 and then when he abdicated ten months later amid a constitutional crisis.

In early January 1936, Averill Furness died. She passed away in a Nairobi nursing home and was buried quietly alongside her husband in the African bush. She was only twenty-seven years old. The utter waste of such a bright and adventurous life could hardly be captured in the succinct reports that appeared in newspapers on both sides of the Atlantic while her father, through intermediaries, could only say that he was too devastated to pay tribute to his daughter.

Most believed she had died of a broken heart (the official cause of death was acute heart failure) while the less charitable version offered by some was that she had drunk herself to an early grave. The one published comment, by an unnamed friend, about her marriage to Andrew Rattray and their life in the Kenyan wilderness—'They were absurdly happy together'—only highlighted the tragedy.

Duke could not be consoled. Over the years he had assured himself it would just be a matter of time before Averill would see the error of her ways and come home—home to the money.

But Averill was not interested in money. In fact she eschewed it and her estate, which she left to her brother Dick, amounted to just £1200, a pittance compared to the Furness family wealth.

Dick was a popular figure at Burrough Court when he came to visit. Pat recalled his bonhomie and acceptance of his father's third wife and her children. A tall and dashing cavalry officer with the Welsh Guards, he seemed to fill every day with some sort of adventure. He would take Pat on long rides, during which they risked injury and parental wrath to leap brush fences while he cried 'tally-ho', or he and Pat would track a mother fox in the winter snow to its lair and then lie quietly to watch her with her cubs before creeping away, leaving them untouched.

Dick had his issues with his father, and they were partly of his own making. During Duke's absences he would use Burrough Court as a location for drug-fuelled parties and orgies. All this came to a head one night when he and some of his guests decided to go fishing in the giant fish tanks that lined the billiard room. When the carnage was discovered, Duke banned his son from the house and threatened to disinherit him.

Enid calmed her husband down so far as the inheritance was concerned, but Dick never again set foot inside Burrough Court. This inevitable estrangement would later come back to haunt the older man.

Anthony, Duke's son with Thelma Morgan, was treated worse, if that was possible. Enid, having put aside her differences with Thelma, arranged for the boy to visit Burrough Court in 1937 and see his father for the first time since his parents' divorce. But Duke refused to meet 'the bastard', clinging to his belief that Tony, as he would become known, was not his son. He then turned on Enid, insisting that she shift her children, Pat and Caryll, to an apartment in Mayfair and that any visits by them to Burrough Court were made when he was away.

The death of Averill had made Marmaduke Furness shrink more into his hardened shell of self-loathing. His money gave him less and less pleasure, it seemed, as he descended into a darkening world, self-medicated by drugs and alcohol.

Things became even more complicated when Enid injured her back in a riding accident that left her bedridden for months and with a permanent 'knob' on her vertebrae that would remain a problem for the rest of her life. The injury caused another, more serious problem. Enid, who had always been teetotal, was given morphine for pain relief. Not only did she become addicted to the drug—an all-too-common response in the 1930s, by those who could afford it—but Marmaduke used the opportunity to find a doctor willing to prescribe morphine on demand, thereby gaining easier access. Fearing for his safety, Enid tried to get Scotland Yard involved but Duke, as a wealthy man, was able to find other means of obtaining what he needed.

Although Enid would eventually wean herself off opiates by seeking help, Duke persisted using them. What had begun as a romance of adulation with his wife had now become skewed into an almost constant fit of jealous rage. Where once he had adored men being mesmerised by Enid's grand entrances into a casino, he now saw only potential suitors—men like Hugh Grosvenor, the Duke of Westminster.

Bendor, as he was known, was a notorious womaniser who would marry four times and had a habit of placing diamonds under the pillow of his mistresses, among them the French fashion queen Coco Chanel, with whom he had a ten-year affair. Now aged in his mid-fifties, he had been living apart from his third wife, Loelia Ponsonby, for many years, and felt free to seduce other women, married or not.

Bendor had indeed been showering attention on Enid Furness who, while happy to encourage his interest, had resisted his advances. At least so far. Furness didn't believe it, and was particularly angry because his apparent rival not only carried one of the most senior aristocratic titles—unlike his own bestowed moniker—but was also one of the few men in England wealthier than him.

His anger finally bubbled over on 12 May 1937, as he and Enid prepared to attend the coronation of George VI. Enid, in particular, was excited at being one of the peeresses inside Westminster Abbey, herself regally dressed in flowing coronet robes of ermine and crimson velvet and a tiara of diamonds and pearls.

But Furness chose this moment to explode in a rage and to confront his wife over the alleged affair and then, when she dismissed the accusation, he went into a sulk and refused to attend. Enid's response was to declare that if he refused to accompany her then she would simply go on the arm of someone else—Hugh Grosvenor. She was in no mood to be judged by Marmaduke when she knew that he was playing games—with Thelma Morgan, with whom he had been socialising on the quiet.

'I left my husband when his divorced wife, Thelma, returned to him,' she would explain years later in interviews reported by several newspapers. 'He turned my two children out of the house. There wasn't room for the two of us, so I went to America.'

❦

Thelma Morgan was only too happy to let slip to the American media that her successor's marriage was on the rocks, or at least seemed to be going that way. By the time Enid arrived in New York in 1938, with Pat (Caryll was at boarding school) and a retinue of staff in tow, gossip columnists such as Maury Paul of the *San Francisco Examiner* were already speculating about her marriage and whether she would become the next Duchess of Westminster.

'If what I hear across the sea is true, prepare for some startling news in the household of Lord and Lady Furness,' he wrote. 'Matters are none too rosy with Lord Furness and his third wife, whom he wed following his divorce from the beautiful Thelma Morgan, sister of Mrs Reginald C. Vanderbilt. And they do say the discord in the Furness marital lute may—mind you, they say *may*—reach the British divorce courts. Should a divorce take place, they do say Lady Furness will annex another title, one even more glamorous than that of Furness.'

The barbs were easy enough for Enid to ignore, distracted by her chance meeting aboard the *Queen Mary* with film actor Gary Cooper, who struck up a conversation with Enid about their shared love of Kenya. The meeting turned into an invitation to Hollywood, where Pat was entranced when she saw Cooper filming a jungle scene for his latest movie; she recalled also watching Joan Crawford and Norma Shearer on the set of the film, *The Women*, which followed a group of rich Manhattan women and their worries about the fidelity of their husbands. The irony was lost on the thirteen-year-old.

But it was the wilds of America, rather than its man-made glamour, that would have the biggest impact on the teenager as her mother sought to relive her own arrival into the country more than twenty years before when she and her new husband, Roderick Cameron, took stagecoaches and trains across the vast continent and she became captivated by its natural beauty.

This was a cathartic journey for Enid in many ways: it was her first substantial contact with the surviving Cameron sisters, Catherine and Anne, since the death of their brother. Catherine—or Aunt Nanny, as Pat called her—would accompany them on their travels across America over the next few months. This included climbing down on horseback into the Grand Canyon, where they camped out for the night, and venturing into the Redwood forests of the Canadian Rockies, where they were confronted by a giant brown bear.

By the time they reached San Francisco in the early spring of 1939, the *San Francisco Examiner* had forgotten all about Enid's marital problems:

> Sinking with a sigh of relief into inviting arm chairs at the Palace, Thursday evening, were Mrs Robert Hays Smith and her two great friends, Lady Furness and Mrs Tiffany of Gotham,

who had returned to the hostelry after a full day of sightseeing under the able guidance of Sue Smith. I don't know if many persons are aware of the fact that Mrs Anne Cameron Tiffany and the beautiful Lady Furness are ex relations-in-law, for Enid Furness was at one time married to Mrs Tiffany's brother. This titled woman is an artist of considerable ability and her town house in London contains some murals executed by her own hand, which never fails to bring forth praise from guests and critics. In the house, too, is to be found the famous collection of Waterford glasses which Lord Furness has been many years in assembling and which is now considered about the finest in existence. Mrs Tiffany and Lady Furness left yesterday morning for Canada where they will tarry only briefly, for the latter is sailing shortly for England.

15

THE STING

Long before the French Riviera became a summer mecca for the well-heeled and lavishly oiled it was a place of winter rest and recuperation. Initially its fresh air was supposed to be ideal for tuberculosis sufferers, like the novelist and travel writer Tobias Smollett who, after an accidental visit in 1763, described Nice as 'sunshine paradise'.

A century later it had become a favourite escape from London's slate-grey skies, the place to be seen, even for a dour monarch like Queen Victoria, who arrived in 1882 with a retinue of a hundred staff and food supplies, and rode in a wagon pulled by a rescued donkey she named Jacquot. Her son, Edward VII, followed as did various European heads of state, aristocratic and political.

By the early twentieth century the rich and famous from all over Europe had bought many of the hillside farms and turned them into magnificent villas. Many of them travelled from London to Dover by the overnight sleeper from Victoria Station and then the ferry to Calais. From there they took the Calais-Mediterranée Express (now known as Le Train Bleu) south to Lyon, where they changed trains to head south to the coastal cities of Cannes, Nice and Monte Carlo. There, they spent their days playing golf or croquet, and their evenings in the casinos.

Even when sunbaking became popular, the winter season remained a favourite and it was here, in the overly warm January of 1939, that the Morgan sisters, Thelma and Gloria, rented a villa called Piccola Bella perched on the escarpment above Cannes and overlooking the Côte d'Azur.

It had been a difficult few years for the Morgan sisters, both of them entrenched in court battles over marriages and children. Gloria, especially, had been through a rough time; she was involved in an unseemly legal tussle over custody of her daughter, Gloria Jnr, whom she was accused of abandoning after the death of her husband, Reginald Vanderbilt.

This was true, at least to an extent. For much of the past five years she had left 'Little Gloria' in the care of a nanny and her sister-in-law, Gertrude Whitney, while she pursued her social agenda and hunt for a new beau. But when she formally applied to confirm her status as legal guardian, her own mother, Laura, objected. 'I'm doing this for the child's sake,' she told Gloria, warning her daughter not to fight against it because she had Vanderbilt money behind her.

The seven-week trial was a sensation. Gloria (her real name was Maria, but she adopted this new persona as a teenager, after becoming captivated by the sultry actress Gloria Swanson) was portrayed as a sex-mad and cocktail-crazed alcoholic, who wore silk pyjamas while reading pornography with rich boyfriends.

Laura Morgan, clutching a crucifix, testified to her daughter's 'shame'. She expressed fear that Gloria and one of her boyfriends, a German prince named Gottfried 'Friedel' Hohenlohe-Langenburg, to whom she was briefly engaged, were secretly plotting to orchestrate the death of her granddaughter so they could get their hands on her inheritance.

Then came the testimony of a series of staff—among them the butler, a maid and the nanny—who told stories of debauched behaviour observed through keyholes and open doors. The most damning story came from a maid who one morning saw Gloria in bed reading a newspaper while being kissed by another woman, Lady Milford-Haven, who immediately denied the suggestion of a lesbian affair.

The newspapers lapped it up, not only gleefully publishing the salacious details of Gloria's alleged behaviour—'an erotic interest in women'—but splashing on their front pages photographs of the distressed ten-year-old girl—a 'solemn-eyed pawn', as one writer described her—forcing her way through crowds to get into the courtroom.

It was a haunting memory that would remain with the young girl, through into her mid-nineties: 'I had no one to talk to except through lawyers', she said in a newspaper interview in

2012. 'It was difficult and horrible and took a long time to get over.'

And her mother? Was she as bad as the Vanderbilts suggested? 'I really never knew my mother. I never bonded with her unfortunately. She told me that she was always afraid to pick me up as a baby because I might break.'

When the court decided to make the girl a ward of the state and grant custody to the Vanderbilt family, Gloria was labelled an unfit mother who could only be trusted with her daughter on weekends. The decision also left her without a secure income from her daughter's trust fund, which was worth $US4 million (the modern equivalent would be around $US400 million). Gloria's meal ticket—as she regarded her daughter, the cynics suggested—was no more.

But not everyone was against her. The *New York Journal America* published a ditty that picked up on the hypocrisy of the decision:

Rockabye baby
up on a writ,
Monday to Friday
mother's unfit,
As the week ends she rises in virtue,
Saturdays, Sundays, mother won't hurt you.

Thelma too relied on motherhood for financial security. But, unlike her sister, Lady Furness had not only retained the use of her married name when she divorced Marmaduke Furness but also the custody of her son, Tony, who was now almost ten years old. As his guardian, she received a healthy income from her 1933 divorce settlement.

But it was not enough to cover their extravagant lifestyles. Thelma, in particular, was frequently travelling between London and New York. 'They practically commute across the Atlantic,' one newspaper profile gushed. 'The sisters are constantly on the front pages and continue to be wooed by men of wealth and position.'

They went into business with a dressmaker named Sonia Rosenberg, who designed and made expensive gowns. The role of Thelma and Gloria was as 'pullers-in', organising swank parties at which their rich friends would buy dresses. But their attempts to cash in on their fame fell flat.

It proved a tough sell in the middle of the Great Depression and the business collapsed in 1938 with the sisters and Sonia Rosenberg blaming each other for the failure. This would lead to yet another court case, during which their partying habits were again exposed; they were accused of turning up drunk to the New York shop and taking dresses for their own use.

The judge reserved his decision so he could ponder it over the 1938 Yuletide and so the sisters had withdrawn to Cannes to contemplate their situation and their futures. Now aged in their mid-thirties, the identical beauties were both young enough to catch a new husband, if only their reputations—one a twice-divorced seductress and the other a merry widow—could be put aside. It seemed to run in the family. Their older sister, Consuelo, had similar form: her first marriage to a French count ended in divorce because of her affair with a US diplomat, whom she wed six months later. Unlike her sisters, she had no children but she still referred to herself as a countess.

But here in Europe the Morgan sisters were not judged. After all, the adulterous games they played were par for the course among the elite. Marriages were often regarded as no more than contracts of convenience between families or a means to have children. Love and lust were another matter, if treated with discretion.

By March, Gloria had been lured back to New York but Thelma was in no mood to return to a cold and empty London. Instead she remained basking in the Mediterranean warmth and the explosion of colour as the mimosa trees bloomed early and covered the hillsides in gold. 'The skies had never been so blue, the sun never so bright,' she would write.

According to her later memoir, Thelma received a telephone call from Marmaduke Furness one evening in April. Enid had left him and gone to America with her daughter, he declared, and he had decided to go to Cannes. What a happy coincidence that Thelma was close by. He was staying at the Carlton Hotel and, if he sent his car the next day to pick her up, would she have lunch with him?

This version was, of course, manufactured. Thelma had known about Enid's departure many months before and had almost certainly alerted the American media to it. The phone call from Duke was hardly a surprise, given that one of the reasons for Enid's trip was because of Thelma's renewed friendship with him.

But her account of what occurred on this day was true. Of course, she would love to have lunch with her ex-husband, she told Duke. After all, how could she ignore the opportunity to talk about the woman who had taken her place and bask in Enid and Duke's marital woes.

As promised, the car was sent and took her to the same restaurant, the Réserve de Beaulieu, between Monaco and Nice, they had frequented on their honeymoon more than a decade before. A divorce with Enid was in the offing, Duke told her as they sat down, but he gave no more details, although he was clearly upset at the notion.

Thelma decided not to press for more information and the matter was dropped for the rest of the lunch, which was spent talking about family, friends and good times. Thelma felt as if their past troubles were behind them as they got back into Duke's car for the return trip to Cannes, but then things suddenly changed.

Duke became agitated. The cool persona over lunch was replaced by a jittery man who appeared to be in pain, nervously reaching inside his sleeve and fiddling with his kerchief. She asked what was wrong, but he refused to say and the further they drove the worse things became. Was it a sudden illness? she wondered.

When Duke began to bite his knuckles, she asked what was wrong again, but he turned away, his brow now soaked in sweat. Instead of accepting a ride back to Piccola Bella, Thelma determinedly followed him to his hotel suite, where he began calling for his valet. When the man did not appear, Duke took off his jacket and rolled up his sleeve. He turned to his former wife. 'Can you give me a *piqure*,' he asked, using the French drug addict parlance for an injection of morphine—a *sting*.

Thelma panicked when he offered her a hypodermic needle. She backed away. 'I can't, Duke. I can't do it.'

Duke held out the syringe again. 'Please, Thelma. I need it. Please help me.'

It was frightening for Thelma to see him like this—a man normally so decisive and powerful, if overly angry, now reduced to a pleading mess. 'I don't know how,' she said. 'What do I do?'

Duke gave up. He needed the injection now. 'Just pinch my arm here and I'll insert the needle.'

Thelma complied, tentatively, and was grateful to see the needle sink into his arm. Duke sighed and sank back onto a couch. The pain had passed, at least temporarily. When the missing valet appeared a few minutes later, he took Duke into the bedroom, where he drifted off to sleep.

Over the next few weeks Thelma visited Duke almost daily as he remained holed up in his hotel room. It was clear that he was ill, mentally and physically, and that the marriage problems with Enid were exacerbating his condition. He was also a man haunted by his own failures as a father: the loss of his daughter and the growing distance between him and his eldest son.

Thelma resisted raising the issue of their son, Tony, who Duke still refused to acknowledge or see. Likewise, he refused to address the issues raised by the morphine injections or his drinking habits. There seemed little she could do.

They were having lunch one day when the phone rang. It was Duke's secretary in London—Enid was on her way back.

16

AN ULTIMATUM

When Enid returned to Burrough Court she had been told that Duke was gambling in the casinos of Le Touquet. Rather than follow him to France, as he might have expected, she wanted her husband to come grovelling to her.

In spite of their troubles, she wanted the marriage to continue. She believed that he loved her, or at least desired her, and that was enough because, despite his faults, she loved him too and their life which was a constant whirr of adventures. Besides, she was trapped by her ill-considered decision to hand over the Cameron fortune in return for Duke's financial support. Divorce was difficult enough, especially for women, without the fear that she might forfeit her financial lifeline.

Enid arranged, via her loyal secretary, for a telegram to be wired to Duke informing him that she had returned and was distraught by his absence. She then ensured that concerned friends rang him to say they were worried about her state of mind, even hinting that she was about to do herself harm. Having laid the bait, she disappeared.

Enid was miffed more than distraught, and wanted to test Duke's feelings and responses to her manufactured plight. She had no intention of self-harm. On the contrary, she checked into a London clinic for cosmetic surgery.

'Beauty surgery' had become the rage among the wealthy and famous, lured by the promise of almost instant revitalised youth and comforted by testimonies from stage actresses that recovery from surgery was a matter of days, sometimes just hours.

The techniques had grown out of work pioneered by New Zealand surgeon Harold Gillies, who'd been knighted for his restorative work on soldiers injured during the Great War, rebuilding and remoulding thousands of faces twisted and reduced to shapeless pulp in the horrors of trench warfare.

After the war Gillies and a handful of other surgeons, including his cousin Archibald McIndoe, turned their skills to private practice, not just to treat medical deformities and the victims of accidents but for purely cosmetic reasons, arguing to cynical colleagues that it was a legitimate way of keeping the practice alive and developing.

By the mid-1930s prominent members of society, including the aristocracy, were paying hefty fees for this Cinderella surgery, correcting double chins, reshaping noses and smoothing wrinkles and creases, even having stomach tucks. Their reasons varied: from sheer vanity to a professional need to look youthful rather than jaded. Ageing wives feared being cast aside by errant husbands searching for a younger model.

Enid fell somewhere in between. She was a 47-year-old woman who had always relied on her physical beauty, but now sensed the inevitable waning of those powers. She had the discomforting notion that she might lose a third husband, one who had laid the world at her feet but was now wavering.

She could use clothes to accentuate her still-lithe figure and to hide her body's signs of ageing. Makeup was an effective cover for skin flaws and beautiful jewellery distracted and flattered, as did an attitude that radiated confidence and style. But ultimately Enid would be betrayed by something that couldn't be concealed—her eyes. What previously had been her most striking physical assets were changing, not in colour but in shape and vitality.

The solution was a process called blepharoplasty. It was relatively simple surgery, she had been told, in which the skin above the eyes was slit open like a small bag so the excess fat inside could be removed. Each lid was then sewn up and tightened so it had the effect of causing the lid to lift, hiding any scarring and removing the hooded or droopy eyelids that were a tell-tale sign of age.

The surgery went ahead without a hitch but the next morning Archibald McIndoe got the shock of his life when he walked into the clinic ward to find his patient in bed with a pair of foxes curled up on the pillow. Enid was making herself at home, wallowing in the luxury of being pampered by an army of clinic staff and in no hurry to leave. Although there would soon be reason to do so.

Later that day Enid had another visitor. The chastened Duke, informed that his wife was in hospital, had returned home.

❧

Although they were back together, the trust on both sides had been worn to a thread. Duke was now wary and Thelma was taking delight in exploring the fragility of the relationship, particularly the gulf that lay between her former husband and Enid's children, who rarely saw their stepfather.

Enid's healthy relationship with her children frustrated Duke, particularly her closeness to her eldest son Rory, who was now twenty-five; he behaved more like a confidant and his mother's protector than a son. It made the older man jealous, not only because it seemed to create a barrier between him and his wife but because it was in such marked contrast to his own, distant relationship with his son Dick, who was a similar age.

Duke was also jealous of Enid's relationship with Pat. It was a painful reminder of his unnecessary estrangement from the tragic Averill, whose death hung over him like a pall.

In spite of their doubts and troubles, Enid persuaded Duke to head back to Le Touquet, where she would have a better chance of keeping him away from drugs and in particular a man named Motz who was now his main supplier. She had reported Motz to the police but it seemed there was little they could do other than warn him off.

In Le Touquet, she could keep Duke distracted as they mingled with the glitterati who gathered there each year for champagne summers in hotels such as the Royal Picardy, dubbed the world's most beautiful hotel with its 500 rooms, private staff, riding trails and swimming pools.

It was here that the Prince of Wales was filmed dancing with Mrs Simpson; the novelist H.G. Wells stole away with Amber Reeves, one of his mistresses; and a young Princess Elizabeth learned how to sand-yacht. Crazy airmen scattered the crowds along the beach with daredevil manoeuvres and the Dolly Sisters, the most famous vaudeville act of the day, strolled on the boardwalk with pet tortoises, flashing matching four-carat blue diamond rings.

But there was no togetherness for Enid and Duke. Instead, he returned to the casino tables while Enid took sanctuary at the golf club and entertained her brother Grant and his wife who had been in Europe on a six-month holiday.

Duke favoured the prestige and extravagance of the Barrière Casino, in the centre of the town; its rococo interiors of white and gilt and its heavy curtains to keep out the daylight would later inspire the fictional *Casino Royale* setting for the James Bond novel by Ian Fleming. The casino building had twice been rebuilt after mysterious fires—not unlike Duke's own matrimonial history.

It was also the place where he'd first met and been entranced by a vampish Enid, although that irony would likely have been lost in his bad mood as he buried his self-pity in the fug of cigar smoke and the low lights of the roulette tables, where he watched young and idle aristocrats frittering away their family fortunes. Duke played as a means of distraction from an otherwise meaningless life, rather than from a compulsion to gamble.

Caryll and Pat went to Le Touquet too and, as usual, travelled separately from their mother and stepfather. Pat recalled being picked up at the back gate of Burrough Court, where they had been making a rare visit, by a limousine and driven to the airstrip at the back of the property. As the plane took off, their governess, Miss Unger, told Pat and her brother to look out of the window: 'Take one last look at Burrough Court,' she said, 'because you will never see it again.'

Although Pat, aged fourteen, didn't recognise it at the time, Miss Unger's comment was a prediction about the impact of a looming war, which was only a few weeks from being declared. And she was right.

Wealthy British holidaymakers had ignored the doomsayers and travelled to France for the summer of 1939, preferring to believe that Adolf Hitler was merely a political upstart, whose aspirations to invade Poland would be dealt with quickly. Besides, they were protected by the Maginot Line, a series of concrete fortifications and gun positions built at the French borders with Italy, Switzerland, Germany and Luxembourg to thwart any invasion attempt by Germany. It would prove to be a false sense of security.

Enid and Duke counted the author P.G. Wodehouse, creator of the iconic Jeeves and Wooster novels, and his wife Ethel among their close circle of friends in Le Touquet. The Wodehouses, who lived next door, had both recently made headlines: Ethel winning handsomely at the roulette table while her husband lost.

Not that they needed money. Although far from as wealthy as Furness, Wodehouse was reputedly earning £100,000 a year in royalties and busy writing his forty-fourth novel, *Joy in the Morning*, which marked the return of his famous Bertie Wooster stories.

The Wodehouses would be among the few English residents of the town to refuse to leave when the war began. This was a decision that almost destroyed the novelist's career because it was later interpreted, wrongly, as the act of a Nazi sympathiser. The reason they stayed behind was because they didn't want to leave Fred, their pet dachshund.

Pat and Caryll spent their days riding horses through the pine forests that bordered the house or motoring with Rory, who joined them in a rare visit, through nearby towns. One morning while riding on the beach with her groom, Pat watched as a Hurricane aircraft, stationed at a nearby RAF base, crash-landed on the sands nearby. The pilot crawled from the wreckage and ran towards them, trying to shed his burning flying jacket, which had turned him into a human torch. The groom tried to smother the flames, but the pilot died.

Pat saw little of her stepfather, whose rare appearances only made her feel anxious. On one particular day he arranged to have one of her dogs put down because it was making too much noise. Her mother intervened and stopped the killing, but the dog had to be given away so Duke wouldn't find out it had been spared. 'I had always disliked him but now I hated him,' Pat wrote.

It was no surprise that Furness was absent from a family portrait, later published in the social pages of the *Sydney Morning Herald*, in which Enid posed outside the villa with

Rory, now taller than his mother, at her shoulder and her arms protectively around two hesitant teenagers, Pat and Caryll.

A few days after the photograph was taken, she and Duke left the children in the care of Miss Unger and set out for Monte Carlo; it was supposed to be a chance for them to be alone and sort out their differences. They booked into the Hôtel de Paris, which kept a portrait of Enid at the foot of its main staircase, but it was only a matter of time before Furness's jealousy reared its head.

One night at the casino he became enraged when he saw another gambler flirting with Enid, a situation he once enjoyed. Unbelievably, he challenged the man to a duel—pistols at dawn—and intended going through with the ultimatum.

According to his personal staff, he kept repeating 'I'm going to shoot the bugger' over and over as he stomped around the hotel suite. They told Pat about this when she and Caryll arrived at the hotel a few days later.

Their normally serene mother was distraught. Duke, now aged 55, had been practising with a pistol; he was apparently a good shot and he planned to wound rather than kill his alleged love rival. But his hands were shaking terribly, as much from alcohol and drug abuse as from rage, and Enid feared it would affect his aim.

For once, she wasn't guilty of flirting, Enid told her daughter. The man in question was a well-known ladies' man and had indeed been pursuing her around the casino, but she had given him no encouragement.

Desperate to end the conflict, she delivered an ultimatum to Duke. She had rented a villa near the city of Nice and she would take the children there for the rest of the summer. Duke could follow if he wished, or stay and carry out his threat. But if he did stay, then the marriage was finally over, even if she had to risk losing the Cameron money.

17

LA FIORENTINA

Marmaduke Furness had relented in his threat to shoot a man, put his pistols away and trailed after his wife, offering to buy her a summer palace as a sign of his love. There was another version of this story, that Enid had won £20,000 at the casino one night and decided to invest by buying a house on the Riviera.

Either way, Enid had set her sights on one of the most spectacular villas on the Riviera. La Leopolda, built into a hillside above the seafront village of Beaulieu-sur-Mer between Nice and Monaco, was for sale, as were numerous others, their wealthy owners now fearful of losing everything as the war loomed closer.

But the villa once owned by King Leopold II of Belgium wasn't for Enid. Too formal and too far from the sea, she decided within a week of arriving. As Rory would recall: 'Properties on the Riviera in the late thirties were easy to find and the prices comparatively reasonable. It was a question, really, of elimination and on what part of the coast one wanted to be. It took my mother about six weeks to find her ideal; a house right at the end of Pointe de Saint-Hospice with enough land around it to assure complete privacy.'

Enid's choice would change her life. La Fiorentina stood on the edge of the world, or so it appeared, perched on the cliff edge of Cap Ferrat, a forested peninsula jutting out into the Mediterranean between Nice and Monte Carlo.

There was also an Australian connection. The villa had been owned by Sir Edmund Davis, a Melbourne-born diamond magnate who had died a few months before at the age of seventy-six. His widow had no love of the Riviera and no use for the grandeur, so the villa was for sale.

La Fiorentina was a wild paradise, the grounds covered with pines, citrus and olive trees, built in the last years of the Great War by a French countess named Thérèse de Beauchamp who had dreamed of a seafront palace.

The main house was designed to make the most of the view: a loggia of arcades and belvedere turrets, and grand reception rooms with views across the Ligurian Sea toward the coastline of northern Italy. Outside there were not one, but two swimming pools surrounded by thematic, sculptured gardens and cloisters; the back of the house faced the open sea and there were other views toward a sheltered bay and across to the beaches of Nice and the famous Promenade des Anglais.

The rear gardens were dominated by an avenue of cypress pines guarding a great marble staircase that descended to the water's edge, ending in what Rory, in his 1975 memoir *The Golden Riviera*, described as 'a tangle of stone pines tortured by the wind into weird Rackham-like shapes', referring to Arthur Rackham's famously haunting Brothers Grimm illustrations. 'It was for these trees that I believe my mother really bought the place,' he noted.

Countess de Beauchamp had named the villa Fiorentina in homage to her father, Count Philippe Vitali of Nice, whose own home shared the same name, but the villa's construction would be marred by family tragedy. Her son Francois was killed at Verdun in 1917 and then, in the last days of the war, her husband, Robert, also died on the battlefield.

It is not surprising then that, by the time La Fiorentina was completed in 1920, Countess de Beauchamp had grown tired and disillusioned of her dream and it was sold to Davis, who used it as a summer residence until age and ill-health limited his travel. The magnificent property was left fully furnished and empty until Enid Lindeman drove through the gates, still emblazoned with the de Beauchamp family motto, 'Destiny rules the world'. She fell in love with it immediately.

There were several houses on the property which, in Duke's now paranoid mind, created a physical barrier between his wife and any future suitor, who might have bought one of the neighbouring villas to be near her. The children were moved into one of the smaller houses, an old stone farmhouse called Le Clos, out of sight while Duke and Enid occupied the main building.

Duke was now very clearly a sick man—drug-addled and depressed. He was fuelled by the paranoid belief that Enid would be taken from him by a younger, richer or more handsome man. He spent his days in the darkness of his new bedroom, uninterested in the spectacular surroundings; his nights were spent drinking and gambling in the local casinos.

But his mood lifted as summer turned to autumn and as Enid persuaded him to begin entertaining at home with quiet dinner parties. She invited guests to stay, often for a week or more.

If Le Touquet felt like a British holiday camp then the Riviera was its sophisticated European cousin. There were English visitors, of course, mostly from the world of arts and politics; among them were Charlie Chaplin and the novelist Somerset Maugham, both of whom had bought nearby villas, and the playwright Noël Coward, who penned one of his most famous songs, 'I Went to a Marvellous Party', based on five parties he attended at Cap Ferrat hosted by the American social queen Elsa Maxwell and attended by Belgravia's visiting glitterati and neighbours including Enid. The lyrics reveal the wild and carefree nature of the drug and alcohol-fuelled events—'with Maud at Cap Ferrat'—where nobody cared what was worn, and sexual abandonment was common.

Maud, of course, was Enid's middle name.

Pat, aged fourteen and almost forgotten in the adult drama unfolding around her, would bury herself through her teenage years in the Regency romantic novels of writers like Georgette Heyer and Jean Plaidy, and thrilled at the Western adventures of Zane Grey and the Scarlet Pimpernel stories of Baroness Orczy. 'I immersed myself in these books,' she would write many years later. 'They were a refuge for a shy girl in a household with such larger-than-life figures as Furness, my beautiful mother and my bossy and sophisticated brother Rory.'

She spent her days cycling and roaming the fishing village of Saint-Jean-Cap-Ferrat at the base of the peninsula, sometimes with a young English maid named Hannah, where they would flirt with the young fishermen, in the first flush of teenage love. In the evenings she would ride back up to the main house to have dinner with her mother while her stepfather kept to his room.

Pat watched, intrigued and alarmed at the strange procession of guests who would pass through the house that year, including a Belgian couple—Jews who had fled south to escape the German Army. They would not be the last refugees to whom Enid offered sanctuary, either oblivious to the risks she was taking by being identified as a Jewish supporter or, more likely, relishing the audacity and refusing to bow to oppression.

There were many visitors. Enid loved to invite artists, writers and musicians. The stranger the better, like Leonor Fini, the famed Argentinian surrealist painter and friend of Salvador Dali. She arrived with two male lovers, one black and the other white, and was given two bedrooms to accommodate her sexual habits. At night Leonor dressed in long white clinging dresses and walked around the house, captivated by her own voluptuous reflection in the giant mirrors adorning each room.

She painted Enid's portrait as a thank you: a wild and powerful image of a defiant woman with steel-blue eyes and set jaw, her arms folded and hands gloved, as if prepared for a fight. Her silken gown and silver hair were tugged by the wind that sometimes blew across the bay. Was this a stand against Germany or an observation by Fini, known for her portraits of powerful women, about the challenges Enid faced in her private life?

More confronting was a woman friend of Duke's, a countess who began behaving more and more strangely. One day Pat found her crawling around the main reception room, salivating and calling out: '*Mon Dieu, mon Dieu, c'est cache.*' The woman was a morphine addict and desperate for a hit but Enid, in her efforts to nurse Duke back to health, had cut off any drug supplies.

The purchase of La Fiorentina and its three outbuildings for only £20,000 was completed just before Germany invaded Poland. But rather than flee back to London, Enid and Duke made the decision to remain, believing they were safe for the moment. The house needed renovations and there was always the option of returning to England by boat from Marseilles if events became more serious. Many of their new friends and neighbours, including 'Willy' Maugham, made the same decision.

Caryll was sent back to London when his new school year began while Rory, an American citizen, decided to go to the States and enlist. He would later be transferred to the Office of Strategic Services, the forerunner of the CIA, and was stationed in London where he joined British Intelligence because he spoke fluent French and German.

It would be three years before Pat saw either of her brothers again.

18

LOOKING-GLASS WORLD

Christopher 'Dick' Furness arrived in Cannes in early June 1939, not to see his father but to stay with his former stepmother.

Years later Thelma Morgan would write of her delight at the moment when he arrived at Piccola Bella: 'As spring gave way to summer, Dick arrived by car with his valet. My handsome, gay, debonair stepson seemed more charming than ever.'

Life was about to take a dangerous turn, if it hadn't already done so. Dick, who had recently turned twenty-seven, was only seven years younger than his father's ex-wife and, if her later musings about him were any indication, then there was a clear physical attraction between them, one that had been brewing for some time if not already consummated.

Hints of the future affair are evident when she reminisces about their first meeting in 1926, when she was aged twenty-one and had just begun a relationship with his father: 'When we entered the drawing room, the only person there was a handsome boy of fourteen, tall and slender with the merriest blue eyes and reddest red hair,' she wrote in her autobiography before detailing how the pair had chatted over a breakfast of porridge, kippers and hot scones—'I ate almost as much as Dick did [and] for some reason this pleased him'—and then walked together to view a new stag pony his father had bought him. She was entranced, not just by his looks but by his open nature: 'This boy I was to get to know and love so much.'

And now Dick was a boy no longer; and Thelma was no longer his stepmother. Despite her history with older men—of loving them, being squired by them and marrying them—she had now fallen for a younger man and one who, by social convention, should have been off-limits.

Dick would stay for almost two months, during which he even threw a surprise party for her thirty-fifth birthday. He was apparently unconcerned about the response of friends to their relationship or, worse, that Duke might find out about the affair.

'It was a gala party,' Thelma recalled two decades later, adding, 'the last we would know on the Riviera for a long, long while.' But any hopes for a bright future ended the next morning, when Dick appeared at breakfast with a telegram in his hand; he was being ordered to return immediately to London, where he was expected to report to his regiment, the Welsh Guards.

Dick and Thelma left the villa and drove back to Paris, where they got caught up in the crush to get out of Europe. There would be no transport for a week, until the British Ambassador to France, Sir Eric Phipps, intervened and managed to get them aboard an already overcrowded boat filled with fleeing families. They spent an uncomfortable night on deck as the unsteady boat made its way across the Channel.

Men wielding loudspeakers greeted them at the Dover docks the next morning, blaring news of an imminent declaration of war as Dick and Thelma disembarked and hurried back to London. Here the lovers parted; he would leave for France a few weeks later.

Thelma would not see Dick for five months, until one morning in early March 1940 when he returned for two weeks' leave. 'My maid announced that Lieutenant Furness was downstairs. I rushed to Dick and threw myself into his arms.'

'Can you put me up?' he asked her.

'Could I? As if I would let you stay in any place but my home.'

Although her words could be read simply, as an adoring and somewhat smitten former stepmother, the fact that Dick chose to spend his leave with Thelma suggests otherwise. This was a full-blown love affair. Duke believed so when he eventually found out, going into a fit of rage and, once again, threatening to disinherit his son.

Thelma seemed to blame the surreal nature of war for her relationship with Dick. 'The war had turned everything into a queer, unreal, looking-glass world, with everybody and everything topsy-turvy,' she wrote later, 'yet Dick seemed the same old Dick—gay, happy, without a care in the world. Whatever he saw was "a jolly good show", even the war.'

Petrol rationing meant they couldn't escape from the quiet

gloom of London, whose inhabitants waited, fearfully, for the expected German bombardment. Instead, they took long walks around the city and along the Thames, happy in each other's company. The two weeks passed quickly and he prepared to head back to the front in the Somme, where the British Army lay in wait for the enemy.

'I saw him off,' she would write in her memoir. 'How handsome he looked in his uniform, leaning out of the train window waving his cap, the wind rumpling his auburn hair.'

According to one newspaper interview she gave later, the pair had even discussed marriage. A date was set for late July 1940, when Dick was next due to take leave.

Dick Furness's leave had ended just as Germany began its invasion of Belgium and France. He was immediately sent to the battlefront, a lieutenant in command of a carrier platoon of the Welsh Guards which formed part of the garrison at Arras, a key town in northern France. It was from here that the Allied forces were attempting, through a series of counter-attacks, to frustrate German advances.

On 17 May 1940 Dick spent his twenty-eighth birthday patrolling the Allied perimeter, where there were frequent exchanges of tank- and gunfire. Every day could be his last. His actions prompted this official assessment: 'Lieutenant Furness displayed the highest qualities of leadership and dash on all these occasions and imbued his command with a magnificent offensive spirit.'

On the evening of 23 May, Dick was wounded, shot in the arm while on patrol, but he refused to be evacuated. The moment was critical because German reinforcements had arrived and, with growing confidence, had begun to encircle the town. The Allied forces were in danger of being trapped, their only escape route being toward the town of Douai, 25 kilometres to the east.

Just before midnight, commanding officers received orders to evacuate. The withdrawal was set for 2 a.m.—orders issued to 'Wake up, get up, pack up'—and plans set to walk the men and their equipment out of the town without alerting the enemy. The key was to leave quietly and avoid alerting the German units, which were on the move.

The garrison had all left Arras before daybreak. The convoy then split up, with the Northumberland Fusiliers using a side road while the main body of troops, several hundred in number and including Dick's platoon, stayed on the widest road so as to accommodate their forty or so heavy vehicles.

They had been lucky. The previous few nights had been lit by a full moon and clear skies but on this morning there was a thick mist over the River Scarpe, which the road followed. But how long would it last?

The convoy had travelled 5 kilometres out of the town when it was suddenly halted by the sound of gunfire from up ahead. It came from an outlying German machine-gun post, which had begun firing as the first line of Allied soldiers appeared through the mist.

The Germans had dug into high ground overlooking the

road, wedged between a copse and ringed by barbed wire. It would take valuable time to take them out, time the Allied soldiers could ill afford because the German Army behind had begun to advance on Arras and would soon discover the town had been abandoned. They had to find another way out before the sun rose and the skies cleared.

It was then that Dick Furness stepped forward, offering to distract the enemy ahead while the convoy turned around on the rutted track and made their escape using the same road as the Fusiliers. The quartermaster would later report that Furness told him: 'Don't worry about Jerry. I'll go and shoot him up and keep him busy while you turn and get out.'

'Then he went off in the direction of the firing,' the officer added.

In spite of his own wounds, Lieutenant Furness personally led the attack, crouched inside the first of three armoured personnel carriers, each armed with a Bren gun that could be fired through a slit in the carrier's metal plating. Machines normally used for carrying soldiers and towing equipment across difficult ground had suddenly become attack vehicles. They rumbled toward the German line while several small tanks provided cover fire from a distance.

The audacity of the move took the Germans by surprise and they fell back, giving the Allied main column the breathing space it needed to begin turning the convoy. But the lull did not last long, and the Germans soon opened up with heavy machine-gun fire and anti-tank guns, disabling the tanks, which burst into flames.

Furness did not pull back. Instead, he drove his carrier forward. The other two followed and, despite the continued bombardment, they managed to reach the German position, which they began circling and firing at, 'causing heavy losses on the enemy', according to one account.

But it was just a matter of time. The other two carriers were hit, and their crews killed or wounded and later taken prisoner. Dick's carrier was then hit, killing the 22-year-old driver, James Berry, and twenty-year-old gunner, John Daley.

Dick Furness survived. Now alone, he scrambled clear of the wreck. One soldier saw him lying on top of the carrier, firing the Bren gun before he stood up and charged the German post in a gallant but futile attempt to overpower the remaining enemy soldiers.

Dick would be awarded the highest of honours, the Victoria Cross, for his bravery—'gallantry in the presence of the enemy'. The citation would say of his final moments: 'He then engaged the enemy in personal hand-to-hand combat until he was killed. His magnificent act of self-sacrifice against hopeless odds, and when already wounded, made the enemy withdraw for the time being and enabled the large column of vehicles to get clear unmolested and covered the evacuation of some of the wounded of his own Carrier Platoon and the light tanks.'

In his 1946 book *Welsh Guards at War*, Major Lionel Ellis concluded: 'The fight of the carriers had not been in vain, for while it was taking place the company of the Fusiliers was extricated and the transport of the 1st Battalion Welsh Guards moved safely to another road.' Lieutenant the Honourable

Christopher Furness and his men had sacrificed their own lives to save their battalion from being wiped out.

But was he dead?

At first Dick was reported as missing in action and, although it seemed clear to those few witnesses that he was fighting to the death, there was always the possibility that he might have been captured.

Duke was bedridden at La Fiorentina, so Enid took hold of the telegram when it arrived a week later with its news that Dick was missing, presumed dead. She knew that, despite his previous anger about his son, her husband would take the news badly. Was it better to tell him now or wait until Dick's death had been confirmed? She decided to wait until the news was more definitive.

19

RIVIERA REFUGEES

When German Panzer tanks rumbled beneath the Arc de Triomphe and down the Champs-Élysées on 14 June 1940 the reality of Adolf Hitler's power finally hit home to the foreigners living in the south of France.

Until now, life under the cloud of war on the Riviera had been pleasant enough. Rationing had been less severe than in Paris or London and, as the weather warmed toward summer, the bars, casinos and hotels began to reopen to a clientele of French holidaymakers, British and American tourists and soldiers on leave. Such was the optimism that city officials even ran competitions to attract visitors while the English fashion designer Edward Molyneux released a new pleated frock for the season.

But the fall of Paris changed everything. The forlorn hope that Hitler could be stopped had gone. The French Army had been decimated and 338,000 British soldiers rescued from the beaches of Dunkirk by a flotilla of 800 boats.

The world was dark, even on the beaches of the Riviera, which would soon be under siege. The bright lights of Nice, Cannes and Monte Carlo were flicked off and the usual sound of revelry was replaced by the noise of warplanes and heavy gunfire from the Italian coast.

Somerset Maugham was still in his villa at Cap Ferrat when the news broke. It was time to leave. The British Government was sending two ships to Cannes to bring back its last 1300 or so citizens from southern France and he intended to be on it.

Maugham was worried that others, including Duke and Enid, with whom he had become close, might hold out. He pleaded with Enid to join him, insisting that the risk to Duke's health was not as great as the likelihood that they would be interned. And she also had her daughter's safety to consider.

The novelist would recall his increasingly desperate conversations with neighbours at this time in *Strictly Personal*, a memoir he wrote the following year: 'When I was asked, point-blank, what I thought was the likelihood of our reaching England safely, I was obliged to say that I didn't think there was more than a fifty-fifty chance; but I pointed out that if they stayed there was the risk of internment; it would be impossible for them to get money and there might be a shortage of food. I left them to decide for themselves whether they thought the risk was worth taking. I went home.'

Maugham's entreaty worked. Enid and a reluctant Duke agreed to leave. Restrictions on the boat from Cannes meant they were allowed only one suitcase and a blanket each, as well as provisions for three days. For a woman who often travelled with a dozen cases, it meant that most of Enid's possessions would have to be left at La Fiorentina in the care of their local staff and in the faint hope that she might one day be able to return.

On the morning of their departure, Furness was carried to the Bentley by his chauffeur and slumped in the back, drinking from a hipflask. Pat hadn't seen him for weeks and he looked terrible. He was normally so careful about his appearance, dressed by his valet every morning in a new shirt with a matching tie, and yet he barely noticed that he was spilling brandy on his sleeve.

Once they reached Cannes, they sat in the Carlton Hotel eating lunch and waiting to board one of two cargo ships that had docked in the port across the bay. Furness was becoming more agitated as time went by, his hand shaking so badly that the crockery rattled.

Enid began feeding her husband soup and tried to calm him. 'Darling, don't get so upset,' she soothed. 'Once we are onboard it won't be so bad. At least we will be amongst friends.'

Furness looked angrily at his wife. 'They're not my fucking friends,' he barked. 'They are all your bloody friends and that is not a ship; it is a fucking cargo boat. If you are so worried about your safety, you can go with your bloody friends and take that little bitch with you. I'm not going.'

He was referring to Pat, who sat at the table. It was one of the few times she had ever shared a meal with her stepfather and she had been transfixed by his neat hands and nails, which were buffed three times a day by his valet. Although she was used to his swearing, the words stung.

Enid persuaded her daughter to leave the room and wait in another lounge. When she joined her, Enid had decided to stay behind and send Pat back to London with Maugham. 'Darling, you must understand that I cannot leave Duke. He is too ill to travel and he wouldn't survive the trip. Willy is to take care of you on the boat and see you get to safety back at Burrough Court.'

Pat could not believe that her mother would make her go alone and began screaming. 'The thought of having to leave my beloved mother was more than I could bear,' she remembered. 'I clung to her in such a frenzy of despair that Mummy, in the end, had to agree to let me stay. Once she had promised I could remain, nothing else mattered.'

Maugham ended up onboard the smaller of the two ships with 500 others, most of whom had escaped with little but the clothes they were wearing. The ships, which had been commandeered after dropping loads of coal at Marseilles, were not equipped or prepared for hundreds of passengers, who had to sleep on the decks and in the holds below.

The elderly suffered most from the coal dust, and there was a water and food shortage. As Maugham recalled in *Strictly Personal*, published in 1942: 'It was queer to see women queuing up for a piece of bully beef, a plate or a can in their grubby hands, with rings on their fingers and a pearl necklace around their necks. They wore their jewellery because they had to, there being no other place to put it.'

The danger was clear on the second day at sea, when Italian submarines were spotted. There were only life rafts and vests for thirty-eight crew-members. Maugham realised that most of the passengers would die if the ship was sunk. He sought the advice of a neighbour, a retired doctor, about how to drown with the least distress. 'Don't struggle,' the doctor told him. 'Open your mouth and the water pouring into your throat will bring on unconsciousness in less than a minute.'

'This I made up my mind to do,' he wrote. 'I thought I could stand anything for a minute.'

It would take twenty days for the cargo ships to reach London safely, while back in France there would be one last chance for Enid, Duke and Pat. A luxury boat, *Sister Anne*, lay at anchor off Cap Ferrat. It was owned by the socialite and fashion icon Daisy Fellowes, who had already gone back to London. On 20 June the boat's captain was ordered by local authorities to scuttle the vessel but he refused, instead opting to leave and offering to take anyone left ashore back to London.

There were thirty-two 'Riviera refugees' who would take up his offer, including a famous film director and a British consul aide, but Duke again refused to leave and, from the marble steps of La Fiorentina, Enid watched the vessel sail.

The journey back for the *Sister Anne* was more hazardous than for the coal carriers: it threatened to capsize in the wild Atlantic Ocean as it avoided enemy submarines and aircraft. But it reached London safely on 13 July, prompting one relieved passenger to quip: 'Our armaments amounted to a child's catapult and [Ethiopian Emperor] Haile Selassie's sword, which he had presented to Mrs Fellowes.'

Thelma Morgan had had enough of London. The public parks were being dug up to fill sandbags with soil; the ornate iron railings were being cut off and melted down to make bombs; people were scurrying, rather than strolling, around the streets, most of them carrying gasmasks as she might carry a handbag. The skies above the city were scarred with balloon barrages to trap aerial attacks and the nights had become claustrophobic blackouts as the city waited in trepidation for an unseen enemy.

The constant fear of a German bombardment was taking its toll, psychologically as much as physically. Thelma was worried, not only about her own safety and home near Hyde Park in the centre of London but whether her son, Tony, was safe at his boarding school, Summer Fields, located outside Oxford.

The basement of her Mayfair home had been turned into an air-raid shelter. It was large enough to be declared a public facility so that, when the air-raid sirens began sounding in June, she saw people fleeing down her steps from the street to huddle, frightened, inside, sometimes fifty or sixty at a time.

Her lawyer had pleaded with her to withdraw Tony from school and go to New York to wait out the war in safety. At first she had refused but, as the summer months of 1940 drew to a close, she relented: she packed her most precious possessions into boxes to be stacked downstairs and left the house in the hands of her chauffeur and his wife. This decision would be vindicated a few months later, when a bomb landed nearby and the damage caused her basement to fill with drain water.

The first leg of Thelma and Tony's voyage was a channel boat to the south of France, where she booked tickets on one of the steamships that still made regular passage to the US from Monte Carlo. It meant a week's layover, during which time they stayed with her brother, Harry, who was living in Cannes, 55 kilometres to the south-west. Unlike the English, Americans were still safe in France.

While she waited, Thelma decided to contact Duke. Despite the fact that Tony had had almost no contact with his father, she wanted the boy to see him again before they left. It was also her excuse to make mischief once more.

Duke sounded tired over the phone but he agreed to make the trip to Cannes, telling Enid he was going to see a dentist and insisting that he travel alone. Although suspicious and fearing that he might be searching for a source of morphine, she didn't argue.

When he turned up at Harry's house he looked pale and unhappy. Thelma was worried: 'I said "Oh Duke, what are you doing here? Come to America with us." "I only wish I might but that is impossible," he said. "My place is in England but I am too ill to go there now."'

The next day Duke came again, this time to a hotel where she was having a farewell lunch with friends. Thelma tried again to persuade him to leave France. 'I'd never seen a man look so frail, so mixed up, so ill,' she would write. 'I cried "Oh Duke, if only I could put you in my pocket and take you away." Tears spilled down his cheeks. "If you only could, Thelma," he said sadly. Tony and I never saw him again.'

Thelma would tell a different story to the newspapers a few years later, claiming she had visited La Fiorentina while Enid was absent and had been shocked by Duke's condition. She said he had refused to see Tony because he did not want his son to see him ill, but had reassured her that he had been provided for in his will.

Marmaduke Furness expected to die before the war had run its course.

20

RESISTANCE

All the boats had gone, and with them went the only immediate route to the relative safety of London. At La Fiorentina Enid realised that her life was now on a knife edge. There was no guarantee of safety, even here in the south of France where life had seemed to be more secure.

Enid wondered if she had made the right decision in allowing Pat to stay, happy that her daughter was by her side but worried about what dangers lay ahead. But Pat had been insistent, so she would have to make the best of it.

Duke was clearly desperately ill; the now regulated shots of morphine were not enough to quell his constant pain. Although she would not admit it, Enid knew deep down that her husband was dying. It was just a matter of time and she arranged, as best she could, full-time nursing care at his bedside in the now largely silent and cavernous house. What had been bought as a castle of love now seemed like a tomb.

The English staff had all gone, and food was now scarce and sold for ridiculous prices on the black market. One house guest, a famous woman tennis player who had settled in France and refused to evacuate, was found to have been stealing food from the kitchen, hiding it under her corset and stockpiling it in her room in one of the houses on the estate. Enid reluctantly asked her to leave.

The sun still shone brightly and the waters sparkled, but this was no ordinary Côte d'Azur summer. The beaches were empty, the seafront boardwalk void of evening strollers and the gardens of the largely shuttered grand hotels overgrown.

The cinema stayed open, as did some restaurants, but there were rumours that the chefs were using dogs, cats and even rats to make their stews and soups. Not that people went out much anymore. Petrol was being rationed. Instead, horses and carriages and bicycles filled the streets. The food scarcity worsened, if that were possible, with people queuing for up to three days for basic supplies.

Enid resorted to keeping goats and milking them herself to make cheese, butter and milk, much of which she gave away to struggling villagers. Essentials such as soap were impossible to find so she began making her own from a mixture of boiled candles and grease, which were then set into bars. They were dark in colour, furry to touch and produced almost no lather but at least they allowed the nurses to wash her now bedridden husband twice a day. A man who once sat on golden toilet seats, and wiped his arse with £5 notes when he ran out of toilet paper, was now scraped clean with second-hand boiled wax and fat.

Enid was mixing up a soap slurry in the basement kitchen one day when a maid called her to go upstairs. The doctor had arrived to see her husband. 'Duke needs me so I must go up,' she told Pat, who sat nearby watching her mother. 'Darling, keep an eye on the saucepans to make sure the grease does not boil over onto the stove.'

When she didn't return after an hour, Pat knew something was desperately wrong. Eventually she took the simmering pots off the stovetop and went to find her mother, who was still upstairs. Pat had never ventured near Duke's rooms before, but this was different. She climbed the stairs and stood outside the bedroom door, trying to make sense of a muffled conversation inside the room. She could hear her mother's voice, but not what was being said; eventually she decided against knocking, instead waiting in a silent and darkening house lit mostly by candle stubs.

Marmaduke Furness died later that night, 6 October 1940. Any ill will Pat felt for her stepfather melted away at the sight of her mother sitting on her bed, arms wrapped around her knees and weeping uncontrollably. Whatever their problems, Enid had not wished for him to suffer or to die.

'Lost in misery, she did not hear me come in so I tip-toed out again,' she would write. 'I knew she would hate anyone to witness her despair. She was a great believer in never showing a weakness.'

The death of Marmaduke Furness, one of the richest men in England, was greeted with underwhelming headlines back home, coming as it did the same day that the British Government announced a financial incentive to encourage young mothers to leave the city, which was now under nightly siege from German bombers.

The Blitz had begun a month earlier and would continue for another seven months and yet the departure from the bombing zone by mothers and their children had slowed. 'There is no need for mothers to be in the capital,' the health minister warned, adding that people who offered shelter in the country would be paid five shillings a week to house a woman and another three or five shillings for each child, depending on their age.

Most papers carried a concise report of the Viscount's death, stating he had succumbed to pneumonia. In truth he had died from cirrhosis of the liver, caused by his alcohol and drug addiction.

Duke was only fifty-six years old. He had achieved great success in business and horseracing but his personal life was largely one of sadness and regret. His eldest child, Averill, was dead, Dick was reported missing in action, presumed dead, and he had never acknowledged Tony as his son. He had buried one wife at sea and divorced another. The third, Enid, was at his bedside when he died; as the papers reported, his life of opulence and power had withered, and he died in isolation and distress.

In the months and years ahead, there would be debate, anger and accusations about Duke's death and who should inherit his millions. Dick had died a war hero and his younger son Tony was in New York with his mother, Thelma, who would almost certainly lay claim to at least some of the inheritance.

But the immediate problem for his widow, Enid, was to find a way to get through the war financially. She and Pat were relatively safe in the south of France, at least for the moment and mainly because Enid was an American citizen, courtesy of the passport she had obtained as a result of her marriage to Roderick Cameron.

The US was a safety net financially as well. The British courts refused to release any money from the Furness will to her because she was deemed to be behind enemy lines. Instead, the US Consulate agreed to provide her with a small weekly stipend but it was a long way short of the money she was used to spending.

France had been cut in half by an armistice. The north, including Paris, was occupied by the German Army while most of the south had been declared a 'Free Zone', under the control of the new French state led by the 84-year-old Marshal Henri Philippe Pétain and based in the city of Vichy, 400 kilometres south of the French capital.

Vichy France, as it became known, would be a puppet government. On 24 October 1940, barely three weeks after Furness's death, Pétain met Adolf Hitler in the city of Montoire-sur-le-Loir and, with an infamous handshake that became a symbol of German propaganda, formalised the Vichy regime's collaboration with Nazi Germany.

Pétain was an authoritarian ruler who abolished political parties and fundamental freedoms. Even the French national motto, '*Liberté, Égalité, Fraternité*' (Liberty, Equality, Fraternity), was replaced with a new mantra—'*Travail, Famille, Patrie*' (Work, Family, Fatherland).

In Nice he launched *L'Alerte*, a weekly 'magazine of French renovation'. While its competitors were restricted by new laws to four pages per edition, *L'Alerte* was twenty-four pages of Pétain pro-Fascist and anti-Semitic propaganda.

A *Daily Mail* correspondent, reporting from the Franco-Spanish frontier, summed up the bleak atmosphere: 'Instead of representing the height of fashion, the Riviera has become a deserted string of provincial places. Monte Carlo, Cannes and Nice have been transformed into gloomy towns with empty beaches and silent casinos. In addition to imposing puritanical regulations in beach dress—they recently banned sun bathing—the new French rulers are developing a hostility to all foreigners. They are particularly assailing what they call the "English atmosphere". This, they say, must not be revived after the war.'

The Pétain government began rounding up and imprisoning Allied servicemen, many of them inside Fort de la Revère, an imposing nineteenth-century fortress high above the village of Eze and overlooking the coastline beyond the Cap Ferrat peninsula. Here conditions were overcrowded and water scarce but the building itself was also ripe for escape, as thirty-nine men did one night in September 1941.

Pat turned fifteen a week or so after the coal carriers left for London. She had outgrown her shoes and was forced to wear wooden clogs, made by a gardener, and cut-down dresses created by her mother. Most of the time she roamed around the village barefoot, the life of wealth and privilege gone.

She was captivated by the idea of imprisoned men and would sit on the walls of the village harbour trying to signal to the prisoners with a hand mirror and wondering what their lives were like inside. It was a teenage game to pass the time, but it became all too real when her mother offered the villa to the French Resistance as a safe house to help smuggle soldiers across the Pyrenees to Spain and then on to Gibraltar, where they could be evacuated to London.

Over the next two years, men would appear occasionally and stay, mostly for a few days and sometimes for a week or more, until they could be moved on to the next stopping point on the hazardous journey to the Spanish border.

Given its prominence and splendour, La Fiorentina had become an unlikely, and therefore valuable, link in the chain of an operation run by the famed Belgian resistance fighter Albert Guérisse who, going by the nom de guerre Pat O'Leary, had established several lines of escape through central and southern France.

Enid's involvement was clandestine by necessity and dangerous. She was not above suspicion and on more than one occasion Vichy police raided the property, arriving one day while an escapee was staying at the house. Enid reacted swiftly and, after ordering the staff to take their time answering the police demands to enter the property, she hurriedly dressed the man as a maid.

It was enough to fool the police and would become a frequent subterfuge as her involvement with the resistance became more brazen.

A Welsh guardsman named Jim Lewis was one of the first to stay at the villa. He had been wounded and captured in Boulogne in June 1940, but managed to escape from a hospital in Liège. He made his way south, posing as a chauffeur before finding himself in Marseilles, where he was picked up by the Resistance and smuggled into La Fiorentina just a few weeks after Marmaduke's death. Here he waited for a fortnight before being led to the Spanish border and on to London. Lewis would re-enter the fray in 1944 as part of the D-Day landings and be awarded a Distinguished Service Order with bar and a Military Cross.

One day Enid asked Pat to help with a ruse by riding her bicycle into Nice with an airman who was dressed as a gardener, in the belief that riding with a teenage girl gave him more cover. The disguise worked: they were waved through several patrols before arriving in the back streets of Nice and the next safe house. Pat rode back to La Fiorentina alone. Despite the success, Enid probably regretted her initial decision and never involved her daughter again.

During this time, the only Allied fighter's name Pat ever heard was Wing Commander Whitney Straight, a well-known racing car driver and decorated airman, who had been shot down in northern France in July 1941. A fluent French speaker, Straight managed to evade capture, hiding aboard trains and buses and even swimming a river, as he made his way south toward Spain. But he was caught near the Spanish border and imprisoned at Fort de la Revère, which now housed almost four hundred Allied soldiers, mainly pilots.

Realising that his capture would be a propaganda victory for the Germans, Straight concealed his rank and claimed he was a captain with the Royal Army Service Corps. Word of his survival and then capture reached the War Office in London, which arranged an escape orchestrated by O'Leary. In June 1942, a year after his plane crashed, Straight and two other officers walked out of the prison hospital and were smuggled under the cover of darkness into La Fiorentina, where they remained for two nights as police hunted for them.

As the search moved south, the men were moved down the coastline to the town of Saint-Pierre-la-Mer where, in an operation dubbed 'Bluebottle', they were put aboard a French fishing trawler and taken to Gibraltar and then on to London.

Much to Enid's disappointment, Straight did not express his gratitude when they met again some years later.

❧

Whitney Straight's escape was the turning point for Enid. Soon afterwards, the local police made it clear that they suspected she was harbouring escaped Allied servicemen and were determined to expose her as a Resistance member. It was just a matter of time before she was caught and the consequences would be dire, not just for her but for Pat.

Besides, the American entry into the war after the bombing of Pearl Harbor in December 1941 had complicated matters, turning US citizens like Enid from neutrals to enemy aliens. Even without evidence of collusion, they could be interned at any moment. It also seemed inevitable that the Free Zone would collapse, and the German and Italian armies would come marching into Nice.

It was time to go back to the safety of London, a decision confirmed when she and Pat were given three days to get out of France or face arrest. The local authorities, who for two years had refused to give her safe passage, had now changed their minds. 'The Germans want you out,' they told her.

The journey back to London would be dangerous, even for two women who were not being actively sought by authorities. To stay alive, Enid traded on the black market most of the jewels she had taken to France for US banknotes. On the night before their hurried departure, Enid sat rolling Pat's long hair into a series of curls, each concealing the last of their remaining paper money. A beret then covered her handiwork.

The only way out of Vichy France was a dash across the Spanish border and then a three-day journey to the Portuguese capital of Lisbon in a cramped train carriage with little food and water. They arrived, tired but safe. It would then take another fortnight in Lisbon before Enid could cajole and bribe her way aboard a flying boat that would make the perilous flight to London.

The plane left under the cover of darkness with no lights, relying instead on the moon's reflection on the blackened sea as the plane skimmed low over the surface to avoid detection by the German Air Force radar. Despite being a civilian aircraft, the journey was always under threat. Three days after their flight, another plane was shot down.

Enid and Pat finally made it back to London and were reunited with Caryll who had been boarding at Eton. But their wartime problems were far from over.

21

WHERE THERE'S A WILL . . .

Enid's arrival back in London caused a sensation. She was a returning heroine of sorts: a woman who had remained in her home, defiant of Nazi Germany until the last possible moment and providing aid to the Resistance movement. But she was also a woman with a cloud of suspicion over her head about the death of her wealthy husband and his will.

She fed the conjecture by taking a suite at the Dorchester in Mayfair, where newspaper reporters flocked to sit and jot down her stories. She spoke particularly of her attempts to help the French, who were being crushed spiritually and slowly starved to death by an uncompromising enemy aided by a compliant government.

The Australian media, eager to remind readers Enid was one of their own, lapped up the details: one reporter even declared that she couldn't divulge the 'astonishing story' because of secrecy provisions. 'All of her beautiful jewels have long since been sold to further her work of mercy in surroundings where to be merciful was to court death,' the journalist from the *Women's Weekly* breathed in admiration.

The hardships she witnessed were real. Enid had seen babies born without fingernails, their bones warped because of their mothers' hunger during pregnancy. 'Every day you hear of someone dying from hunger,' she said, breaking into tears as she remembered the discovery, the day before she left, of the emaciated bodies of a woman and her seven children in a nearby apartment.

Food had been scarce and bread rationed to a quarter of a loaf per day. Women in ragged dresses were forced to wait in queues for hours every morning to get a few small potatoes. Enid had provided milk for twenty local families from a small farm she had created in a corner of the estate, but her chickens did not lay eggs because of the lack of grain. Meat was almost impossible to get, other than on the black market, which was controlled by the Germans 'for profit and to destroy the morale of the French'.

She had watched one night as a basket of ham, bacon and olives was auctioned off for an outrageous sum while German tourists flocked south, oblivious to the distress around them, and were welcomed into hotels and restaurants where French locals were banned.

Vichy France may not have been occupied, and was still under a French leader, Marshal Pétain, but the nation was being squeezed into submission. And it wasn't just physical hardship.

French culture was dying: music and dance were banned as individual freedoms were removed. Clothing, like food, was all but impossible to buy.

'Never have women been so badly dressed,' Enid observed, unable to ignore the destruction of French fashion. There were no stockings, no new materials or leather. Shoes had disappeared, which meant most women walked about in wooden clogs. 'At the end of last winter, the French people were threadbare. How they'll stand another winter I don't know. There's not even firewood left.'

And yet there was a spirit of defiance. This was evident from small moments, like the time she witnessed a mother on a bus rebuffing the advances of a German soldier, despite the risk to her of arrest for dissent.

'Every person I talked to, particularly the women, said that when our troops land they will help them fight the Germans, with their hands if they have no weapons. Despite these hardships, the women of France are maintaining a wonderful spirit. When the Japanese were threatening Australia, even in the midst of their own terrible troubles, they found time to sympathise with me.'

Then there was her husband's death twenty months before, and news that Thelma Morgan was contesting the will on behalf of her twelve-year-old son. At the heart of the challenge were two codicils added to the will in the final weeks of Duke's life, the last of which left almost the entire estate to Enid. Thelma was not only accusing Enid of influencing Duke's decision to change the will, but accusing her of having had a hand in his death.

'I've been accused of practically everything short of murder,' Enid complained in one interview. 'And I'm not too sure I'm not even accused of that. I'm concerned that my friends in Sydney should know I'm still the same. There's not a shred of truth in the [Hearst American newspapers] article.'

It was a rare moment of vulnerability for a woman whose mantra was never to show weakness. The journalists had become therapists of sorts, as if she were unburdening herself to a confidant when she talked of her marriage troubles with Marmaduke Furness, their squabbles over money and love affairs, and how he had turned the children out of the house and forced her to live between two houses. The privacy of their marriage was being shredded in a looming battle over money.

Thelma Morgan, Enid insisted, was the cause of much of the disharmony between herself and Duke. Far from being the rescuer of a stricken man, as Thelma had declared, it was her constant appearance in London and her interference in their affairs that had ultimately prompted Enid to flee to America.

Enid only agreed to come back when Furness begged her forgiveness. She returned to find a man who was deeply troubled and unwell, dependent on morphine and in the thrall of a confidant—Motz—who simply fed his habit.

Although she had eventually succeeded in convincing Scotland Yard detectives to warn off Motz, it would be a hollow victory. Her last, desperate bid to save Duke was to shift the family to France. Even with the threat of war it felt like the only place where he might be able to recover. Instead, he withered and died inside La Fiorentina.

Given the sequence of events, it was galling to be accused of hiding him away and orchestrating his demise. It beggared belief, she said. Why would she put herself and her own daughter in harm's way?

'I've been accused of influencing Lord Furness to leave me most of his money to the exclusion of his son. The charge is baseless. No provision was made by the will for my children. Later Lord Furness altered his will without saying anything to me.

'[I am accused] of being a woman who married only for money. I was happily married to Brigadier-General Cavendish for sixteen [*sic*] years before he died. He never had a penny, except his pay, and was a poor man. I am going to fight this case, no matter what it costs in pain and publicity.'

Thelma Morgan had been feeding the American media with her version of events, particularly through the stable of newspapers owned by the publishing magnate William Randolph Hearst, a champion of so-called 'yellow' journalism—the art of sensational headlines and scandal-mongering.

The *San Antonio Light* in Texas and the *San Francisco Examiner* were two of a number of Hearst papers across the country that published a double-page feature titled 'Thelma Morgan tears the shroud from Viscount Furness's tragic life', in which she unleashed on Enid, the woman who had taken her place. She blamed her for Duke's estrangement from his children, Averill, Dick and now Tony.

He had been killed by 'drink, drugs and sinister influences', she claimed. She made public Duke's problem with alcohol, which had begun after Daisy Hogg's death, and how, when told by his doctors that he was slowly drinking himself to death, he traded in the bottle for a needle. Her argument was that a man 'steeped in drugs' could not be held responsible for his actions and therefore the late codicils to his will, which disinherited his sons and left his estate to Enid, should not be recognised as valid.

As for Enid, Thelma regarded her as an 'evil star', who married for money and social position, charges that appeared hypocritical given her own marital record and flirtations with the Prince of Wales and the Aga Khan.

Enid was accused of abandoning Duke when he was desperately ill and going to America; she had then 'vetoed' Furness's escape from France by rejecting an offer from Daisy Fellowes to sail back to England aboard her yacht, before orchestrating the late change to his will.

It was a sensational accusation and one which the papers revelled in reporting in dramatic detail, even commissioning an artist's impression of Duke's deathbed entreaties to his dead children, Averill and Dick, while Enid mopped his perspiring brow.

Thelma helped them paint the portrait of Duke's last hours, complete with ghosts and regrets. As Viscount Furness lay dying, his body was tortured by fantasies created by his drug-addled mind, in which he would see two ghostly figures standing at the foot of his bed.

'"Averill, Averill," he would call to the vision of his daughter, long since in her grave, and then he would call out to his other invisible visitor: "Dick! You're alive! Are you? Speak lad, speak up. I can't hear you."'

Although the account was twisted by Thelma's bias, the conclusion was accurate: 'The Furness fortune is not quite in Enid's hands yet and, if Thelma's long array of witnesses are believed, she may never enjoy but a small fraction of the fortune that is hers on paper.'

❧

The will was indeed complicated, given the ups and downs of Duke and Enid's marriage and his ever-fluctuating relationships with his children. Its main text had been written in early February 1936, two and a half years after his marriage to Enid, and clearly sparked by Averill's sudden death in Kenya.

It left the bulk of the vast estate, estimated to be worth around £10 million, and held mostly in great swathes of land and parcels of shares in various shipping companies, to his eldest son, Dick, and a smaller share—one-eighth—to younger son Tony, despite Duke's reservations about actually being the boy's father.

There was also money for his trusted advisers and staff, including his valet, Price; his stud groom, Tomlinson; and his chauffeur, Davis, who would each get £1000. Employees in his London office would also be paid the equivalent of two years' wages and several close friends stood to inherit bundles of shares in businesses and even London clubs.

Enid's share was substantial and included a one-off £10,000 payment plus £5500 per year for life which, in effect, returned the money she had handed over from the Cameron estate. She would also get the Grosvenor Square residence, all the furniture and her husband's fleet of motor cars as well as the racing stud at Gillingham. There was also money for Caryll and Pat, despite Furness's clear disdain for his wife's children. Both would receive the income generated by £10,000 trust funds.

One provision stood out—'that my said wife arrange for my favourite horses which are known to her to be shot'. Such was his narcissism that Duke wanted to be accompanied to the afterlife, like some sort of Egyptian pharaoh, with animals he purportedly adored.

There was a clear warning by Furness at the bottom of the document. If any benefactor challenged the will then they would be immediately disinherited and forfeit their share. The distinction between a benefactor and a bystander was an important one, given that Thelma was not mentioned in the will and, therefore, could raise a legal challenge on behalf of her son without affecting his claims.

The will remained unaltered until early 1939, when cracks had appeared in Duke's marriage to Enid. Angry at her friendship with Bendor, the Duke of Westminster, Furness called in his lawyers and executed a covenant which stripped her £5500 annuity in favour of a private arrangement in which he had agreed to pay her an income of £6800 a year while he was still alive and £8640 after he died. It appeared as if he was laying the groundwork for a divorce settlement.

Six months later, when Enid returned from America and the marriage was eventually patched up, things changed again. Although the details of her annuity would remain unchanged, a clause was added that would give Enid control of the estate in the event of the death of Dick and Tony. On the surface it appeared an insignificant item, given that the sons would likely survive their stepmother, but it was a clear indication that the marriage had steadied and that Thelma was on the outer.

Duke's attitude toward his former wife hardened further in July 1940, a few weeks after the coal carriers had sailed, marooning the family in France. Despite his failing health and angry manner, Duke added a codicil that effectively disinherited Tony and, because of the apparent death of Dick two months before, would hand the entire estate to Enid. If he only learned of Dick's disappearance later, he made no attempt to reverse the codicil.

There would be one final change to his will, written just ten days before he died, adding La Fiorentina to the list of assets that Enid would inherit, as well as a healthy fund of £100,000 to renovate the property. But the document, witnessed by a lawyer in Nice, did not include his usual, bold signature—*Furness*—instead it was marked with a faint *F*, clearly indicating his ill-heath and raising questions about its legitimacy.

And to complicate matters, how could anyone be sure that Dick Furness, now missing in action for two years, was actually dead? The Probate Court hesitated when asked to make a decision and issue a death certificate so the estate could be finalised. Mr Justice Hodson declared 'Yes and no': he was presumed dead as far as his personal assets were concerned, but still alive in terms of his claim to his father's title and estate.

The judge argued that French peasants had been known to hide English soldiers at their own peril. It was only a slight chance, he knew, but Dick might be among them. What if the war ended and he suddenly emerged?

22

THE FAIRY QUEEN OF LEES PLACE

Enid found a bank manager willing to lend her money in the expectation that she would be given access to the annuity she had been promised in the Furness will, now that she was back in England.

It was enough to pay Caryll's school fees at Eton and hire the small household staff needed to run a large townhouse in Lees Place just off Grosvenor Square, bought some years before for her and the children to separate them from Marmaduke Furness. War had changed the relationship between mistress and household: the butlers and housemaids were no longer simply paid staff; they were men and women with their own lives and hardship stories.

There was Collins, the butler, whose hands were so arthritic that he struggled to pull white gloves over his swollen knuckles; and a lady's maid named Maureen, who'd been buried alive in the rubble of a German bombing but survived because she'd had time to hide under a bed. While she waited to be rescued, Maureen had to listen to the cries and moans of her sister, lying crushed nearby; they only ceased some hours later, when she died.

Hannah, the head housemaid, had a beautiful singing voice that filled the house each day as she brushed clean the yellow carpeted staircase, and the under-maid, Mary, had a penchant for American GIs and became pregnant to a man she would never again see. Enid let her move into the house with her illegitimate son and use the kitchen table to change nappies on; they were then dried near the Aga stove. The cook kept the baby entertained and well fed while his mother completed her tasks upstairs.

Before the war, Duke had kept five footmen but now there was just one, a young man named Walter who had not followed his mates to war because he had been born with one leg shorter than the other. Enid also kept on the chauffeur, Arthur, despite the fact that the cars never left the garage because of petrol rationing. Instead, Arthur spent his days polishing the Buick and the Rolls-Royce until they shone like mirrors.

It was an eclectic if slightly eccentric household and one that seemed to suit Enid, who accepted that compromise was required. Besides, her life in London was luxury compared with the past two years at Cap Ferrat.

On a typical morning Enid, a notorious late riser, would brief the cook on the day's menu at 11 a.m. while she sat in bed eating her breakfast. There were no fresh eggs available, so she had to be content with powdered eggs, scrambled, with her coffee, which was one of the few items not rationed during the war. But Enid, always a stickler for ceremony and manners, expected her breakfast tray to arrive with starched linen, Dresden china, silver cutlery and fresh flowers.

Enid's wartime experiences in France had made her realise that she could be useful, so she took a job at a nearby armaments factory as a member of the assembly line making radio parts for aeroplanes. Although she invariably arrived late every day, the factory management accepted her efforts and raised no objection when she began taking unfinished projects home, so she could spend her evenings completing these tasks behind the blackout curtains.

One night Pat, worried by an eerie sound and flashes of light, peeked through her mother's bedroom door. Enid was crouched by the bed, with welding glasses over her eyes and clutching the glowing welding rod over one of her assemblies. She was surrounded by a blaze of sparks and the industrial equipment and goggles contrasted dramatically with her pale blue nightgown and negligee trimmed with ostrich feathers. Her mother looked magical, 'a fairy queen attended by fireflies'.

Pat then noticed another figure reclining on the floor by her mother's side. It was Enid's latest boyfriend, an American businessman whose name she could never remember, who was holding Enid's free hand and kissing her fingers. Pat fled, afraid of being discovered.

Encouraged by her new-found skills, Enid began looking for projects around the house. One day she tried to fix a loose handle on the door of a guest room occupied by her friend, the Countess Drogheda, who was staying for a few days, but she only managed to weld the door shut and lock the countess inside the room. Staff tried to coax the countess onto a rickety ladder to climb down an outside wall but she refused and spent the day inside the room until a handyman could be found to unlock the door.

The countess was one of Enid's closest friends, a doe-eyed beauty who dressed like a gypsy and was famous for her love of the occult, often holding seances at Enid's townhouse. She had been a lover of Duke's before he met and fell in love with Enid, and often told the story of how she made him take his private yacht to China so she could fill the hold with artefacts, including a collection of Tang Dynasty horses, a symbol of prosperity. Instead of being rivals, she and Enid had become firm friends.

Enid and Pat had witnessed several bombing raids while in France. On one occasion they had made a rare visit to the Carlton Hotel in Cannes. Soon after checking in to their room they heard screaming and the sound of a plane, followed by an explosion from the harbour. They flung open the curtains and looked outside. The plane, presumably German or Italian, had disappeared but panic remained in the streets, with people fleeing in all directions. It was a similar scene downstairs at the Carlton: its lobby was filled with frightened guests screaming and shouting. Some had even fainted. Enid had surveyed the scene calmly. 'Well, I don't know what all this is supposed to accomplish,' she had said disdainfully as she and Pat went back to their room.

The two of them had missed the devastation of the Blitz but the air-raid sirens continued to sound frequently. In an act of defiance, instead of descending to their basement shelter, Enid and Pat would dash up to the balcony to view the German bombers against the night sky.

Enid invented a crazy game of counting the falling bombs. They both had to call out aloud, watching as the bomb bays opened and the shells appeared. Enid invariably ensured that Pat counted a few more, doling out a one-pound note for each extra bomb counted. Pat realised later that it was her mother's way of protecting her by creating a distraction from the terror, although it almost backfired one night when one of the bombs appeared to be heading for their house. The missile hurtled past and landed on the roof of the garage where, miraculously, it did not explode.

Enid didn't bother to report the incident for several months. When she did, nearby Grosvenor Square was evacuated while the removal squad deactivated the enormous device. Enid insisted that Pat watch from the balcony, arguing that if British soldiers were going to risk their lives to disconnect *our bomb* then they were going to share the experience, declaring: 'We are not going to take the cowards' way out and abandon them.'

There would be frequent reminders about the dangers of daily life in London, particularly when the Germans began using flying bombs fired at the capital from beachfront ramps along the French coast. They were nicknamed 'buzz bombs' or 'doodlebugs' because of the noise made by the overhead engines that propelled the torpedo. When it went silent, it meant the engine had died and the bomb was falling. Those underneath its path had just twelve seconds to flee.

Enid and Pat's main source of entertainment was the cinema. They were at a city theatre one day when a doodlebug landed outside in the middle of a lunchtime crowd. They emerged through the shattered foyer to witness the bloody scene of torn bodies, heads and arms and legs. Two buses had been ripped apart. Dozens were killed and hundreds more injured. Pat wondered whether staying at Cap Ferrat might have been safer.

Peregrine Francis Adelbert Cust, the sixth Baron of Brownlow, was Enid's first boyfriend after the death of Duke. Enid had met the baron, known more commonly by his friends as Perry Brownlow, in the 1930s when he became a key figure in the relationship between the Prince of Wales and Mrs Simpson. Perry was good friends with the prince, who often used the Cust family's ancestral home, Belton House in Lincolnshire, as a weekend retreat. When the crisis emerged over the prince's plan to marry Wallis, Perry escorted her to France, where he tried to dissuade her from going through with the marriage.

Lord Brownlow was married and had three children but it wasn't his infidelity that bothered Enid, rather that he began to haunt Lees Place, appearing more frequently than she expected, or wanted. After experiencing Duke's jealousy, she didn't like the feeling of being trapped by an obsessed suitor and Perry was quickly shown the door. Likewise, the doting American businessman Pat spied on her mother's bedroom floor came and went swiftly.

Enid was changing men as casually as she might switch handbags or nightwear, which had always been her habit. When she took her bath each night, the maids would lay out a negligee and nightgown to match the colour of the bedsheets, which were changed daily and sprayed with her favourite eau de parfum, Jean Patou's 'Joy'. A second set would also be laid out 'in case Lady Enid wants to change during the night'.

Not all of her male friends were lovers. Francis Stapleton-Cotton, the fourth Viscount Combermere of Bhurtpore, had been in the regiment of her second husband, Frederick Cavendish. They became reacquainted when Enid began spending weekends on a property in Wales she'd bought on the banks of the River Wye. The viscount lived nearby; on her weekend visits, the pair would spend hours standing in freezing Welsh rivers fishing for salmon and trout.

Enid loved the attention and company of men but at the age of fifty she was looking for security rather than a passionate affair. Both now arrived in the rather large figure of Valentine Castlerosse, with whom she had cavorted in Paris in the summer of 1916.

In the years since, Castlerosse had established himself as one of the most popular newspaper columnists in the city, writing the cutting 'Londoner's Log' in the *Sunday Express* owned by his mate, Lord Beaverbrook. It followed the social misdeeds of many of his friends, including himself.

His larger-than-life persona was now matched by his physical size. Fed by a hedonistic lifestyle, his weight had ballooned to over 300 pounds (136 kilograms); this prompted cruel stories, including that he had once sat on the family dog and killed it.

'I don't know how it started,' he tried to explain, according to biographer Leonard Moseley, 'except that I began to get hungrier and hungrier. I found that I needed vast quantities of food to sustain me, and my thirst for alcoholic liquors was practically unquenchable.'

Accounts of his meals were legendary. A friend once watched as he downed three treble martinis and demolished a game pie while waiting for a lunch of smoked salmon, chump chops, a bottle of claret and five brandies. And the editor of the *Express* sat open-mouthed as he ate an entire ham washed down with three large red-peppered vodkas, an imperial pint of champagne in a tankard and a bottle of brandy.

When his father died in 1941, Castlerosse had become the sixth Earl of Kenmare. The Browne family's landed history stretched back over four centuries and centred on the rich green fields of Killarney, around the shores of Loch Leane in County Kerry, Ireland. It was here in 1587 that Sir Valentine Browne, the surveyor-general of Ireland appointed by Queen Elizabeth I, was granted 6500 acres in return for his loyalty to the throne (hence the family motto, 'Loyal is Everything').

The family was granted a coveted earldom in 1801, when the United Kingdom of Great Britain and Ireland was formally recognised, and by the mid-nineteenth century their land holdings had increased to more than 117,000 acres across three counties, equating to almost 500 square kilometres. But the Browne family's fortunes would be changed dramatically by the Land Wars of the 1870s, when tenants rebelled against high rents, and land was gradually sold off to pay debts.

Still, by the time the sixth earl assumed his place at the head of the family, it still held vast tracts of land around the town of Killarney although, like many great landed families, they were struggling to maintain the façade of wealth.

Enid and Castlerosse had kept in touch over the years, and even considered rekindling their fleeting romance but, as Enid told author Leonard Mosley, 'his wife or my husband got in the way'.

When they met again in London in 1942, their situations had changed. Enid had been a widow for almost two years and Castlerosse had been divorced from his wife, the socialite Doris Delevingne, for more than four years. Not only were both free from other relationships, but each had something the other desired.

Despite his steady income from journalism, Castlerosse needed money to bankroll his lifestyle and Enid, apparently on the verge of acquiring a substantial share of the Furness estate, could be his financial meal ticket. It was as practical as it was mercenary.

Enid didn't need a financial backer so much as a social patron, and in the ranks of British peerage an earl ranked as the third most senior title—below a duke and a marquess, but above a viscount and a baron. Valentine Browne was therefore a step up the social ladder from Viscount Marmaduke Furness.

They seemed to be the perfect match. At least that's what they told each other.

23

THE STOREKEEPER'S DAUGHTER

She had the best legs in London and a reputation as the city's most voracious man-eater. Doris Delevingne was a woman who would capture attention and controversy as frequently as she beguiled and courted men. She was not born inside society's privileged tent, but was determined to force her way in and be noticed.

Doris was the daughter of a suburban haberdasher. Showing her independent streak, she broke away from the family business and started selling second-hand evening dresses to chorus girls in the West End. It was here that she became friends with the stage actress Gertrude Lawrence, who was dating Captain Philip Astley, a close friend of Edward the Prince of Wales, and frequently found the prince and his friends in her dressing-room.

Doris had her entrée to society.

The two young women flatted together in Mayfair, where they confided their aspirations to each other. 'I'm going to be the most celebrated actress in London,' Gertrude declared. 'I'm going to marry a lord,' Doris retorted. They were both right.

Doris made the most of her best assets—her long legs and blue-eyed honey-blonde beauty—to advance her life as a contemporary courtesan. Her looks were wrapped in an unabashedly liberal attitude to sex. According to author Lyndsy Spence in her 2016 biography of Delevingne, *The Mistress of Mayfair*, Doris allegedly once declared that a woman's bed was her castle, and she was happy to trade favours for Italian shoes and a new pair of French silk stockings. The men she bedded were boyfriends rather than clients; this was not prostitution, but a declaration of self-worth in a misogynistic society.

When Doris walked into dress designer Victor Stiebel's shop one day, he commented that he liked her shoes, to which she replied: 'Thank God. I'm just back from Italy and I've bought 250 pairs of the damn things. It's idiotic to wear shoes more than three or four times.'

Doris met her conquests at private parties or in a job she took as a hostess at one of the city's dubious gentlemen's clubs. The fact that many of her admirers were married made them more attractive in many ways—they were men who would lavish her with gifts and money without the need for commitment. Besides, she had a specific requirement in a husband—a title with clout.

She met Valentine Castlerosse one night in late 1926. He was in the St James nightclub bemoaning his ill luck at the racetrack when he spied Doris and was instantly smitten, telling her that he was 'exhilarated' by her presence. It was a familiar and tragic pattern in Castlerosse's love-life, given that he had met Jacqueline Forzane in largely the same setting and manner a decade before.

Doris was less enthusiastic about Castlerosse, whose enormous green waistcoat was once cruelly described as a tennis court. But what he lacked in beauty, Castlerosse made up for with personality. He was famous and successful and, most importantly, as the eldest son of a lord, he would one day inherit his father's title.

Doris thought he was easy to manipulate and accepted his advances and gifts but she became concerned when he stole a key to her apartment and began pestering her. As the relationship developed, so did their disagreements; it became clear that they were both strong personalities and were probably ill-suited.

But they both ignored the danger signs. He was besotted, and she wanted his title and fame. Ignoring warnings from friends that the relationship would not last, they married in 1928 in a Hammersmith registry office ceremony held in secret because Castlerosse was apparently afraid of telling his parents. His mother, when she found out, cut Castlerosse off from the family finances, worsening his already precarious position.

As predicted, the union did not last long, at least in the pledge of fidelity that they had made to each other. Castlerosse was a victim of his own excesses—overweight and balding and with significant health problems, including ulcerative colitis. A photograph of them on a summer holiday summed up their physical differences; he is grossly fat and frowning while she, blonde, svelte and youthful, smiles at the photographer, seemingly oblivious to Castlerosse's attempts to hold her hand so he can lever himself out of the water.

Doris could live with an ugly man, after all she had already slept with many and once complained: 'You may think it fun to make love. But if you had to make love to dirty old men like I do, you would think again.' But a poor man was a different matter.

So Lady Castlerosse, the storekeeper's daughter from Beckenham, continued her pursuit of other, more moneyed, men, including a brief fling with Winston Churchill and a longer affair with his son, Randolph, with whom Castlerosse had a heated telephone exchange.

'Are you living with my wife?' Castlerosse demanded.

'Yes, I am, which is more than you have the courtesy to do,' Randolph Churchill replied, equally angry.

In his 1934 autobiography, *Valentine's Days*, Castlerosse wrote of marriage: 'It is a mistake to marry a woman with a past. That type of union is like life insurance—for the benefit of other people.' Doris and he fought in private and in public, often resulting in one or both of them bearing the scars of their angry stoush.

Beaverbrook once admonished his friend after a fight had left Doris with bruises. Castlerosse replied by rolling up his trouser leg to show his own injuries, inflicted by his wife. 'That's still no reason to belt her,' Beaverbrook told him.

Individually, they were literary inspirations. Simon Balcairn, the newspaper columnist in Evelyn Waugh's satirical novel *Vile Bodies*, was based on Castlerosse; Doris was said to be the model for Michael Arlen's character Iris Storm in his novel *The Green Hat*.

Private Lives, one of Noël Coward's most popular plays, would mimic the tempestuous nature of their relationship which Coward, a friend of Doris's, had witnessed first-hand. Coward and Gertrude Lawrence, Doris's former flatmate, took the lead roles when the play debuted in London in 1930. When questioned afterwards by a patron about the reality of a husband and wife rolling around the floor fighting, Coward replied: 'You don't know the Castlerosses.'

The marriage would last ten years, although in name only as they lived separately after the first year. Castlerosse sometimes stood forlornly outside her apartment in Mayfair, waving his blackthorn cane at any man who dared walk toward the door.

The stories of Doris's sexual exploits seemed endless. Many of the quotes attributed to her seem too good to be true: 'There's no such thing as an impotent man, just an incompetent woman,' she is said to have remarked.

The affair with Winston Churchill, who twice painted her portrait, happened in the summer of 1933 at the Riviera villa Chateau de l'Horizon, owned by the actress Maxine Elliott. It was the only time in his marriage that Winston strayed. There are some family members who deny it happened, but Winston and Doris were certainly there at the same time because there is a photograph of them together sitting on the rocky beach below the villa. Churchill is smoking a pipe and lounging in a dressing-gown, seemingly after a swim. 'Doris, you could make a corpse come,' he supposedly told her after sex, according to author Lyndsy Spence.

She was said to have boasted about her mastery of a sexual technique called Cleopatra's Grip in which the vaginal muscles are tightened around a man's penis during climax. She even tried to 'cure' one of London's best-known homosexuals, Robert Heber-Percy, by providing a prostitute and telling him to 'whip the wench'. When he refused, she picked up the whip herself: 'I haven't wasted my money for this. Here, let me show you how it's done.'

And it wasn't just men on whom Doris practised her art. In the mid-1930s she began a lesbian relationship with Margot Hoffman, a married New York socialite, who was also smitten and bought Doris the Palazzo Venier dei Leoni in Venice, an unfinished palace where she harboured dreams of becoming a great salonnière in the style of the seventeenth-century French hosts who entertained and promoted writers, artists and philosophers.

Back in London, Castlerosse was finalising divorce proceedings, citing the incident with Heber-Percy as evidence of her infidelity. When the decree nisi came through, he announced it in his column. Doris replied sharply: 'We were married for ten years and lived together for one,' adding: 'I much prefer the life I am leading. It takes half the effort and earns twice the money.'

While Castlerosse steamed, she began hosting guests at the palazzo (it now houses the Peggy Guggenheim Museum). The glitzy guest lists included the movie star Douglas Fairbanks and a young Prince Philip of Greece, the future husband of Queen Elizabeth II. But her dreams would fizzle with the declaration of war and instead of heading back to London, Doris fled to the US with Margot.

It was there that her life began to fall apart. Margot ended the relationship and Doris found herself in a country where she had few options and no ready means of funding her extravagant lifestyle. By 1942 she was running out of friends and money; the Venice palazzo was now behind enemy lines and useless, having been taken over by soldiers. She had no other choice than to sell off some of her jewellery.

Desperate to return home, Doris sought the help of Winston Churchill. He arranged a flight to get her across the Atlantic and she arrived back in London in early December, to be greeted at a blacked-out Waterloo Station by Castlerosse, with whom she had kept in contact.

Doris was under the impression that Castlerosse had promised to take her back but that he reneged when she stepped into the light at the Dorchester Hotel and he saw that middle age and stress had stolen her good looks. He would later deny making any such promise. He should be believed, given that he was already involved in a serious relationship with Lady Enid Furness.

Castlerosse and Doris had dinner that night; he then went home to Enid while Doris went upstairs to send a telegram to her pawnbroker in New York to check on the unsold diamonds. She was broke and desperate. What she didn't realise was that it was illegal to sell diamonds during wartime and Scotland Yard was monitoring all civilian communications.

According to Lyndsy Spence's account, when detectives turned up at the Dorchester, she was distraught and panic-stricken. In desperation she telephoned a bookmaker friend and asked to borrow £500. When the man said he could only manage £200, she replied: 'If I can't borrow £500 from an old friend when I need it, then it really is time I left this vale of tears.'

There was no answer a few hours later when a messenger carrying the £200 knocked on the door of her hotel room. Doris was found unconscious, having taken an overdose of barbiturates prescribed to her for insomnia; she was rushed to hospital, where she died a few days later.

An inquest could not decide if it was suicide, concluding: 'The drug was self-administered in circumstances not fully disclosed by the evidence.'

Castlerosse, who had sat by his ex-wife's bedside until she died, had no doubt that Doris killed herself. In a letter to Lord Beaverbrook, he wrote that he had found her company 'a strain, filled with sorrow and sadness that would dim the sun itself'.

'There is no logic to love. I loved Doris with a folly and a fatality that passes belief. Without doubt, she treated me ill, as badly maybe as a woman ever treated a man, yet this argument to me bears no strength for if a man is not full and generous in forgiveness then there can be no place among the angels for him.'

Castlerosse was unaware of the police investigation into

Doris's diamond sales because the visit to the Dorchester by Scotland Yard was concealed by the Official Secrets Act. Instead, he blamed himself for her death: 'Often enough has death beckoned me and I have heard oblivion calling and it sounds so sweet. How then, with my past and with the knowledge that I had so painfully acquired, that I did not see that a crisis had arisen. I was blind, wickedly and criminally blind. I could have lifted Doris up, given her hope but I did not. I let her die all because for once I was going to be wise.'

Six weeks later he married Enid in a ceremony at the Brompton Oratory, the spectacular Roman Catholic church in Knightsbridge. Unlike his marriage to Doris Delevingne, this time the church was full of Castlerosse's family and friends, including his mother who had hosted a party the night before. Pat served as bridesmaid and Caryll gave his mother away—who looked 'chic, vulnerable and paper-thin', according to one observer—because Rory was still in the States.

There were politicians, businessmen, journalists, horseracing celebrities as well as a clutch of lords with names like Rosebery, Portal, McGowan, Ashfield, Brownlow (her annoying former boyfriend), Queensberry, Kemsley, Camrose and Cranbourne. One reporter described the ceremony as 'taking place in a night club setting for all the titled crooks and rogues of London'.

In a letter to a woman friend, Castlerosse wrote: 'I happened to be passing Brompton Church in the company of a woman you will adore when I heard a voice saying: "Don't leave this church until you are one hundred and ten per cent married", so you see, my dear princess, I had no option. We went to Ireland

and had our honeymoon and now I am pointed out as the ideal husband.'

The British newspapers drooled over the union and its attendant drama, a story with equal parts of love and death, complicated by money and mystery. In America, Hearst newspapers again went to town on Enid with headlines like 'Penniless peeress and her 300lbs of new love' that rehashed the story about the battle over the Furness will and her inevitable climb up the social ladder. 'She has moved up another rung, which she had a sort of Jacob's dream about in girlhood and has been busy climbing ever since,' it claimed erroneously. 'Her first husband was a commoner, her second a general, her third a Viscount and now she is getting close to the top with an Earl.'

The newlyweds had gone to Killarney, where they braved the New Year cold to go fishing on the lake and take walks through the deer park. But Castlerosse pulled out of a planned round of golf, a game he adored, because he felt too tired. The next day he suffered what was described as a mild heart attack by a local doctor who advised him to cut down on his eating and drinking, or die.

It was good advice.

24

THE EXCESSIVELY LARGE GENTLEMAN

Enid felt she had been hustled into her fourth marriage. The death of Doris Delevingne had been unsettling and she was surprised when Val, as she preferred calling her new husband, insisted on announcing their engagement just three weeks later.

Betrothal was one thing but marriage seemed a step too far, at least for the moment. There was no hurry, she had told him, preferring to wait until her own financial affairs with the Furness estate had been settled. At least then, they could both be clear and confident about their life ahead.

But Val insisted, worried that his 76-year-old mother, who was ill, might die and leave him frozen out of the will. The dowager Lady Kenmare had still not forgiven her eldest son for marrying Doris and would have much preferred that her second eldest surviving son, Gerald, became the new Lord Kenmare.

Castlerosse hoped that marrying Enid would mend the relationship with his mother and solve, at least partially, money worries which he had largely kept hidden from his fiancée. Despite the fact that he was almost broke, he had promised to pay £3000 into Enid's account the day after they married, a dowry of sorts, so she could settle her own debts with the bank. As she would discover, it was money that he did not have.

He had also told Enid that he earned £8000 a year from his work as a journalist and was owed another £30,000 from the script he had written for a movie about the pilot Amy Johnson. Neither sum was accurate. Instead, he was gambling his future on what Enid could bring in from the Furness estate.

By contrast, Enid insisted she had been open about her financial difficulties, as she told Lord Beaverbrook in a letter explaining their relationship: 'I wanted Val to know exactly the state of my affairs and sent him to Goddard, my solicitor, with instructions to keep nothing from him, so Val knew exactly what I would have if I lost the case and how well off I should be if I won it,' she wrote. 'I wanted to announce our engagement only and wait till my affairs were settled before getting married but he wouldn't hear of it and the moment our engagement was announced I was rushed into a marriage before I had time to find out the true state of his affairs.'

There was another complication. The week after Doris's death, Enid had enjoyed a rare piece of good news when Justice Farwell of the Chancery Division of the High Court, which had blocked any payments from the Furness estate while she was in France, cleared the way for her to be paid the annuity which

Marmaduke Furness's infamous Kenya safaris included a dozen Rolls-Royces and hillsides littered with empty champagne bottles. *Cavendish family collection*

Averill Furness riding one of the Grévy's zebras brought to Burrough Court by Andrew Rattray. Averill and Andrew, her father's employee, would become tragic lovers.
Author's collection

Thelma, the self-styled Lady Furness, in New York with her son Anthony, the boy Marmaduke Furness refused to acknowledge. *Author's collection*

Enid's official portrait for the 1937 coronation of King George VI. The evening would mark a turn in her marriage to Marmaduke Furness. *Cavendish family collection*

War hero: Lieutenant Christopher 'Dick' Furness would be awarded a posthumous Victoria Cross for bravery. *Cavendish family collection*

Rory was Enid's eldest son, whose American birth certificate kept him safe from active duty for most of World War II. *Cavendish family collection*

La Fiorentina, pictured in 2014 when it was marketed as the world's most expensive house and sold for US$525 million. *Unknown*

The fourth marriage: Enid marries Valentine Castlerosse in 1942. He would die a year later from a heart attack. *Author's collection*

Somerset Maugham, pictured here at La Fiorentina, was Enid's neighbour, bridge partner and the person who nicknamed Enid as 'Lady Killmore', a joke that she would come to rue. *Cavendish family collection*

Fred Astaire was among the many Hollywood stars who came to stay at La Fiorentina. *Cavendish family collection*

Enid (left) hosts a glamorous ball at La Fiorentina in the 1960s. *Cavendish family collection*

When she wasn't hosting lavish dinners at La Fiorentina, Enid could usually be found painting, often dressed in her negligee. *Cavendish family collection*

After World War II, Enid and her children spent much time in Africa, especially at son Caryll's Equator Farm in Kenya, named because the equator ran through the living room. *Cavendish family collection*

Enid with son Rory (left). They loved to travel together and explore the ancient world. *Cavendish family collection*

Even aged in her seventies, Enid cut a cool figure, often with a hyrax or parrot on her shoulder. *Cavendish family collection*

Enid, now bowed in later life from back problems, leads her namesake Miss Lindeman back to scale after a race win in the early 1970s. *Cavendish family collection*

had been stipulated in one of the first codicils written into Duke's will, before there was any question about his mental and physical state.

The money had previously been withheld because she was technically deemed to be an 'enemy' as she was living in France. But her return to London had changed things, Justice Farwell ruled, and she was now entitled to the money and two years of back payments.

But before a penny had been paid Thelma Morgan intervened and, against the advice of her own lawyers, appealed the decision. It was a spiteful tactic by Thelma, with little chance of success, but it meant that her adversary would be forced to suffer for longer and perhaps be willing to cut a deal on the main body of the will.

Now desperate, and with the banks demanding payment, Enid considered selling off more jewellery and even taking a job. At face value, it seemed the whole premise for her marriage to Castlerosse was skewed, something he had warned about in his memoir written years before: 'Marrying for money often means spiritual bankruptcy, marrying for position is a cul-de-sac but marrying because you love a woman is right, reasonable and justifiable.'

But Enid insisted that, although money was a driving force in their relationship, they were also 'fearfully happy' together. Even in their sex life. When advised by a doctor to withhold sex, because Castlerosse's heart might not take it, she refused: 'It was one of the only pleasures left to him in life, so how could I ration him?'

She adored being on the Killarney estate in Ireland with him and, likewise, Castlerosse had fallen in love with her cottage in Wales, although his delight had created its own set of problems when he began spending money on the property, ordering the installation of electricity throughout the house and turning the sitting room into a study where he could work, aided by 200 bottles of champagne. This was money they didn't have.

Before she knew it, they had racked up a new £1000 debt, not to mention the railway fares she funded for her husband and his secretary and valet. In desperation, she went to see the Killarney estate manager.

'I began to feel terribly nervous and spoke to Mr Bevan who said he would pay me £75 a month for Val's share of expenses. Well, as his drinks bill came to £76 a month and his cable and phone bill £50 without any other living expenses, I saw that something had to be done. Mr Bevan then told me that Val didn't have even 3000 shillings and instead of being able to pay me £3000, they were trying to find money as he owed debts everywhere.'

When the newlyweds returned from their honeymoon, Castlerosse moved into Enid's house in Lees Place but he didn't stay long. The unexploded German shell was still wedged in the garage roof, and he demanded that it be removed and the family evacuate the house while it was deactivated. When Enid refused and took Pat to stand on the balcony to watch proceedings, he declared them 'all mad', left the house and booked into

Claridge's where he often kept a room. Friends found him lying on a sweat-stained bed, clearly unwell.

Castlerosse's comings and goings from Lees Place became the norm. He disliked the staircases, claiming they would be the death of him because of his bad heart, 'if the sex doesn't finish me off first'. But he was clearly happy with Enid, who was content to stay at home with him and invite friends around, in contrast to Doris's habit of flitting off to attend parties by herself or suddenly disappearing overseas with a group of friends. The compromise in their living arrangement was that Castlerosse would mostly stay in a flat in nearby Grosvenor Square owned by her former suitor Bendor, the Duke of Westminster, who had remained a friend and frequent dinner guest.

The Lees Place dining room became the centre of their world, with an endless stream of visitors for lunch or dinner parties during which Castlerosse invariably held court, frequently demanding that his guests relate stories of their daily lives that would later appear, often in exaggerated form, in his columns.

Pat viewed the marriage with a mixture of trepidation and excitement. Her new stepfather was an imposing figure physically but his presence invigorated the house and her mother, whom she once found at the dining table with the former Air Chief Marshal Hugh 'Stuffy' Dowding in the midst of a séance session, in which he was communicating with restless dead RAF pilots killed during the Battle of Britain. Viscount Cherwell, the physicist and wartime science adviser to Winston Churchill, was another visitor, particularly at musical evenings, during which he played the piano while Enid played the flute.

Pat came to adore Castlerosse, or Valentine as she referred to him. After spending most of her teen years in a house with Marmaduke Furness, a man who despised her presence, she discovered that the loud and 'excessively large gentleman' who had married her mother was a devoted step-parent.

'I had always found that my mother's generation were hopeless with the young,' she would write. 'I realised that I was ugly, tongue-tied and painfully shy but they behaved as if I was a creature from another planet. As I was of no interest to them, I was ignored. They talked over me and around me but never to me. Valentine, on the contrary, was marvellous with young people. Mummy kept sending me to him with messages and I realise now that she did it on purpose so that I would get to know him.'

Initially she was reticent about entering Castlerosse's private domain where he wrote and roared at people in equal measure. But his insistence that she stay and talk, often involving her in discussions about his work or books she might enjoy, won her over.

She found herself accompanying him most afternoons when, on the orders of his wife and doctor, he went for a walk around Hyde Park. He grumbled to her: 'The trouble with your mother being a beautiful woman is that she invariably gets her own way. Not only does she hide all the food and starve me to death but she has now got it into her head that I have to be exercised into my grave.'

One night in early June 1943, after Castlerosse had gone to one of his clubs for the evening, Enid decided on the spur of the moment to take Pat and Caryll out to a cinema in Leicester Square. In no hurry, they had dinner at the Savoy afterwards and arrived back home around midnight to what Pat described as chaos. The house was darkened by the nightly blackouts, but clothes were being flung from an open window on the second floor.

The noise grew louder as they entered. Its source was clearly Castlerosse, upset and bellowing like an enraged elephant. Pat followed her mother upstairs and peeked inside the bedroom, where furniture lay in pieces.

At the sight of his wife, Castlerosse roared again and flung a chair across the room. 'You whore,' he thundered. 'Who is he? Who is the bastard who is fucking my pregnant wife? I'll kill him.'

It was the first Pat had heard about her mother being pregnant, but it was Enid's response that made her gasp: 'I might be a whore, but it seems to me that I'm the one paying for your servicing.'

'I'm not going to father someone else's bastard,' Castlerosse retorted. The cause of his anger wasn't that her mother was pregnant, but that he believed she had been out with another man that night.

Enid told Pat to fetch the cinema ticket stubs from her purse and tried to calm her husband, who was now collapsed in a corner, sobbing. Any anger she had for his accusation was gone, replaced by concern for a man who, driven by self-disgust and the behaviour of his previous wife, had convinced himself that he was inadequate and couldn't possibly have sired a child.

Pat returned with the stubs, which proved they had been at the cinema. Enid then rang the restaurant and insisted that Castlerosse speak to the maître d'hôtel, who confirmed that she, Pat and Caryll had dined together. As Pat crept out of the room, she saw her mother comforting her husband, giggling softly and telling him that she loved him.

Despite his anger, Castlerosse was delighted about the pregnancy, as unlikely as it was. He had always wanted children but his own ill-health and the disastrous relationship with Doris, who was not interested in a family, had put paid to his chances, or so he'd thought.

It was also unexpected because of Enid's age. She had turned fifty-one a few weeks before their wedding, which made conception rare and the delivery of a healthy child uncertain. Privately, she didn't expect the child to be born, although she kept her doubts to herself.

Others expressed doubt that it could be true, accusing Enid of concocting the pregnancy to ensure she kept control of the Kenmare estate, even though this made no sense if a child was never born. As it was, she stood to gain nothing from a false story.

Castlerosse may have been pleased, but the same could not be said for his mother. Lady Kenmare, far from being on her deathbed as he had feared, was angry. Very angry. Her wayward eldest son's marriage to Enid was one thing, but having a child complicated the line of succession.

While others enjoyed Castlerosse's largesse and buffoonery, Lady Kenmare saw it as a weakness which had cost the family money and reputation. Having long preferred that his brother, Gerald, inherit the title, she now saw a potential grandson preventing that happy event.

In the old lady's distress, she demanded confirmation that her daughter-in-law was pregnant from not one, but two doctors. 'After all that has happened he has done this,' she cried. 'He loses our fortune, he ruins our lives and now this.' Her response when both doctors verified Enid's claim was to demand that she abort the pregnancy. After all, she noted to Enid, any child born to a woman of her age was bound to be an idiot.

25

THE TOUCH OF DEATH

In the summer of 1943, Castlerosse abandoned London, preferring the peaceful climes of Killarney to the capital's muggy anxiety. He left Enid alone to wrestle with morning sickness. He was working on a new movie script, but his real focus was on a bigger project, the completion of a golf course on the estate.

Work had begun in 1937, with the course expected to open in the early autumn of 1939, but the declaration of war had halted work and the project was shelved. Castlerosse had stewed for the next two years but when his father died in 1941, the new Earl of Kenmare decided to renew work on his dream and now he stood ready to show it off.

Golf had long been Castlerosse's passion, a game that even a man of his girth could play. In fact, he had once been a very good golfer and boasted a free-flowing and long-hitting swing when he was a young, and much slimmer, man before the Great

War. As he grew older, wider and more famous, he frequently attracted an audience to watch his match play against other celebrities such as Edward, Prince of Wales. It was also a passion he shared with his new wife, who had been a regular player at Le Touquet during the summer months.

Of all the stories about Castlerosse's golf exploits, the one that best captured the audacity and character of the man occurred in the US during one of his visits in the mid-1930s. He was drawn to play a round of golf with the legendary Gene Sarazen, one of the sport's greats at that time, at the Sleepy Hollow course outside New York.

Sarazen and the other two players, both prominent amateurs, stood at the first tee waiting for their guest. He was late, and the crowd was becoming restless. Ten minutes went by before the door of the caddie master's shed, adjacent to the tee, burst open and Castlerosse emerged, dressed in a purple jersey, plus-eights, green stockings with tassels and smoking a giant cigar.

Sarazen hit off first, straight and long, followed by the other two, who also found the fairway with their drives. Then Castlerosse stepped up, insisting that his caddie place the ball on the tee rather than bend down himself, before sending the ball flying with a satisfying click 20 yards past the seven-time majors winner.

The crowd oohed at the sight and swarmed around the lumbering figure as he strode down the fairway, all but ignoring Sarazen. The contest continued in that vein as the round went on, with Castlerosse and his partner winning the match and earning a headline in the local paper the next day which read: 'How the Lord humbled Sarazen'.

Years later, Sarazen would visit Killarney and play on Castlerosse's visionary course. He described the eighteenth hole, which golfers needed to play across water to a green nestled on the shores of the lake, as one of the most beautiful holes he had ever played.

Castlerosse was close friends with Henry Longhurst, the golf writer and commentator, who had helped with the course design. In late August 1943, Castlerosse wrote to Longhurst, asking him to come to Killarney; he extolled the virtues of their creation, which drew together the hills and rolling landscape of the estate down to the lake's edge.

'At least you and I have made a golf course in colour,' he wrote. 'We have acres of hybrid rhododendrons, hydrangeas, azaleas, camellias, white heather and countless flowering shrubs and trees. If a man makes a beautiful garden—well, it is just a beautiful garden. Likewise, if a man makes a fine golf course, well it is just a fine golf course. But if a man makes a startling golf course in still more startling colour, well that is news and all the world will have to come and see it. To discuss a golf course in wartime is something akin to sacrilege and any publicity on this subject now would infuriate folks, and yet I have been through quite a deal of war and I am certain that the time will come when men's souls cry for peace—not peace as opposed to war—but real peace, where the beat of an engine is not heard nor the loudspeaker nor the radio. Now that is what I am striving for.'

At the bottom of the letter he added a dour note: 'I do not know how long I have for this world, but I should like the work to go on.'

Castlerosse began discussing death long before it was due to come knocking on his door. At times he seemed preoccupied by a self-loathing that was a direct result of his upbringing; his parents never spared him their disappointment with his physical challenges.

His largesse was legendary, such as the day he walked into the Alfred Dunhill pipe shop and filled his pockets with two dozen of the most expensive pipes available, and then walked through the West End giving one to each of his friends. But his 1934 autobiography, *Valentine's Days*, was littered with references that belied his public image as a man who enjoyed life and its trappings, even when he couldn't afford them.

Behind his bonhomie lay a darkness. 'It is reasonable to cuddle close to the circumstances of happiness,' he noted. 'But many of us who find more misery than joy in life, why should we not welcome death? The touch of Death is not terrible. I think it must be a gentle, light caress which brings peace and soothes the pain of a fevered brow . . . Death is always calling like a mother to her children. One day we will answer, and our troubles will be over.'

He often raised the subject of death in his missives to Beaverbrook, as he did in the early spring of 1939. Castlerosse was unwell and frustrated by his doctors who, he believed, were not being frank with him.

'Am I going to die, slowly or swiftly? Is my heart all bust up? Because it is beginning to look precious like it. I cannot clean my teeth without the damn thing giving an imitation of an airplane engine, and it seems to get worse daily. Doctors won't tell because it upsets most patients if you inform them that they are going to pop off; but really, I am quite different. You see Max, I am telling you the truth—I have never lied to you and I am not going to now—death means nothing to me. That really is a fact. It would no doubt annoy me if I possessed a horse that was going to win the Derby or if there was some other great event to look forward to but . . . as it is, it is a matter of complete indifference to me whether I die now or in thirty years' time.'

But life with Enid seemed to soften his perspective. After his initial pang of jealousy, he had settled into the idea of being a father. Despite Enid's reservations and his mother's protestations, he had spread the word among the locals at Killarney. Their joyous response was heartening. The prospect of being a father with a new wife were reasons to live. If only they could find a solution to their money problems.

Enid and the children had spent a few weeks at Killarney in the early summer, but she had been forced back to London to deal with her financial problems. Having sold most of her jewellery, and with the bank demanding repayments, she had put the cottage in Wales on the market and taken a job behind the counter in the clothing department of Debenhams in Knightsbridge.

Enid was proud to be working but this job would only last a month before workers' representatives, shocked at the sight of a member of the aristocracy working alongside their members, demanded that she be removed because she was taking money out of their mouths.

The only asset left was the house in Lees Place, so she and Pat moved into Claridge's while they arranged to sell the furniture before renting the property to meet the bank's new terms. The plan was to move to Ireland and live at Killarney, where they would wait for the Furness estate to be finalised.

Enid had remained quiet about her troubles, but they were revealed by Castlerosse in a long letter to Beaverbrook on 17 September, which detailed not only his own desperate financial state—'Here I live cheaply. There is no rent to pay and the food comes off the estate'—but the outrageous delaying tactics used by Thelma Morgan and her lawyers to deny Enid a share of Duke's will.

'Lady Furness has no earthly chance of upsetting Enid's right to her original contention to half of the life interest in the Will. Lady Furness's actions are naught but what almost amounts to blackmail.'

The newspapers were right—Enid was a penniless millionaire.

The case had reached a stalemate and was unlikely to be resolved until the war ended because Thelma had declared that she could produce witnesses—staff at La Fiorentina—who would testify that Enid had played a role in Furness's death. If proven, this would extinguish her claim to the estate.

The allegation seemed preposterous. After all, Thelma had never been to La Fiorentina, which was behind enemy lines;

she could not have had contact with the French staff, who were all loyal to Enid and knew that Furness had died as a result of his own battle with booze and drugs. It was a deliberate move to delay and cause grief but with Thelma's lawyer pressing and the judge adamant, there was nothing they could do until, and if, the war was won by the Allies. At least Italy had now surrendered.

As it stood, Enid's lawyers believed that she was entitled to half of the earnings from the estate, if not half of the value of the estate itself. The legal advice was clear: 'There remains the question of whether the wife takes half of the income of the residual trust fund for her life or (possibly) some other period only or takes half of the capital of that fund. There is no expressed limit to the time period during which she is to take the income: it is indeed an indefinite gift of income and the rule is that an indefinite gift of income amounts to a gift of capital. We see nothing in this codicil to displace that rule.'

Enid's lawyers had attempted to negotiate a settlement. But Thelma's legal team—headed by Sir Walter Monckton, a legal adviser to royalty who would serve as solicitor general in Winston Churchill's post-war caretaker government—had so far refused. Monckton was a friend of Castlerosse's and had privately offered to quit the case but Enid and Castlerosse begged him to stay on, because his presence gave them hope of a fair outcome.

It would be a long wait.

❧

Pat had turned eighteen on 30 June 1943, an occasion that might once have been celebrated in grandeur and with expensive gifts but, given the family's financial problems, was toasted with a picnic on the banks of Lake Killarney and a ruby eternity ring, one of the last pieces of jewellery retained by her mother.

Not that it bothered the shy teenager, who left Ireland with her mother the next day to return to London and a job in the typing pool of the American embassy, a few minutes' walk across Grosvenor Square from the house. She was keenly aware that she had landed the job thanks largely to the influence of her mother's fleeting romance with the American businessman whose name she couldn't recall. But once inside, she had to make her own way.

A six-month course in a secretarial college was her only experience of the real world outside a privileged but closeted childhood. Caryll had been sent to Eton, but she had been left at home, taught by governesses and surrounded by nannies and house staff rather than friends her own age, with her social experience limited to carefully arranged small groups of people.

Inspired by the busty screen actress Lana Turner, she decided it was time to step out of the shadows of her famous mother who, despite her reputation as a femme fatale, was a conservative dresser who preferred elegance to *vulgarity*. Pat thought differently and stuffed her bust bodice with cottonwool to give herself curves, à la Turner. The effect was immediate and confronting: for the first time she enjoyed the attention of men as she walked across the square.

But it also brought unwanted attention when one of the older women in the office beckoned her into a room to confide that she had fallen pregnant. 'Do you know how I can arrange an abortion?' she asked. Pat, still a virgin, was taken aback but assured her she could find out. That night she innocently asked her mother, who was pregnant herself.

'I will never forget the deathly silence and look of total horror on her face,' Pat recalled. 'It suddenly dawned on me that my beloved mother thought that it was me who was pregnant. I couldn't believe how long it took for me to disabuse her of this assumption. I was getting frantic. Mummy could now see sex maniacs popping up from under every desk in the embassy. The more I explained, the more suspicious she got.'

Enid eventually calmed down and provided Pat with some suggestions, which she passed on to her colleague the next day. 'In a funny way, that abortion did me a great service at the embassy,' she wrote. 'Word must have leaked out that Patricia Cavendish, the lowly typist, was the daughter of a peeress and world-famous beauty and acquaintance of Castlerosse, well known for his sharp and funny newspaper column. In no time at all, my typing skills were demanded by all and sundry.'

Pat was at her desk one afternoon in late September 1943 when she got a call from Collins, the butler. 'You'd better come,' he said. 'Your mother is very upset. Lord Kenmare has been found dead.'

Just three days after his long missive to Lord Beaverbrook, Castlerosse had got his death wish and was struck down by a massive heart attack. That morning at Killarney he had sent an invitation to some friends, inviting them for dinner and to stay the night; he had then gone out to the garden to pick some roses for the table. When he suddenly felt a pain in his chest, he went inside to telephone Enid.

'The pain has not gone away,' he told her. Enid knew he was in trouble and ordered him to put the phone down immediately and call a doctor. She rang the doctor herself and then started making arrangements to travel from London the next day.

In the meantime, Castlerosse ordered the car to be brought around to the front of the house before going to his room to lie down and rest. A few minutes later, his valet heard the sound of Castlerosse's bedside buzzer and rushed to the room, where he found the earl unconscious. He died before a doctor could arrive.

Enid Lindeman had been left a widow for the fourth time.

26

THE NEWSPRINT KNIGHT

An estimated seven thousand people—*all friends*, as one voice in the crowd noted—watched Valentine Browne's body being lowered into the family crypt at Killarney a week after his death. Such was his weight that at one point the casket threatened to slip from the grasp of pallbearers, to crash and burst open on top of his forebears.

Somehow, they regained control and the ceremony was completed with appropriate grace and sweaty brows. A few mourners thought they heard the sound of Castlerosse's high-pitched laughter echoing from the Gothic vault above, one final joke from a man who had made irreverence his trademark.

Enid was overwhelmed by the scene. 'If Val had been able to see what was going on today he would have known how many people really loved him,' she wrote to a friend a few days later. 'If you could have seen his servants, Tim and Dennis, and all those that worked on his plan in the golf links you would have seen something which was even more than love. They worshipped Val, and not only those men but all the townsfolk. Really, I could never describe to you, you would have had to see that devotion to believe it.'

In London a few days later, hundreds more of his friends, contemporaries and colleagues attended a commemorative service held at Westminster Cathedral. Lord Revelstoke, the uncle who had quashed his relationship with Jacqueline Forzane, was more generous about his nephew in death than he had ever been during his lifetime, reading out a verse he'd written that summarised how everyone felt about Castlerosse's passing. It read:

The stupid world,
a shade more dull and grey,
Goes rolling on
for Valentine's away.

For Enid, the experience was not only one of grief but of trepidation, at the prospect of having to face the ire of her late husband's family. At the funeral she had stood alongside Lady Kenmare and her gormless son Gerald, their grim countenances more about the battle to come over the treasured title than the loss of a son and brother.

After the service the family members adjourned to read the will. It was short. Almost everything went to Enid, although in reality, *everything* meant mostly personal effects because there was no money, only debts that she would later pay to square a ledger her husband had always intended to meet.

In a curious bequest, Castlerosse had left his monogrammed silk shirts and pyjamas to the Convent of the Presentation in Killarney. Some years later, while working on his biography, Leonard Mosley visited the mother superior to ask if it was true. The exchange that followed was priceless.

'But of course, it is,' she smiled. 'The good Lord Castlerosse always remembered us. We were most grateful for the gifts of his shirts and silks, and we are still wearing them.'

She smiled suddenly. 'Did you know he left us his slippers too. His feet were very small. Look.' From beneath her robe she thrust out a foot. On it was a black silk slipper, a snug fit, and it was embossed with a scarlet C. 'Dear Lord Castlerosse,' she said. 'He was a good son of the church.'

The most valuable assets, the title and the estate, were not Val's to give away; they were a matter of male descent. The family wanted to immediately declare Gerald as the next Earl of Kenmare until Enid stepped forward: 'But gentlemen I am going to have a baby, so the property must come to me if it is a son.'

The room went cold and silent, the men measuring Enid's words. Was this pregnancy real or was this woman trying to hijack the title by pretending to be pregnant? Word had already spread by the time she stepped outside the church, where four women accused her of deceit.

The allegation made little sense because, if it was true, then all she had accomplished was to have delayed the inevitable and the shame of being branded a liar, which would have had serious ramifications in the on-going saga of the Furness estate, in which she might be called as a witness.

The meeting with Val's family broke up without resolution. The management of the estate was in Enid's hands for the moment, much to the annoyance of the dowager, who sat beside Enid on the journey back to London by ferry and train. In Pat's words, she began to haunt Lees Place 'like a sinister black crow'.

Shaken by the experience, Enid sat down to write to the only person she thought might be able to help her with her plight—Lord Beaverbrook. They had met on numerous occasions since her marriage to Val but they still hardly knew each other, despite the fact that both had met Castlerosse in Paris during the Great War.

'I wonder if you mind my writing to you,' she began tentatively before asking him to be empathetic: 'I want you to try and put yourself in my place just for a few minutes and then you will understand me a little better than you do. You see, I can't feel you are a stranger to me as I am to you because not one single day has gone by since I have lived with Val that he hasn't spoken about you. I have heard long conversations, very intimate, that you and Val had in front of me so . . . please be a little gentle on me and don't misunderstand things I have said or am going to say.'

The hostility of the four accusers outside the church had been the most confronting for her, she told Beaverbrook, and since her return to London, Lady Kenmare had not let up in her demands for an abortion. It was wearing Enid down to the point where she might cave in.

'This world is a desperate and cruel place for a woman in my position,' she wrote. 'I want nothing from anyone except to be left in peace. So many of these people said I married Val to get into society but that is the last thing in the world I want.

'As for the child, I didn't want Val to say a word about it in such early stages, but he was so terribly excited that he couldn't keep quiet, and anyway I was feeling so ill and getting up early in the morning that other friends could not help knowing how sick I was, so it couldn't be kept quiet. I don't think for one moment in the world that anything will come of it, my nerves are in a dreadful, dreadful state but for other people to joke about it and say I'm using it to put one across the family is such a wicked accusation. Please forgive me and don't bother to answer, just let me feel for a little time that you do understand me.'

Even though he had frequently predicted his own demise, Castlerosse's death had still been a shock. Of course she realised her grief at the loss of an obese, middle-aged aristocrat paled when compared to the grief of thousands of women across Britain who, each passing day, were mourning the death of much younger brothers, sons and husbands killed fighting for their country in the war.

'It really is unbearable to have Val taken from me so soon. I was not prepared for this great shock although now, looking back, I should have known it. I don't think I have slept for more than two hours a night since Val died and I know too I have no right to look upon my own suffering when so many women and fathers are all in the same boat and taking it much better than I am.

'Yes, I am ashamed at myself, but I loved his faults as well as his good points. His faults were such human ones and he had such an enormous capacity for giving his love to others, as he did to both you and me. Bless you and please be patient with me for just a little longer, then I won't bother you anymore. Enid.'

❧

Lord Beaverbrook would become Enid's knight in shining armour, as he had been for Castlerosse. A man noted for his hard-headed business dealings, for his rough-and-tumble politics and for his willingness to use his newspapers for revenge against opponents now showed a kinder side, offering guidance and a period of financial security. He could afford it and, after all, it was simply an extension of the help he'd been giving his friend Castlerosse for the past two decades.

'On the surface no two men could be more utterly different than Castlerosse and me,' he wrote in his newspaper, the *Sunday Express*. 'I had a talent for hard work and in consequence I made money. Castlerosse had a supernatural talent for getting rid of it. He was an enchanting and warm-hearted companion.'

In private, Beaverbrook was generous to Enid, who was surprised and grateful for his words and financial support: 'I cannot get over what you said to me on the phone,' she wrote in early October. 'It is the kindest, most thoughtful thing that has ever happened to me in my life and I just can't understand it.'

Her missives, kept among Beaverbrook's personal papers now stored in the Westminster Parliamentary archives, came thick and fast in the last months of 1943, at first thanking him for flowers and then offering a few mementos. Castlerosse's watch and chain had gone to his batman, and his cigar case and cutter to his chauffeur but there was still an engraved matchbox and a pencil and silver notebook in which Castlerosse had pencilled all his thoughts. It was full of his ideas, and Enid felt Beaverbrook might appreciate the personal nature of them.

She also attempted to explain their relationship and marriage, 'in case you might be wondering'. They were not in love, as such, but had deep affection for each other, 'which I think means more than being in love'.

Castlerosse had come into her life at a time when she felt down and out. He didn't provide a financial fillip or increase her social position as much as he eased her anxieties by taking responsibility for negotiations with her lawyers about the Furness will. And she, in turn, eased his self-loathing, feelings that had developed since the age of eight when he decided his mother hated him.

'I knew I could make him happy and give him the affection he always craved for, and not only affection but I was proud of him too. He may have wasted his life, but he has brought so much laughter, love and gaiety into people's lives and that means so much in a world of strife and hate.

'Val married me because I am this God-damned stupidest woman he has ever met but even in spite of that he was proud of me. Isn't that reason enough? I knew he had no money and he knew I had none now but hoped I would win the case and then we would have had enough to be happy.'

The dowager Lady Kenmare had treated Enid well until she became pregnant. Rather than a potential grandson being a joy, it had reignited her anger at Castlerosse's irresponsible behaviour with money. Her husband, the late earl, had been forced to pay £100,000 to keep him out of bankruptcy and, in doing so, had created financial problems for the family. There was also a lien over the estate for money that Castlerosse had borrowed in recent years. Lady Kenmare had written her eldest son out of her will and had no intention of changing it. Castlerosse wouldn't have got a penny if she had died before him.

Enid believed that, given time, she could have changed her husband's ways, but it was academic now that he had died. All she could do was soften his legacy by paying his outstanding bills. She sold a gold bracelet Val had given her as a wedding present and used the proceeds to honour his long-standing debt to a wine merchant. It seemed the right thing to do and, after all, 'Val always did enjoy his port and brandy.'

'I regret nothing,' she wrote. 'It has all been worthwhile, just being married to him and having his love and affection and knowing what fun and pleasure he brought into other people's lives. My life was much richer for his company and there will never be another. Val was a law unto himself. May God rest his soul, and may he help me for I feel my path now is a tough one.'

A few weeks after the funeral, Enid travelled back to Killarney to sort through Val's personal papers; here she discovered a diary that detailed the fractured relationship with his mother.

She decided to keep the contents secret, unwilling to upset Lady Kenmare, but she could not resist sharing her sadness in one letter to Beaverbrook:

'It would be most distressing for her to read it as there are so many entries in which he would write "My mother hates me" on and on again,' she wrote, adding that Castlerosse believed it had badly affected his life.

But Lady Kenmare wanted no reminder of her son: 'I now know direct from his mother that she does not want me to have the child and is most anxious for things to be settled so Gerald can call himself the Earl of Kenmare and live at Killarney. I have had so many shocks that my feelings are past being hurt.'

On her return to London, Enid called her children together, including Rory who was now based in London where he was working with British Intelligence. Pat would recall her mother standing at the sitting-room fireplace still dressed in mourning black, her silver hair shining in the flickering light.

Lady Kenmare was pressing her to have an abortion, she told them. *Adamant* was the word the dowager had used, as if she had the right to make such a demand. Enid was too old, as far as Lady Kenmare was concerned; she already had a grown family and did not *need* another child. Besides, Enid was a Protestant and, therefore, could not raise the child 'in the Catholic way', as the Kenmare family would have wished.

Then there was the issue of the earldom: it was selfish to keep Gerald from assuming the title that was rightfully his. This argument ignored the fact that Gerald was forty-seven years old and a confirmed bachelor who, as Castlerosse once noted, seemed to enjoy the company of horses and dogs rather than human beings. Lady Kenmare had overlooked, or chosen to ignore, the fact that, as unlikely as it seemed, the family's only hope of securing the title and estate beyond Gerald's lifetime was if Enid bore a son.

Enid told her children: 'She knows [when the Furness will is declared] that I will be able to afford to maintain Kenmare a great deal better than Gerald but when she asked me if I intended to make it my permanent home, I had to tell her that in all probability I would return to France after the war. It is now up to you to help me make the right decision.'

Pat wanted her mother to have the baby, but Rory's views held sway. If Castlerosse had still been alive, it would have been different, but as things stood, he agreed with Lady Kenmare that his mother was too old to have another child. 'Mummy always did what Rory told her so between Rory and the old dowager, she chose to have an abortion,' Pat would write. 'Tragically, the child was a boy.'

Gerald Browne never married and died nine years later. The titles of Kenmare and Castlerosse became extinct on 14 February 1952. It was St Valentine's Day.

27

THE WAITING GAME

Lord Beaverbrook would help keep Enid and her household afloat through the latter years of the war. Her diamonds and pearls, baubles of Duke's flailing indulgence, may have been sold off but her bedrock asset, the Lees Place home and its staff, remained, thanks to a drip-feed of new bank loans secured by Beaverbrook's patronage.

She wished she didn't need a helping hand, Enid reminded him frequently, in letters she signed 'Enid Kenmare'. She revealed in one missive that she missed the guidance of her former mentor, Bernard Baruch, who was busy with matters of state on both sides of the Atlantic—as an economic adviser to US President Franklin D. Roosevelt, and a friend and confidant of Winston Churchill.

'If Bernard Baruch was here I wouldn't be asking for a helping hand from you. He knows me so well and has been the greatest comfort in my life ever since my first husband died. He has always guided me and his hand has been near me for support, but all letters are censored and he is too far away.'

She intended to repay Beaverbrook's kindness, but it was just a matter of when. It was clear that the Furness estate could not be settled until the war was over and France reclaimed. The Chancery Court insisted that Thelma Morgan's claims of skulduggery had to be tested; this meant tracking down the unnamed staff member who, according to Lady Furness, as Thelma still insisted on being called, would attest to Enid's crimes.

Enid, forever optimistic about life, realised that patience was now her best friend although she withdrew socially, the loss of Castlerosse weighing heavier than she might have expected, given that it was a rekindled wartime romance. In April 1944 *Tatler* noted that Enid was stepping out for the first time since her husband's death seven months before. The 'event' was not a glamorous ball, but Caryll's sports day at Eton; the coverage included a photograph of him in the 120-yards hurdles, frozen in a gazelle-like motion across the last fence, his eyes fixed firmly on the finishing line ahead as he won.

But, as usual, all eyes were on his mother who arrived in a bespoke outfit—made before the war by her friend Coco Chanel—and then created a stir when her butler and footman unloaded a picnic hamper complete with silver cutlery, Royal Worcester crockery and vases of flowers. The champagne and wine—largely for show since Enid was a teetotaller—was consumed by uniformed men who crowded around the now 52-year-old beauty, much to Caryll's horror.

'That day was one of the most embarrassing in Caryll's life,' Pat would recall. 'He used to long for Mummy to be a normal, tweedy matron. His life was made miserable at Eton by the number of his friends' fathers who had been her lovers and the gossip this created. In later years, he accepted with pride the knowledge that our adored and famously beautiful parent would, with her legions of distinguished lovers and husbands as well as her eccentric lifestyle, always be the subject of gossip and hearsay.'

Pat was right. Her mother would continue to be hounded by clumsy innuendo and outright accusation in equal measure, created by rivals and an insatiable media appetite for upper-class scandal.

In early 1944, the US media picked up on a dispute between Enid and Gerald Browne, now the Earl of Kenmare, over the running of the family estate. Enid had objected to Gerald's decision to sack the workers who were completing Val's golf course. He hadn't even bothered to visit the property and see for himself his brother's vision. To compound matters, Gerald had also wanted to summarily dismiss the house staff loyal to Val.

Although she had terminated her pregnancy and Gerald was the heir presumptive, a legal technicality meant that he could not take over the title of Lord Kenmare and ownership of the 10,000-acre estate until eleven months after his brother's death. Enid still had the final say and vetoed the order. Enid found herself having to rein in demands by Gerald to make changes; these only eased when Val's mother died in May 1944.

The *San Francisco Examiner*, a Hearst publication that had been foremost in the publicity battle waged by Thelma Morgan in the immediate aftermath of Marmaduke Furness's death, pounced on the dispute and ran a full-page feature with the provocative headline 'Heir Hoax of the Penniless Princess'.

The paper repeated the accusation hurled at Enid as she left the church after Val's funeral: that she had invented her pregnancy in order to frustrate Gerald's rightful ascension to Earl of Kenmare. The paper scoffed at the idea of a woman in her fifties having a baby—'improbable but not impossible'—before launching into a fictional series of events and a confession.

'Before long, Enid's friends were writing, phoning and cabling—for heaven's sake, why hadn't she told them? The situation became so embarrassing that she finally admitted that it was all an inadvertent hoax. She hated so much giving up those lovely [Killarney] lakes that she'd invented the "wishful-thinking baby" on the spur of the moment, just to take Gerald down a peg and keep him wondering.'

The article, which included a cartoonish piece of artwork depicting Enid standing triumphantly on her four husbands piled on top of one another, went on to dismiss her as a money-grubbing social climber who had plotted her path 'to a dizzy level of social prominence' at the age of eighteen and had been 'rescued' financially by her marriage to Castlerosse. This ignored the fact that it was he who was broke.

'How much it would have meant to her to have the advantage that would have been hers as the mother of a wealthy earl can best be understood by a glimpse of her marital career. His death last Fall left her again in financial and social doldrums—all of which helps to explain her impulsive invention of that baby.'

There seemed to be little point raising an objection about her treatment by the media because it would only highlight her discomfort and almost certainly encourage the tabloid press to pursue her further. Enid decided to ignore the bullies and wait.

❧

Burrough Court, the grand hunting lodge of Marmaduke Furness where an English king had started on his path to his own demise, was no more. On the night of 1 February 1944, the building was burned to the ground when Canadian airmen, using the house as a billet, tried to dynamite open the cellar and help themselves to the wine stocks.

There was little the local fire brigade—its ranks and equipment depleted by war—could do to combat the ensuing blaze. Only the courtyard and groom's quarters were left intact as the soldiers scurried back and forth, ignoring the valuable paintings, fine chinaware and silver, and preferring to drag out the crates of wine and bits of furniture, including a grand piano.

When all was clearly lost, one man was seen sitting at the piano and playing the Vera Lynn classic, 'I Don't Want to Set the World on Fire', his figure silhouetted against the raging flames. Later the same day, as if in mournful harmony, the steam yacht *Sapphire*, on which Daisy Hogg had died, sank in a Scottish loch after colliding with a submarine. The boat was not considered worth raising from the lake floor.

A soldier named Coleman was charged with stealing 128 bottles of spirits and thirty-nine bottles of wine from the Burrough Court cellar, but he was let off by a magistrate after he was described by his superiors as a good soldier who had simply let temptation get in the way.

And that seemed that. One of the last physical reminders of the Furness family was gone. Marmaduke and his first wife, Daisy, were dead and so too were their children, the tragic Averill and the war hero Dick. The famous horse stud and beautiful thoroughbreds had been sold off to the Aga Khan, who would go on to create the most famous horse stud in Britain.

The luxury private plane, with its armchair seats and bar, had not been flown for five years and remained locked in a hangar at the end of an overgrown runway where the Prime Minister Neville Chamberlain had taken off in September 1938 on a secret mission to talk appeasement with Adolf Hitler in his Bavarian mountain retreat, Berchtesgaden.

A few months after the fire, there was an auction of what was left of the livestock on the main 500-acre farm, including a dozen Percheron draught horses and a herd of dairy cows as well as pigs, goats and poultry. There was hunting saddlery for twenty horses and a selection of idle farm machinery and motor vehicles of varying sizes and types. No mention was made of the exotic collection of zoo animals which, it was rumoured, had been given to the London Zoo several years before.

The sell-off continued when a large parcel of land attached to the estate was put up for private treaty sale. It was known as Adam's Gorse: several miles of undulating fields and fences, interlaced with pretty woodland trails through which Lord Furness had led many of his famous fox hunts with guests such as the Prince of Wales and his brother, the Duke of Gloucester. The proceeds would all be tipped into the pot of the, as-yet unresolved, Furness estate.

The trustee, Mr Wilson, cabled Thelma Morgan in New York to tell her the news: 'Sorry to say the property was destroyed by fire,' he wrote. 'You haven't even got an umbrella left.' Thelma, interpreting the comment as a poor-taste joke, cabled back: 'I never owned one.'

In truth, Thelma cared little about the buildings. Her memories of there were mixed and her dreams of a permanent place in the upper reaches of British aristocratic society ruined by blind ambition and a ruthless friend.

The only thing that mattered to her anymore was that her son Tony—now aged fourteen and ready to finish his education back in Britain, if the God-damned war ever ended—was to be the new Viscount Furness.

On the other hand, the pot of gold that went with the family crown remained intact, even growing if you added the funds from the fire sale of Burrough. However, that remained under threat from the glamorous figure of Enid, Lady Kenmare.

28

A LIE LAID BARE

The city of London swelled with joy on 8 May 1945. Church bells pealed in strange harmony with the tugs and barges whistling and blaring on the Thames as the streets filled with crowds, who danced and cheered in the spring sunshine and called for the king and queen to appear, again and again, on the balcony at Buckingham Palace.

At 3 p.m. Winston Churchill spoke to the nation in a radio broadcast from Downing Street. Germany had surrendered. The war was over. Today was Victory in Europe Day: 'We may allow ourselves a brief period of rejoicing,' he told them. And so, they did. A million or more filled Whitehall, from Nelson's Column to Parliament Square, so tightly packed that it seemed the buildings might have to step back to let them all in. They climbed the Piccadilly Eros and waded into the fountains at Trafalgar Square, furiously waving paper flags and pelting one another with confetti.

As day turned into night, strobe lights lit up the top of Big Ben and the St Paul's dome while bonfires glowed bright in parks and squares. A city that had been forced to shelter in darkness against air raids every night for six years was finally free.

Pat was caught up in the celebrations at Berkeley Square in Mayfair where she volunteered to ride her bicycle, daredevil-style, up a wooden ramp and through the flames of a bonfire. She found it wild and wonderful, but she was glad that her mother wasn't there to see it.

Enid was in the city centre, struggling through the crowds to get inside No. 10 Downing Street, where she had been invited to attend the prime minister's private celebrations. Enid had met Churchill at various times before the war, and later briefed him and his staff about conditions in Vichy France when she returned from the Riviera in 1942.

Even though the evening was a sign that she had earned a level of respect in London, she didn't feel as if she truly belonged. The slings and arrows fired at her in the wake of Duke's death, and then again after her brief but tragic marriage to Castlerosse, had hit their mark and left wounds that would not easily heal. She had been accused of orchestrating the death of one husband, and cheating the family of another by inventing a phantom pregnancy.

She would always be an outsider in a city that was insular in its views, hypocritical in its judgement and quick to dismiss interlopers. She was the 'Penniless Peeress', as the press loved to remind her, or the 'Stucco Venus', as the American-born society matron Emerald Cunard observed, a backhanded compliment about her statue-like beauty.

But her impervious image was beginning to crack, revealing a woman of unusual patience; her quiet demeanour had been misunderstood as a countenance of greed. For the most part she had maintained a dignified silence while Thelma happily fed newspapers with innuendos about their tussle over the Furness fortune, even though the coverage ignored entirely the fact that Enid had handed over her own, independent fortune to Duke when they married. She had been married to a jealous tyrant for seven years and was owed a level of financial security after his death.

Enid Lindeman had been raised to be beautiful and desirable, and had succeeded beyond expectation. Love was incidental to her first two marriages, which produced three children. The marriage to Marmaduke Furness was lust on his part and ego on hers. Wealth was their glue, a weak and diluted bond; it was just a matter of time before it gave way. Despite this warped relationship, she grieved his self-destruction and what she regarded as her own failure to save him. The genesis of her marriage to Valentine Castlerosse was security, but it had unexpectedly blossomed into something far more complex. Where once she equated love with having in thrall a man who was prepared to buy her anything she desired, Enid now understood that the greatest gift she could be given was to have a purpose and an equal place alongside, rather than behind, a man. Her description of their affection—'a kind of love'—revealed an evolution in her needs; love was no longer incidental, and it was little wonder that she felt such grief.

The city would soon begin the task of rebuilding and so would she, if only the estate of Duke could be settled once and for all. Enid had been warned by her lawyer, Theodore Goddard QC, that the hearing could get ugly. The courtroom would be lined with newspaper reporters, eager for a scandal, and not only would she have to answer questions about the awful final days of her husband's life, but it was likely that Pat would also be called as a witness.

Goddard had experience in handling scandalous cases, having represented Wallis Simpson in her 1936 divorce proceedings that cleared the way for her to marry Edward VIII, the Prince of Wales, and he gave Enid and Pat a taste of what was to come one evening when he sat Pat down and peppered her with questions about the night that Duke had died.

When Pat recounted the scene when she and her mother made soap in the kitchen, Goddard stopped her. Rather than supportive, he was furious: why was a woman who had servants making her own soap? And why couldn't she recall details like the time? Did her mother tell her to make up this story?

It was clear that Goddard knew nothing about her mother's predicament—forced by war to scramble for food—nor her difficulty in managing her stepfather's volatile nature. Of course Pat couldn't remember specifics: the exact time meant nothing in the darkening kitchen, lit only with candles, and she had no way of knowing that a man who hated her was upstairs dying. The only thing she knew for certain was that her mother had been downstairs when called by the maid, Jeanne, to say that Duke's condition was serious.

Goddard was supposed to be on their side but as he left the house that day Pat wondered if he was the right man for the job and if she had betrayed her mother.

❦

On 11 July 1946, *The Times* reported on its front page that, almost six years after his lonely, tortured death, the estate of Marmaduke Furness, Viscount of Grantley, had finally been decided.

For a case that promised so much in terms of courtroom drama, with stories of alcohol and drug addiction, coerced wills and even the hint of murder, it all ended with a whimper. Furness's duelling wives, Enid and Thelma, were not in court, let alone the promised witnesses who could testify about the alleged skulduggery in the darkened bedroom of La Fiorentina behind enemy lines.

Only their lawyers were present. Wigged and grandiloquent, they fronted the Honourable Justice Gordon Willmer, the umpteenth High Court judge to consider the matter, with the news that there was to be no trial. Instead, a settlement had been thrashed out behind the scenes and the spoils would be divided, if unevenly. It only remained for him to approve the deal and end the matter.

The disgruntled throng of reporters at the back of the room had to be content with the observations of Enid's trial lawyer, Sir Patrick Hastings QC, who spoke on behalf of his colleagues. The only issue remaining was Duke's 'testamentary capacity' when he added two codicils in the weeks before he died. The maid,

Jeanne, would testify that, although he was weak and signed the last codicil with a spidery *F* instead of his name, Furness was aware of his actions. 'The parties are now satisfied,' Hastings announced. 'There is no question of his capacity and there was nothing wrong with his mental condition when he signed.'

The court would also have to be satisfied that the financial interests of Furness's only surviving child, Tony, who had now turned seventeen, were safeguarded: 'The Viscount's counsel as well as the executor's counsel and myself, assure your Lordship that the settlement is entirely in the infant's [Tony's] interests. Therefore, you may think it sufficient without going further into the facts which can interest only curiously minded individuals in what should be regarded as an entirely domestic matter.'

And with that, Hastings sat down. A case that had dragged on for so long had been settled in a matter of minutes. Still, the amount of money involved—the modern equivalent of more than £600 million in relative income—made it news of some import. Although eager reporters would never see the private agreement, the probate documents would ultimately tell the story: 'The Honourable Gordon Willmer, one of the justices of the High Court having on the 11th day of July 1946 pronounced for the force and validity of the said two codicils.'

Enid had won; the codicils that had substantially increased her share of the estate would stand. Enid was entitled to $US10 million and was now one of the richest women in Europe.

Having signed the paperwork on behalf of her son, Thelma took the first plane back to New York to celebrate in style with her sister Gloria at The Colony restaurant off Madison Avenue, which boasted '*saumon fume*, fresh *caviar de Beluga* and *foie gras de Strasbourg*'. Most important, she ensured that they were noticed and reported in the gossip columns, where she claimed to have won the case, insisting that it had been her rival who had succumbed to pressure and backed down.

'Thelma gets her Tony 6 million Furness $$' exclaimed The New York *Daily News*, typical of the headlines that hid the truth of the saga.

The day before the case was due back in court, Enid's lawyers had received a curiously worded letter from one of the solicitors representing Thelma. The letter revealed that the solicitor had written to the French Government the previous September, just as the war ended, in a bid to get access to the witnesses Thelma had promised. Instead of getting the go-ahead to take a statement, he had been rebuffed.

The story was false. Thelma Morgan's lies had been laid bare.

'Now that I know the real facts of this matter I desire to take this earliest opportunity of apologising for having written such a letter,' the solicitor, named George, wrote. 'I now know that there is not the slightest justification for any of the allegations and insinuations the letter contains. That letter was written by me under an entire misconception of the true facts of this case and I hope your client will accept this apology and in asking her to accept it, I wish to express my deep regret for having made these charges. This letter has been shown to my client, Lady Thelma Furness, and I have her full approval and authority for writing it.'

Beneath his name was Thelma's signature.

Later that day, Pat watched a chauffeured Bentley pull up outside the Lees Place house and a tall, elderly man emerge from the back and knock at the door. She asked Collins, the butler, if he knew the man's identity. 'That's Walter Monckton, Thelma's lawyer,' Collins replied. 'I hope he doesn't upset her ladyship.'

The pair waited anxiously until Monckton left before rushing into the drawing room. They expected to see Enid wringing her hands at a new complication that would delay the case.

Instead, they found her smiling. 'He was the most charming man,' Pat remembered her saying. 'He had discovered that the nurse who was Thelma's witness had been bribed. Therefore, he has immediately refused to have anything more to do with the case and felt it his duty to come and apologise to me in person.'

The fight was over, just as the war was over. Germany had surrendered and so had Thelma Morgan. When the conflict had begun six years earlier, Enid was nursing her third husband; by its end, she was mourning the passing of her fourth. It was time to rebuild; even though her critics had backed off in the wake of her court victory and she was now wealthy enough to enjoy the city, Enid was ready to return to France and La Fiorentina.

There was one hurdle before they left. What to do with the dozens of dogs she had rescued over the past three years from bombsites around the city. Eventually they were taken by the Battersea Dogs Home. She would create a new canine collection on the Riviera.

29

FROM THE RUBBLE

In the summer of 1942, a few months after Enid and Pat had fled southern France for the relative safety of London, the German Army had chased away La Fiorentina's loyal staff, moved into the villa and declared it their local general headquarters.

It made sense logistically as part of a defence line along the mountainous coastline of the Riviera, because its position at the end of Cap Ferrat offered uninterrupted views across to Italy. If the worst happened, and Italy was overrun by Allied forces (and it was), then they would be able to see the enemy coming.

But in a conflict whose sole intent was destruction and capitulation, the soldiers cared nothing about the property. The interior of the main house had been trashed, and the furniture scattered and wrecked. Worse, the gardens were flattened, demolished to make way for a concrete sea wall, complete with machine-gun posts. A huge cannon emplacement, big enough to house twenty men, had been sunk into the upper terracing to overlook the bay. Adding to the mess was a reinforced air-raid shelter dug into the ground alongside the house.

It was unlikely that any of the guns had been fired during the Germans' two-year occupation, except perhaps for testing; yet in late 1944, when defeat seemed just a matter of time and they began to retreat, the Germans blew up the fortifications. This was an act of petulance rather than strategy.

The remains of the villa and its rubble-strewn grounds would stand empty for another two years before Enid could return to assess the damage. She had made it plain to Valentine's mother in the wake of his death that she intended to return to France to live after the war. True to her word, Enid had stayed long enough to finalise Duke's estate, and then left for good.

In September 1946 she and Rory stood amid the ruins and wondered if the place was even worth restoring. In many ways it represented the worst times in their life and yet it also symbolised their ability to survive. Rory would admit having doubts: 'It was my mother who deserves the credit for the restoration,' he would write in his 1975 account, *The Golden Riviera*. 'Alone, I would not have had the courage.'

The first job was to clear the grounds of the German concrete. This proved a Herculean task, not only because of the amount of rubble, much of it still embedded deep in the soil, but because it had to be cleared using a pickaxe. Rory would recall that he and Enid were uneasy when the area command assigned the work to a contingent of prisoners of war, who worked silently, like automatons: 'I don't think I ever tried to talk to them, partly, I suppose, from embarrassment.'

It would take six months, as spring approached in 1947, before anything could be planted in the twenty-two hectares. However, the result, when mature, was spectacular: gardens separated by walls of clipped hedges, so visitors could stroll between classical layouts of green shrubs and white blooms and into wild areas that mimicked the local, perfumed maquis. There were great carpets of choisya; mints and myrtles in yellows, blues and silvers; and dirty pinks of the elephant-eared bergenia.

In other parts of the garden, the planting choices had been sourced from beyond the Mediterranean: mature bull bay trees from Carolina and avocado trees from Guatemala, purple devil's trumpets from Latin America, white ginger lilies from India, and Spanish yellow scorpion vetch. Below the loggia, there were terraces of lavender, clipped into neat balls and encircled by hedges of rosemary.

The ocean winds were screened by stands of laurel, and the pergolas were laced with species of jasmine that flooded the garden with their heady scent. The stone pathways were lined with flat pots of white pelargoniums and huge terracotta jars planted with lemon and bergamot. It seemed endless: a riot of colour, shapes and smells.

Beyond the garden, the driveway swept through the middle of a plantation of orange trees, planted four rows deep and in lines of ten, to the front gates where Enid planted clumps of

Australian acacia that exploded in a golden, honey-scented cloud at Christmas—a homage to her birthplace.

If the gardens were a celebration of nature, then the main house and its interiors would be an ode to opulence and grand Italian architecture. The house may have survived the German occupation, but it had been so battered that, at first, knocking it down and building anew seemed to be the best option. No one would have blamed them for doing just that but, instead, Enid and Rory decided to keep the main walls and basic layout, and to gut the rest and redesign so as to better reflect the building as a Florentine villa. They chose Palladian architecture.

The muted exterior contrasted with an interior of rich colour and texture. The walls of the first hall were marbled in pistachio green and pink and a painted blue ceiling patterned with clouds. The second hall was decorated by English artist Martin Battersby, famed for his trompe-l'oeil three-dimensional illusions, who created a series of classical architectural drawings on sheets of simulated calf-skin membrane that appeared to be thumb-tacked to the walls and ceiling.

Just as unusual were the walls of the main dining room, which featured an eighteenth-century Italian fresco, hacked from its original wall in a Piedmont castle, glued to canvas sheeting for preservation and hidden in a London warehouse during the war. When reassembled and attached, it depicted a landscape of wooded hills and distant castles with birds flitting from wall to wall. Enid would later add her own touch, including painting her own murals on the walls of a bedroom in a Japanese-inspired scene of a bamboo forest and birds, while her watercolour studies of the garden and its blooms and fruits, painted with the eye of a botanist, dotted the walls throughout the rest of the house.

With money no longer a concern, Enid ordered hand-knotted Cogolin carpets and rugs to grace the floors and *point de Hongrie* woven curtains to hang beside the eight great windows that framed the view across the garden to the waters beyond.

It was a creation of light that Rory liked in particular: 'The big double doors were always kept open, anchored with elongated stoppers of colourless Venetian glass and, at certain times of the year, the effect was quite extraordinary. The sun setting directly through the portico struck right through the house, reflecting the polished surface of the floors, touching the crystal chandeliers with points of fire. At these moments, the house took on a special atmosphere and could be the precincts of some pagan temple at the auspicious hour of prayer.'

Perhaps the highest praise for their restoration and renewal of La Fiorentina came two decades later when the house was sold and the new owners, American advertising executive Mary Wells Lawrence and her businessman husband Harding, warned their interior decorator, the legendary New York society designer Billy Baldwin, against making too many changes.

'Remember we bought the house because of what it is,' said Mrs Wells Lawrence, the first woman chief executive of a company listed on the New York Stock Exchange. 'Let's not revolutionize it.'

In her 2002 autobiography, *A Big Life in Advertising*, she would explain further:

> Ah. La Fiorentina. Most people who speak of it let out little sighs and look at me curiously, as if, in owning it, I were someone from a mysterious planet. It is so otherworldly beautiful. It is not a house, it is not real estate—it is a fantasy of what Heaven might be if things go right for you. There it sits, on the tip of the peninsula of Cap Ferrat, surrounded by water on three sides. Monte Carlo twinkles a few miles to the left and sometimes you think you see Corsica straight ahead, way out in the distance, in the cobalt-blue Mediterranean. As you gaze out to sea you understand why Cézanne, Renoir, Monet, Matisse, and Bonnard painted such wonders in this one small part of the world.

30

AUSTRALIA

In 1947, Enid decided it was time to visit her birthplace. The last trip she had made to Australia was in 1929, when she returned with Frederick Cavendish and the children for her sister's wedding. Now, as work continued on La Fiorentina, it seemed an opportunity to escape a European winter and introduce her now adult children to a sometimes forgotten part of their heritage.

When she had arrived in Australia eighteen years earlier she was the wife of a decorated but largely unknown British soldier, and widow of a largely unknown American businessman. She was clearly well-to-do, but not excessively so, with a life that revolved around children and the socially conservative expectations of a military wife—hardly the stuff that excited giddy newspaper columnists.

But much had happened in the ensuing years. The woman who stepped ashore from the liner *Orion* in the late spring sunshine of 1947 had been transformed physically. Age had treated Enid well: she was now elegant rather than simply lovely, with her hair a shining silver and cut into soft curls beneath a smart, veiled boater, dressed in the latest Paris couture fashions, offset by diamond-encrusted jewels.

Her story was now riveting and extravagant; her dance from one husband to another, with all the associated controversy of ex-wives, was too delicious for the daily newspapers to ignore. Enid Lindeman had lived up to her schoolyard nickname of Diana—a divine huntress who had returned home with a catch of four husbands, a distinguished title and a fortune that most could not imagine.

The visit had been flagged several months before, revealed in newspaper columns as a royal tour might have been announced, and the reporters were waiting when the ship docked in Fremantle after the voyage across the Indian Ocean from the southern tip of Africa. They all expected a beautiful woman dressed in beautiful clothes and she didn't disappoint, although the colour of her eyes seemed to change as frequently as her couture outfits.

'Quite the most beautiful and elegant woman among the passengers on the *Orion* was the Australian-born Countess of Kenmare,' gushed the *West Australian*. 'She was dressed today in a slim-fitting black suit with a soft, hand-made white blouse. She wore an extremely smart boater in natural straw, trimmed with black ribbon and veiling. Her eyes, which are almost violet in colour, lit up when talking of seeing her mother again.'

The Age covered her stopover in Melbourne: 'Lady Kenmare went ashore wearing a fur coat loosely over a black tailored suit, and her hair caught in a brightly coloured silk Jacqumar scarf.' *The Argus* concurred: 'Most strikingly decorative of these passers-through was the Countess of Kenmare, the former Enid Lindeman of Sydney. Tall, slim, silver-haired with a delicate skin and lovely blue eyes, she looked stunning. Most intriguing was her lapel ornament of a heavy gold dolphin, encrusted with diamonds and with a single huge pearl as the head.'

Enid was making news from the moment she arrived in Sydney on 29 October 1947. The *Sydney Morning Herald* reporter seemed astounded that at the age of fifty-five, she was wearing a short skirt: 'On arrival, the countess wore a plainly tailored frock by Hermes . . . The skirt was quite short, a few inches below the knees. Explaining the contradictory effect of her Paris clothes, the Countess said that she had had all her hemlines shortened for her Australian visit, as she did not think that long skirts were very suitable to wear here.' *The Sun* newspaper went even further with a headline that suggested she was critiquing Paris fashion: 'Paris Frocks too long, says countess'.

The *Women's Weekly* was gushing: 'She had left Australia as one of the most beautiful girls of that or any era since and in international circles she was just as outstanding, not only for her beauty but for her grace and wit as a hostess of great charm. Age seems to have no relation to this lovely woman. She is beautiful in any company and by any standards. Her skin is as smooth as a young girl's, she is slender and tall with beautiful carriage.'

Her clothes matched her beauty, the *Weekly*'s report continued: 'They are always in perfect taste. She has not been seen in any evening frocks in this ship, but she told me she has many by famous Paris couturiers. Nearly all are represented but the majority of her frocks are by Christian Dior and Balenciaga. I asked if she liked the three-quarter-length skirt which Dior, above all couturiers this year, is pushing on the fashion world: "No, and I don't think it will last, but when one spends most of one's time in France one must wear what the French wear. I don't think I'll be able to wear many of them in Australia."'

But for all the platitudes, the reporter noticed something more poignant about Enid that others hadn't seen: 'Lady Kenmare doesn't smile a great deal but is charming when she does. She has cool blue-green eyes and if her slow, grave way of talking has grown out of her tragic personal experiences it is more than understandable.'

Her *tragic personal experiences* were, of course, the death of four husbands. Instead of questions and innuendo about her possible role in their demise, Enid had, for once, found the sympathy normally afforded to a widow.

The trip had been an adventure even before they arrived in Sydney. Enid and the family had spent almost two months in Egypt before boarding the *Orion* at Port Said with 1300 other passengers, mainly post-war British migrants on their way to begin a new life in Australia.

The Egypt stopover had been Rory's idea; he was keen to study ancient ruins to garner architectural concepts for La Fiorentina as well as to contribute to his budding career in design and travel writing. The archaeological splendours of Egypt were all but deserted; their party was among the first Western group to return since the war. They drifted down the Nile in a paddle-steamer before taking a camel train into the Sahara to the Faiyum Oasis, a three-day ride west of Cairo, where Enid caught malaria from a mosquito-infested lake. 'It was a silly thing to do at my age,' she told gobsmacked journalists when she arrived in Perth still feeling the effects.

Their trip would follow a similar pattern, stopping on the way to explore an exotic culture such as India or an African nation before they stayed in Australia for six months, much of which was spent outside Sydney, away from the glitz of social gatherings. For all her love of the trappings of wealth, Enid seemed just as comfortable camping outdoors, whether on safari in Africa, on a houseboat on the Nile or in the Australian Outback.

After a family Christmas in Sydney, they drove more than 1500 kilometres along the often rough road up into north Queensland, where they hired a launch, the *Pacific Star*, and spent three weeks exploring the islands of the southern end of the Great Barrier Reef and the Whitsundays.

Tourism was in its infancy on the reef. There had been efforts throughout the 1930s to encourage economic promotion of the area, but the war had intervened and tour boats had only just begun to venture out again into the largely deserted waterways. Hayman Island, where they anchored each night, had just been bought by aviation king Reginald Ansett (for just £12,000) but its first resort was still three years away from being opened, and it would be another four decades before the reef was recognised internationally.

Pat had only been three years old when they were last in Australia; her most powerful memory was of sitting on a beach building sandcastles while watching a man being dragged from the water with blood pouring out of a leg wound, apparently caused by a shark attack.

The sharks were here again, black fins slicing through the water behind the boat or circling just beyond the shoreline reefs where they searched for shells. But their threatening presence—'sinister', Pat would write—was soon forgotten on a reef that seemed to breathe with life. She could never have imagined such raw, untouched beauty as they spent day after day exploring the seemingly endless chain of islands and atolls.

When they finally returned to the mainland, the local tour operators ensured that the media was fed stories of their visit. 'A countess at the reef' was reported widely, particularly Enid's reputedly spectacular collection of seashells—'the finest collection in the world'—which she had gathered during her travels around the globe and now added to as she waded through reef pools. 'The thrill of personally collecting specimens far outweighs any pleasure received from buying rare specimens,' she told the *Sydney Morning Herald*. The enthusiast was actually Rory, whose collection would adorn one of the bathrooms at La Fiorentina.

The news reports failed to mention that the party had been marooned on an island for several days after their boat, at anchor on yet another shell-collecting trip, was caught in the huge five-metre tides and sprung a hole on a reef. They were forced to camp ashore on an island teeming with mosquitoes and snakes while the embarrassed captain and his crew struggled to plug the boat so they could get back to the port town of Bowen. Enid took it all in her stride.

They had barely settled back in Sydney before Enid organised another trip, this time to the centre of the continent. They flew first to Adelaide and then on to Alice Springs, where they joined a camel train that took them into the hot, dry Aboriginal camps of the MacDonnell Ranges. Alice Springs was 'a small country town with little Victorian houses, verandas and green roofs'—where Albert Namatjira had awakened a national interest in Indigenous art. But Rory was unmoved by Namatjira's work, influenced as it was by Western art.

Back in Adelaide they sought out Daisy Bates, the journalist and anthropologist, known by Aboriginal elders as Kabbarli, or 'grandmotherly person'. She was now eighty-eight years old, with failing eyesight and living in a small suburban home. She who told Rory on parting: 'I am old and I can give you advice. Be good, but if you are you will be dull.' He took the advice to heart.

There was another important person to find before they left Australia. Roslyn Jamieson was the family friend who had introduced a young Enid Lindeman to Roderick Cameron at a society dance many years before.

The physical riches of Roslyn's life were now remnants. She was a *grand dame* of Sydney with a soft voice and gracious manner, her husband and many of her friends long dead. She now lived in a cottage in the grounds of a neglected estate called Mount Pleasant, not in the city but in Bathurst where her father had built a splendid country mansion, shaped like a baronial castle, and entertained city celebrities who made the carriage trip across the Blue Mountains.

The main house stood empty, too big to maintain, which is why she lived frugally in the cottage, called *Strath*, with an ancient chip heater to ward off the bitter winters and no sign of the servants who once attended every whim. Still, she maintained what Rory called an ambience of dignity as they sat down for coffee in a drawing room where Roslyn was grateful that Enid remembered her and the impact that the introduction had on her life: 'My dear Enid,' she began. 'You, who are used to such different things, how sweet of you to come.'

The journey back to France meandered through Southeast and central Asia but their most important stop-off would be New York, a city of mixed emotions for Enid. It had been the first port of call in her roller-coaster life of love and loss; it had been the birthplace of her eldest son and the place to which she fled when things went wrong with her marriage to Marmaduke Furness.

Contrary to media speculation, she had never fallen out with Roderick Cameron's family. In fact, his sister Catherine, whom Pat called Aunt Nanny, was frequently in their lives—a bossy but nonetheless loving influence.

And there was Bernie Baruch, her mentor and lover, who always seemed to be in the background and yet unseen. He was a married man, contentedly so at least on the surface, so it was little wonder that his friendship with Enid remained hidden, yet enduring. The only overt sign was his role as godfather to Pat, which seemed odd given that he was Jewish.

Enid and Pat were visiting him one day at his city office when he took his goddaughter aside. They were out of earshot of her mother. He seemed nervous, as if struggling to find the right words, so they chatted about their shared love of Zane Grey novels. Then he took her hand: 'You seem to be a sensible girl. I want you to promise me that you will always look after your mother.'

Pat was puzzled. Baruch paused, as if reluctant to say anything further, and then decided that he must: 'I first met your mother when she was about your age. She was the most beautiful girl I had ever seen and she is still the loveliest woman I have ever known. I do not know if she ever told you, but I wanted very much to marry her but she always said I was too old for her.'

His love had long since evolved into the kind of adoration that a father might have for his daughter. He worried that she was more vulnerable than she might appear and that, when he was no longer around, she would need someone else to watch over her: 'Enid has so much money and just seems to give it away to whomever she thinks needs it. I don't want her to end up being poor.'

Pat didn't know how to respond to either the request or the admission. Mr Baruch, as she knew him, was almost eighty years old; yet he was suggesting that her much younger mother needed protection. That scenario did not seem real to her, but she nodded anyway to confirm the promise.

31

'DID I REALLY KILL THEM ALL?'

Enid had had her fill of husbands. If she married again, given her record of four dead husbands, then the unlucky groom would undoubtedly die, and sooner rather than later as she told one suitor who quickly withdrew the offer of matrimony. With the notion of pandering to the whims of a lover fading in appeal after the death of Valentine Castlerosse, her desire for adult male companionship was satisfied by the attention of her son Rory, who was as devoted as any husband, and the accidental hiring of a man to be her lady's maid.

The young man in question was Walter, the footman with the short leg, who was asked to fill in when Enid's maid suddenly retired. Rather than be insulted by the notion, Walter had set about his new task with vigour, and was placed in charge of dressing her ladyship each morning, choosing her clothes and advising on style and makeup. He even helped her dress. Enid was happy at Walter's attention to detail and decided to keep him on.

It seemed an odd choice, as Rory quipped when told: 'Darling, how very eccentric of you. I'll bet you are the first woman to have a male lady's maid.' But it just added to the legend of a woman whose excesses had always been the subject of rumour and innuendo.

Caryll would tell the story of a conversation with university friends, during which one woman asked if he knew about a beautiful countess who had two footmen to help her out of the bath. 'Oh yes,' he replied without a hint of sarcasm. 'That's my mother, but she has four footmen, not two, because she gets worried that the floor might be slippery.'

This was not true, of course, but Pat and Caryll had learned to accept and even have fun with the myths of Lady Kenmare, which made it almost impossible to distinguish fact from fiction.

There was the story about an Austrian suitor named Meissner, who met Enid on the ski fields of France and followed her home to London, where he would wait forlornly outside the Mayfair house. When Enid finally insisted that he leave her alone, Meissner blew himself up.

Supposedly another jilted lover, upset that Enid was seeing a rival, threw himself beneath the wheels of Le Train Bleu, the Calais–French Riviera express, while a third had leaped off a boat steaming into Sydney Harbour and drowned, or was eaten by sharks, depending on who was telling the story. 'They couldn't take the strain,' was the tongue-in-cheek explanation.

Life was now centred in the south of France with the

occasional trip to London, where Enid maintained the Lees Place house despite Rory's preference that she sell and stay at the Dorchester when in the city. Although life had moved on, Enid was not yet ready to sever the final link to her last two husbands and their extraordinary lives.

The renovations of La Fiorentina were now essentially complete and work was continuing on the three other houses on the property, Le Clos, La Florida and La Maison Blanche, which would be either let out or used for the overflow of guests who would stream in and out of the property over the next twenty years.

Somerset Maugham had also returned to the Riviera after the war and, like Enid, had spent time restoring his house, La Mauresque, which had been abandoned and left to rot. Willy was an almost permanent fixture at La Fiorentina, where he and Enid would spend hours playing bridge, often with Elvira de la Fuente, the daughter of a Peruvian diplomat. During the war, Elvira had operated as a double agent with the unlikely code name of Bronx, after a popular rum-based cocktail she liked to drink in London casinos and clubs.

Elvira was credited with saving London from a nerve chemical attack in 1943 by telling the Germans, falsely, that the British had the capacity to retaliate if they went ahead with their plans. In 1944 she also played an important background role in the success of the D-Day landings by telling the Germans, in an encoded message about a dentist's appointment, that the landings were scheduled for the Bay of Biscay rather than the beaches of Normandy.

Her deeds remained a secret immediately after the war, when she returned to high-society life in the south of France. Courtesy of Enid, she lived in La Maison Blanche, partly because she played bridge well.

Maugham and Enid carried on like an old couple, according to Elvira, and this was sometimes misread by observers, as if there was a possible romantic liaison between them and the previously married novelist might become husband number five. Given that he was gay and had a long-time partner, his private secretary Alan Searle, this was most unlikely. 'I shall have to go home soon or lose my youth,' Maugham announced once as a late-night dinner dragged on past midnight. 'Well, you should have brought him with you' came the witty reply from one of the guests.

Elvira knew them well enough to insist that Enid had the measure of the notoriously crusty Maugham: 'They were a funny couple, intimate because of bridge. They played all the time. It was companionship and affection but there was no thought of romance. Two people more different you could not find.'

Rory hated the constant smoking around the card table in the main living room, so he had a pavilion built among the trees overlooking the water and moved the card players out of the main home. It was here during one drawn-out bridge session that Maugham gave Enid the nickname by which she would come to be remembered. Wondering aloud about her name—Lady Kenmare—and the fact that all four husbands had died, he suggested that a more apt title would be Lady Killmore.

Over the years, the timing of this conversation would be changed, the most popular being that it took place before the war, when Enid first arrived at Cap Ferrat and before she had met Maugham. Countess Helene de Breteuil's version went like this: 'Maugham arrived at luncheon and said: "Apparently there is a lady on Cap Ferrat who has killed all her husbands." At which Enid turned to her son and asked: "Rory, did I really kill them all?"'

It couldn't have happened this way, of course, given that her name at the time was Lady Furness, that Marmaduke was still alive and she had not reconnected with Valentine Castlerosse, who had not yet inherited the title of Lord Kenmare, the inspiration for the nickname.

Such details did not halt the story and, ever willing to add to her own mythology, Enid would sometimes raise the name herself in conversation: 'Do I look like a murderer? Tell me, do I?' she once asked a guest who interpreted the question as a challenge.

When she arrived in Australia in 1947 a reporter from the *Sydney Morning Herald* asked her how many times she had been married: 'Oh, four or five times,' she replied lazily. 'I don't bother with divorce; it's too messy. I just kill my husbands.'

Pat was shocked: 'Why did you tell them that? It's not true.'

'It doesn't matter,' Enid replied. 'They'll print what they like anyway.'

But the joke had begun to wear thin by the mid-1950s when Enid attended a dinner party on Long Island, outside New York, where the dinner's host, Jimmy Donahue, an heir to the Woolworth fortune and cousin of Enid's great friend Barbara Hutton, asked her directly about the nickname. When she replied that it was a painful story that had caused her much distress, Donahue persisted: 'But why do they say that?' Enid turned to her escort for the evening and asked him to take her back to New York.

A few days later, the situation worsened considerably when a young man named Donald Bloomingdale, grandson of Lyman Bloomingdale, who with his brother Joseph had turned a small ladieswear shop in the Lower East Side into the iconic department store, was invited to attend a dinner party being hosted by Anne Tiffany, Enid's former sister-in-law, in honour of a visit by Enid and Rory.

Donald was married to another scion, Bethsabée de Rothschild of the French banking family, but it was a union in name only to cover for his homosexuality. He was invited as a friend of Rory's and at one point in the evening was introduced to the hostess. The notoriously snobbish Anne Tiffany pondered for a moment over the name: 'Bloomingdale,' she mused as if trying to recall. 'Oh yes, pots and pans.'

But the amusement had a tragic ending. Later that night, back at his hotel, where he kept a room, Donald Bloomingdale died of a drug overdose and his body was discovered the next day by his butler. The story quickly circulated through society that Bloomingdale had died of a heroin overdose, and that he had been given the drugs by Enid, Lady Kenmare. To compound the story, it would be claimed that Enid was rushed out of the country by friends the following day and did not return to New York for some years.

The story of Donald Bloomingdale's death ran in the newspapers for several weeks, with the media intrigued not only by his demise but revelations about his life. The will revealed that he had secretly divorced his wife three years before and that she had not laid claim to any of his estate, which had been left to friends and relatives, including 'specified jewellery and antiques' to his friend Rory Cameron.

Then it was dropped, although society gossips would peddle various versions for years. Eventually, Enid's alleged involvement found its way into the papers in a lengthy article that quoted a number of Enid's friends, all of them anonymously. In part it read:

> One friend of Bloomingdale said with absolute authority that the heroin was delivered in a lace handkerchief with a coronet and Lady Kenmare's initials. Another was equally adamant that the heroin arrived in the back of a silver picture frame containing a photograph of Lady Kenmare. However it was delivered, the dosage proved fatal. Good servant that he was, the valet knew better than to call the police. It was not his first such experience. He called the family lawyer instead. The lace handkerchief with the coronet, or the picture frame, or whatever receptacle the heroin came in, was removed, as were the implements of injection. The family lawyer called the family

doctor, and the cause of death of the rich, handsome young heir was given as a heart attack. Meanwhile, Lady Kenmare, by that time no stranger to whispers of scandal, was spirited out of the country on the afternoon plane. No connection was ever made publicly between her and the death of Donald Bloomingdale. There was no scandal, no hints in the newspapers, simply a death by natural causes—but everybody knew.

Except that none of it was true.

The *New York Times* reported two weeks after the death that the autopsy had concluded Bloomingdale had died from an overdose of barbiturates, and that it was either suicide or a tragic accident. Several tablets and an empty syringe were found on his dresser, and he had been under treatment for a nervous disorder. A nurse named Loretta Wright had been with Bloomingdale in his room until 2.30 a.m., giving him an injection of seconal, a barbiturate prescribed for insomnia. After she left, he was thought to have given himself a second, more powerful injection, hence the empty syringe.

The autopsy found no evidence of heroin in any form, but it didn't stop the gossips.

'She smoked opium, certainly, and took heroin,' insisted Tony Pawson, writer and cricketer who often visited La Fiorentina. 'A lot of these people smoked two pipes of opium a day. If you keep the same amount and don't increase the dosage, it is supposed to rejuvenate one.'

His voice then dropped to a whisper as he told his version of the Bloomingdale story, *off the record*, describing Enid's stash as 'a bad batch'. When asked if she ever spoke about it, Pawson conceded: 'It was always a tricky subject. She didn't talk too much about it because all the rumours were going around.'

Daisy Fellowes enjoyed perpetuating the myth as well. When Enid was late for one of her lunch parties, Daisy snipped: 'Busy with her needle, no doubt.'

❧

The stream of visitors to La Fiorentina seemed constant to Pat, who noted that during the summer months, in particular, the houses were always full of guests. The chef once complained that he was serving three thousand meals a week, with the food often brought by one of the cooking staff on her bicycle and cooked on a coal stove as post-war electricity supplies remained problematic.

A visitors' book was kept to record the social history taking place. The guests, mostly famous or rich, and usually both, either stayed or dined in what had become the most famous house on one of the most famous headlands in the world.

Their names dropped like stardust—the Mitford sisters, Nancy, Pamela and Diana, who stayed a number of times; as did the art and music critic Sacheverell Sitwell; and the explorer and travel writer Freya Stark. There was the artist Graham Sutherland, American fashion photographer Irving Penn, the French composer George Auric, French novelists Louise de Vilmorin and Romain Gary, and the English writer and historian Lesley Blanch.

US senator and future president John F. Kennedy was a dinner guest one summer while the British Prime Minister Winston Churchill and his wife, Clementine, came on more than one occasion, particularly during his time as opposition leader in the late 1940s.

La Fiorentina also became a 'Riviera must-visit' for Hollywood A-listers. Academy Award-winning actress Claudette Colbert was a frequent visitor, as were Fred Astaire and his dance partner, Ginger Rogers. Cary Grant came for lunch, and Marlene Dietrich and Frank Sinatra for dinner; others included Rita Hayworth, for a time married to Prince Aly Khan, son of the Aga Khan, and reputed to keep ice cubes by his bed to 'cool his ardour' during the night.

Royalty—major and minor—visited. Enid had remained friends with Edward, Duke of Windsor, and his wife Wallis Simpson and they mixed socially whenever the Windsors stayed on the Riviera. One day the royal couple arrived for lunch with a select group of friends, among them a young American named Jimmy. It was rumoured that Wallis and Jimmy were having an affair behind the Duke's back, which seemed to be confirmed when Wallis took the young man upstairs to 'show him the lovely view from your point', while the Duke sat talking about 'when I was the monarch . . .' Enid later remarked that Wallis was known for her fellatio techniques, 'learned in Japan'.

From the world of high society came the oft-married Austro-Hungarian Countess Etti Plesch; the Italian jeweller Fulco, Duke of Verdura; party supremo Elsa Maxwell; the American property magnates Rosita and Norman Winston; and Woolworth heiress Barbara Hutton who, like Coco Chanel, had become a close friend of Enid's.

In the early 1960s the debonair David Niven moved to Cap Ferrat, buying a salmon-pink villa, Lo Scoglietto, from the estate of Charlie Chaplin and restoring it. He brought with him a new batch of famous faces, including Grace Kelly and Prince Rainier, who followed Niven to La Fiorentina. When the prince married the Hollywood star in 1956, Enid attended the wedding and was applauded while leaving the church, the crowd under the impression that she was a member of the Royal Family.

The reclusive screen legend Greta Garbo was another guest, although her arrivals were never noted in the visitors' book. Rory was too afraid to ask her to sign after he was told of the time when she had burst into tears after she was asked at a restaurant to inscribe a book. She was a shy woman despite her fame. 'But Garbo loved La Fiorentina,' he would write. 'She felt relaxed and laughed a great deal, throwing her head back. It is difficult to describe the effect she had on one apart from the extraordinary beauty she wore about her that, like royalty, makes one shy.'

The guest lists were eclectic: architects and movie stars, young artists and old politicians, old-money aristocrats and new-money businessmen, flamboyant socialites and bitchy interior designers, often jumbled together in interests and ages. As the architect Charles Sevigny noted: 'Looking through album after album of photographs of life at La Fiorentina, with its constant unending parties, there was not an angry or worried face among them. Any age, any generation, eighteen to sixty-five, in and out of the house—and dogs everywhere.'

There were exceptions of course, such as the night that Elsa Maxwell dined in a crowd that included the Duke of Sutherland and the diplomat and explorer Sir Bede Clifford, the son of the Baron of Chudleigh. The conversation became heated when it turned to entitlement. 'Any man can be born to a title,' Elsa insisted. She was rounded upon by the two titled men, who vigorously defended their birthright. Elsa fumed and left, declaring that 'Mr Onassis's car' was waiting for her.

Enid was the quiet centre of the storm, forever painting or making something, invariably wafting into the room well after the other guests had sat down to dinner, dressed in a long-flowing diaphanous robe, like some Greek goddess. Or she would be in an evening gown, her arms and fingers bedecked in jewellery, ready to head to the casino—but only after she had finished peeling the broad beans for dinner.

32

THE UNFLAPPABLE HOSTESS

In 1990 the American journalist and film producer Dominick Dunne went searching for the Enid Kenmare story. Dunne had styled himself as a celebrity crime writer, driven by the killing eight years before of his daughter, Dominique, an actress most famous for her role in the movie classic *Poltergeist*, who had been strangled to death by her violent boyfriend. John Sweeney served less than four years for his crime, which enraged Dunne.

He would later write about the trial of football star O.J. Simpson and socialite Claus Von Bulow, among other society crimes, and Enid's story seemed to fit the mould of the famous getting away with murder: the story of a beautiful woman who had been married and widowed four times, and been handed at least two fortunes through the deaths of her first and third husbands.

Dunne pulled no punches. 'There are people in fashionable society who, throughout their lives, carry with them the burden of their scandals, as ineradicable from their personalities as a tattoo on their forearm,' he began. 'Such a person, forever notorious, was the beautiful Enid Kenmare, or Lady Kenmare or, to be perfectly correct, Enid, Countess of Kenmare, a mythical figure of the French Riviera and chatelaine of a great house, the villa La Fiorentina, who lost four husbands, all by death.'

Sadly, the quality of Dunne's research left much to be desired. He enthusiastically tracked down and interviewed a dozen or more now-ageing men and women who had known Enid and Rory, and been regular visitors at La Fiorentina; he gave weight to their gossip without bothering to check the accuracy of their accounts.

Still, it made great copy when published by *Tatler* magazine and later in a book compilation of some of his best feature articles. After his death in 2009, at the age of eighty-three, Dunne's papers were archived by the University of Texas, including the typed notes of his various interviews for the Enid Kenmare story.

They paint an intriguing picture of a woman whom none of her guests really understood but, with few exceptions, they liked her and admired her individuality. She was undeniably eccentric, and unquestionably beautiful and statuesque—even as she made her way elegantly into her sixties, and despite the ever-present hyrax called Tikki, which she carried on her shoulder like a piece of jewellery.

'She had a face like porcelain and the most extraordinary skin,' socialite Marguerite Littman, famous for being the model for Truman Capote's Southern heroine Holly Golightly, told Dunne. 'She walked into the dining room wearing Givenchy and earrings and gloves, dressed like she was going to the Ritz.'

'A beauty, her spirit welcomed us with serene joy,' said Mary Wells Lawrence. 'Enid always descended to her candlelit dinners in her pre-war Lucien Lelongs, Robert Piguets, and Lanvins, wearing cabochon emeralds and rubies, always with a monkey or her pet hyrax sitting bright-eyed and upright on her shoulder.'

It was not uncommon for Enid to change during the evening, as one account detailed during an all-night party in the summer of 1952: 'The Countess amused her guests by changing her dress three times during the evening, from full-length black Dior to a white Balmain ballerina-length to a simple little Jacques Fath playsuit to serve bacon and eggs at dawn.'

For some guests, she was a formidable host. The American singer and actress Lena Horne asked to stop at a hotel for a stiff drink on the way to the villa, before she met the 'beautiful but daunting Lady Kenmare'. Rod Coupe, an art critic friend of Rory's who had been sent to pick Horne up, watched as Enid took the frightened guest under her wing: 'She was soon surrounded by Prince and Princess Liechtenstein, Prince Pierre de Polignac and Prince and Princess Chavchavadze, all of whom were paying her court. I could see that she and Enid were getting on famously, and the beautiful Lena Horne had overcome her fright and had settled peacefully among half the minor royalty of Europe.'

To others, Enid was uninterested in the pretensions of being a society hostess; her guest lists seemed thrown together on a whim, as if she either didn't care or was deliberately challenging social practice. 'She was an original,' mused Elvira de la Fuente. 'You could ask her to sit next to a prince or a waiter. It didn't make any difference to her.'

'Decorative. That's the first word that comes to mind,' New York art dealer Solange Herter offered. 'She had a beautiful bearing, very tall with a fantastic posture. When she walked into the casino at night, people would drop their cards or chips to look at her. It wasn't so much that she was superior, but that she was in another sphere almost. She sort of floated.'

In her own 2011 memoir, *No More Tiaras*, Herter went further: 'To me, Lady Kenmare was utterly enchanting, and I was fascinated by her. Even with a score of servants around, when it came to the salad course, Lady Kenmare would get up from the table and make the dressing herself at the sideboard. It was a weird concoction of Coleman's dry mustard and sweet Nestlé condensed milk, which was anathema to the French; but it was actually delicious.'

The interior designer David Nightingale Hicks, married to the daughter of the Earl Mountbatten, also recalled Enid's signature salad dressing: 'We had been invited by Princess Elizabeth Chavchavadze. I was bowled over by the beauty of the house, the garden, the position. We sat down to a wonderful lunch by an Italian pergola. After an hour our hostess appeared, wearing a long dress and a hyrax on her shoulder. She had been painting Chinese wallpaper. "I'm here to do your salad dressing," she said. She took a tin of very sweet condensed milk, olive oil, lemon juice, curry powder and vinegar and made the most extraordinary dressing. Beautiful, but absolutely practical.'

Hicks once flew next to Enid in a small airplane: 'She sat with her head back and her eyes closed. "Tell the pilot we're heading in the wrong direction," she said to me. "Lady Kenmare says you're heading in the wrong direction," I called out to the pilot. "My God, she's right," said the pilot.'

Enid's gambling matched her seemingly unflappable manner; equally unfazed by winning or losing, her interest was apparently not in money, which she carried carelessly in a purse, but in the challenge of beating the house at her two favourite games, chemin de fer and trente et quarante.

Solange Herter watched in amazement as she gave money away to strangers: 'Her attitude about money was extraordinary. She dug in her purse and gave out tips without looking at the money or counting it out. There were always huge amounts of chips. If she lost, she never reacted.'

Jimmy Douglas, a boyfriend of Barbara Hutton's, remembered one night in particular: 'She swept into the casino without showing her passport because she was so well-known. She didn't bring much money, maybe one thousand francs. She had a system and left that night with one million francs.'

On another occasion, he watched the American financier Eddie Gilbert (dubbed 'The Boy Wonder of Wall Street' by *Time* magazine) playing next to Enid, trying to copy her system. 'Go away,' she told him. 'You're bringing me bad luck.'

Even her accent was difficult to pin down. Did she sound Australian?

'She had a slight accent you couldn't quite define. Americanised, but not really American either,' said writer and cricketer Tony Pawson. 'Enid was, of course, beautiful. We all knew that she was one of the most accomplished women. She rode. She shot. She fished. She painted very well. She sculpted. She did beautiful needlework. She cooked marvellously. There was nothing she couldn't do, and she did all those things because she enjoyed doing them. She was always calm about her agitated life. Perhaps serene is a better word. Oh, but she was tough too.'

There were, of course, rivalries, most notably with her Cap Ferrat neighbour Daisy Fellowes, a woman with a notoriously sharp tongue who once described Enid as 'an Australian with a vague pedigree'.

Once in conversation, Enid began a sentence with the phrase 'people of our class'. Daisy raised her hand and stopped the conversation: 'Just a moment, Enid. Your class or mine?'

On another occasion, Daisy boasted of planning a dinner party where all the guests would be murderers: 'I'm going to have six men and six women, and Enid Kenmare will have the place of honour, because she killed the most people of anyone.'

Yves Vidal, another of Rory's designer friends, thought Enid was misunderstood: 'Before anything else, she was a mother. Most of the things she did—marrying all those men—were for the children more than herself. She was always doing something. I remember once watching her run down the steps of

La Fiorentina followed by her dogs. She was very beautiful, and she knew she was very beautiful. What made her life and ruined her life at the same time was her beauty. Until the end, she kept a wonderful allure.'

Vidal paused, considering the woman he regarded as mysterious: 'I think Enid was miscast in the grand life of a chatelaine and hostess of the Riviera. She would rather have been on a farm surrounded by animals.'

It was an astute observation.

33

BARON OF WATERPARK

Given the antiquated formality and demands of the British aristocracy, it is not surprising that families themselves become confused about their ancestors and their deeds, and that once great legacies, lands and houses are often reduced to mere courtesies and sad baubles.

The Cavendish family has experienced many such twists and turns. One of the great noble houses of the United Kingdom, with numerous branches and peerages over the past five hundred years, it has produced great generals and politicians, composers and writers, and even the odd explorer.

But even such families fracture. When young Henry Cavendish argued with his mother, the redoubtable Bess of Hardwick, in the early 1570s over his libertine ways, it ended with him being disinherited and changing the course of his family's history. Instead of being handed the grand title of Duke of Devonshire, held in wardship by his mother since the death of his father when he was seven years old, the title was given to his younger brother.

Henry was left without a title, other than his nickname 'The Common Bull of Derbyshire' for his sexual exploits with commoners. He also became the MP for Derbyshire for more than twenty years, travelled widely and was considered a friend of Mary Queen of Scots.

And when his mother finally died, Henry exacted some revenge by inheriting the family's great home, Chatsworth House, which he promptly sold to brother William for £10,000. It remains the family home of the Dukes of Devonshire, now in its twelfth generation.

Fast-forward almost two hundred years and five generations to another Henry Cavendish. Born in 1707, he had risen to the position of High Sheriff of Derbyshire and Commissioner of Revenue in Ireland when he was made a baronet, the lowest rung on the aristocratic ladder. On his death, the title was handed to his son, yet another Henry, who would become an important political figure, not for his contribution to policy but as a diarist who, using a system of shorthand, recorded more than five million words of speeches made to the British and Irish parliaments that would have otherwise been unreported. The volumes are now in the British Museum.

His contribution was recognised in 1792 when a new title, the Barony of Waterpark, was created not for him but for his wife, Lady Sarah Cavendish, to circumvent a technicality that would have made it impossible for him to continue sitting in the Irish Parliament.

When Baronet Cavendish and Baroness Waterpark died in the first decade of the nineteenth century, their titles were inherited by their eldest son, Richard, along with the family land holdings outside Cork, in Ireland, and an estate in Derbyshire with a grand mansion called Doveridge Hall, set high on a hill above the Dove River amid eighty-five hectares of clipped lawns, hedges and wooded lands.

Over the next five generations the titles would be handed down, as required, to eldest sons, most of whom (surprise, surprise) were also named Henry. The Barons of Waterpark all followed similar career paths: beginning their adult life in the military, before being elected to parliament and serving in some capacity in local government and the local church. All were based at the splendid Doveridge Hall, overflowing with servants and social calendars defined by fox hunts.

Some attained high office, such as the third Baron, Henry Manners Cavendish, who served as Lord of the Bedchamber to Albert Prince Consort and Lord-in-Waiting to Queen Victoria, a curious but nonetheless powerful role as a confidant to the Royal Family. But his heir, Henry Anson Cavendish, was an exception. Described as a 'sportsman', the fourth baron spurned the traditional responsibilities of office and, on acquiring the title, left to go big-game hunting in Africa and India.

The sixth Lord Waterpark was another Henry, and the older brother of Frederick 'Caviar' Cavendish, Enid's second husband. Henry was a soldier and an African explorer who spent very little time at home, which was perhaps why his five marriages all failed. Still, he managed to have three children—all daughters. The lineage of sons had come to an end and, when he died in November 1948 at the age of seventy-two, the title was handed to his nephew—Caryll Cavendish.

Although the title remained, there was little else for Caryll to inherit beyond the family heraldry—a crest featuring a twisted snake (probably indicating wisdom) above two giant stags supporting a shield emblazoned with three bucks' heads and a rather mundane motto, *Cavendo tutus*, meaning 'Secure by caution'.

The powerful royal and government positions had long gone and so had the money, as well as the lands and, sadly, Doveridge Hall itself. Like many wealthy family estates, it had fallen into disuse and disrepair by the latter part of the nineteenth century, the estate sold off in bits and pieces and the hall leased and then sold, too big to be maintained. In 1938, without any reference to the family, the great hall was finally demolished, its mighty stones crushed and used for road fill that would eventually become the base of the motorway A50.

Although there appeared to be no tangible benefits, the title offered a young man who already had access to money and to a large house something far more valuable—a sense of self. Caryll had just turned twenty-two and been discharged from the army after spending the last two years of the war serving in the 1st and 4th battalions of the Grenadier Guards.

The highlight of his experience came in the aftermath of Germany's surrender, when he helped to guard Grand Admiral

Karl Dönitz, commander of the German Navy and successor to Adolf Hitler as President of Germany in the crumbling days of the Third Reich, while he faced trial at Nuremberg.

But, like many young men returning from war, Caryll was searching for his own space in a new world, not to mention a voice within a family of wealth, personality and tragedy in equal measure. A title, however meaningless in a practical sense, presented him with an identity.

While Pat had grown up at the side of her mother, and older brother Rory was the virtual head of the household and a powerful influence over his mother, Caryll had been at times sidelined during his childhood. This was partly due to the social norms of the day, when young men were sent away to boarding school from a young age, but also because of the tantrums of his stepfather.

Like his sister, Caryll would later regale with delight the stories and mythologies of his mother's adventures, her lifestyle and marriages; these were a matter of pride, rather than of shame or regret. But there were also memories that were more painful, like the summer he was forced to stay at school with his housemaster at Eton college because Furness refused to allow him to join the family at The Berries in Le Touquet.

He was not scarred, as such, but the luxury of La Fiorentina offered little for young Lord Waterpark other than lazy summers. Neither did cities like London or Paris. Instead, he chose to follow the lead of two of his predecessors and look for challenges abroad. In late 1949, he boarded a ship, the *Orcades*, with his mother and sister who were headed to Australia for what would become an almost annual trip. But Caryll was only going as far as Port Said, where he disembarked, having convinced his mother to back his decision financially.

He was moving to Kenya.

Pat was also moving out from under her mother's shadow, albeit with some trepidation. Always shy, the product of a life that had cowed her as much as sheltered her from reality, Pat had turned twenty-four in the European summer of 1949, when she suddenly become engaged to a lanky, brooding poet named Richard Murphy.

The son of the British Governor of the Bahamas, Sir William Murphy, Richard had met Pat when she and her mother stayed on the island of Nassau during a lengthy visit to America and Mexico on the way back from their 1948 Australian sojourn.

She had been entranced by what she called his 'Byronic looks' and romantic manner. Theirs had been a whirlwind romance, with his proposal made on a moonlit night between kisses in the back seat of a car.

She and Enid left Nassau a week later, with the wedding set for September. But then Pat had second thoughts after getting back to France and called it off by letter. The idea of marriage suddenly felt like entrapment: 'I needed to feel free and marriage, in my mind, symbolised a loss of freedom,' she wrote later. She was undoubtedly influenced by her mother's experiences and frightened of life outside the walls of La Fiorentina.

But her commitment fears did not last long. Just three months later, onboard the *Orcades* a few days after leaving Caryll on the Port Said docks, she met Australian swimming champion Frank O'Neill.

This time Pat was swept off her feet not by romantic poetry but by the sheer physical beauty of the athlete from Manly who had been in Europe trying, unsuccessfully, to force his way into the Australian Olympic team for the 1948 Games in London. She spied him doing laps in the ship's swimming pool and watched as he emerged, water dripping from him 'and the most indecent bathing suit of a very thin material in navy blue that looked like a second skin'.

By the time the *Orcades* reached Sydney, they were a couple very much in love—she with his physical magnetism and laid-back Australian manner, and he with her demure beauty that seemed at odds with her place in high society.

Their engagement was announced in early 1950, cheered by the crowd at the North Sydney Olympic Pool as Frank stood on the dais after winning the NSW 110-yard freestyle title. This news was greeted by a swathe of headlines about the reverse 'Cinderella' romance, in which a poor boy falls in love with an heiress.

Pat flashed a five-stone turquoise engagement ring, clearly not bought by Frank, who worked as a dental assistant when he wasn't swimming, but by Enid who was asked about her future son-in-law as she boarded a flight back to Europe a few weeks later. 'Frank is a nice boy. I like him tremendously,' she offered.

This time Pat took her betrothed, who had just won two silver medals at the Empire Games, back to La Fiorentina with her. Here, other than training every day by swimming five miles out into the bay, he slipped into the role of swimming coach to the celebrity guests who stayed that summer, including the painfully shy Greta Garbo, who refused to put her face in the water; Ginger Rogers, who insisted on swimming breaststroke; and a 'mad keen' Somerset Maugham, whom he taught to dive.

Frank wrote home frequently in the months before the wedding, starry-eyed at the lifestyle. 'I have never seen anything so beautiful,' he said of La Fiorentina, where he listened to a famous Russian concert pianist before he, Pat and Enid dined with Prince Rainier of Monaco and Baron Rothschild. There was a chauffeured Rolls-Royce to take them to the races—where a man took his jacket, laid his bets and collected his winnings for him—and an apartment in central Paris along with backstage passes to the Folies Bergère.

He escorted Enid to the Monte Carlo casino, where he watched her bet £500 a hand and embarrass a 'thug-like' Egyptian King Farouk, who hated being beaten by a woman: 'Enid is one of the best gamblers there. She still turns heads wherever she goes and she is sixty. I have to pinch myself that this is all real.'

The wedding was a small affair at the British consulate in Nice at the end of September. Pat shunned white to wear a Bordeaux red dress with polka spots and a silver fox fur over her shoulders while Frank's parents, who couldn't afford to make the trip, waited by the phone back in Sydney for news. When the call finally came, Frank kept it brief. 'He was very excited,' his father told the reporters who clamoured for a quote. 'He told us he didn't have much time, but that he was coming home in October.'

Enid's assessment of the marriage was also succinct: 'They are a sensible couple and will make a success of it on their merits,' she offered as the newlyweds left a month later to fly back to Australia, where Frank wanted to defend his national swimming titles.

But Pat would last three months in Manly, fleeing back to France on the pretext that she was missing her dogs—poodles named Bambi, Jeep, Pancho and Greis—which could not be taken to Australia because of quarantine laws. In truth, she struggled to be away from her mother. 'Poor Frank,' she would later write. 'I really was the most unsatisfactory wife. I didn't want to go and live in Australia.'

And Frank didn't want to live a luxurious life in France. 'I'm just an ordinary boy,' he told curious newspaper reporters. 'Although I enjoyed meeting my mother-in-law's friends, including ambassadors, ministers, writers and artists, the social life was strenuous at most times. The simple life is for me. I am only too glad to get back for a stay with Mum and Dad at Manly. It's the home where I was born and reared, and I'll even be back in my own room.'

Despite his reservations, Frank would follow his wife back to Europe, where the marriage floundered. Pat did not accompany Frank when he returned to Australia the following year in his bid to be selected on the team for the 1952 Olympic Games. She wasn't poolside in Helsinki when he captained the swimming squad, nor commiserating when he did not perform as he had hoped and missed medals in his favourite event. Nor was she by his side when he returned to Sydney to announce his retirement from competitive swimming.

When asked about his wife of just two years, Frank told the media that she was back in France with her sick mother and that their plans to settle in Kenya, on the property with his brother-in-law Caryll, had been put on hold because of the Mau Mau Uprising that would drag on for seven years. 'We might go to Kenya later,' he offered.

But it never happened, at least not for Frank. A few weeks later he received a letter from Pat. She wanted a divorce. Things just weren't working out; they lived in different worlds. Frank agreed, although reluctantly. They would not see each other again for seventeen years.

34

A NEW ADVENTURE BECKONS

The term 'jet set' is attributed to an American newspaper society columnist, the pseudonymous Cholly Knickerbocker, who in the mid-1950s used the phrase to describe the response by the wealthy 'cafe society' to the introduction of scheduled flights for commercial airlines, pandering to their desire to fly around the world on a whim.

It fell neatly into the world of Enid, Lady Kenmare, who seemed to be thriving in her new life beyond the company of men, at least in a formal capacity. She continued to have the occasional lover but they were flings rather than romances, as if she were checking her makeup in the mirror, to make sure her lipstick hadn't worn off. And there was no shortage of admirers, as Frank O'Neill had observed.

Now in her mid-sixties, she no longer had to perform as a wife, but was free to indulge in her personal passions and delightful eccentricities. When she wasn't painting, sculpting, tending her beloved animals, playing bridge or cooking for thirty guests or more, she seemed to be in a constant state of travel, anchored socially to La Fiorentina for the European summer before flying to Australia for Christmas. Apart from these trips, her European winters were now usually spent partly in the Bahamas, where she kept a house on Nassau, while in between she flitted off to New York, London or Paris for society dinners or accompanied Rory on his frequent architectural trips into northern Europe or cultural sojourns into the Middle East and India.

Rory was now an acclaimed travel writer-cum-interior designer. He had caused a stir in Sydney around the time of Pat's engagement to Frank O'Neill when his newly released book, *My Travel's History*, lamented that Sydney was 'like a faded beauty one catches a glimpse of what must have been'. The city had become 'dark, ugly and unimpressive . . . a city of liver-coloured bricks, thoroughfares without trees and a harbour smothered with ugly little houses'.

Melbourne also copped a beating—'dark, grimy and somewhat depressing'—while Canberra was 'a capital in search of a city'. Brisbane was a strange city of 'untidy wooden buildings with corrugated iron rooves' and an art gallery that 'looked like it may have served time as a fort'. King's Park was the saving grace for Perth; otherwise, it was Americanised, its hotel cupboards 'reek of departed commercial travellers, the food tasteless but the oysters are excellent'. Only Adelaide was praised in full—'the finest of Australia's cities. It's gay, it's clean and abounds in trees, statues, ornamental waters, parks, museums and libraries.'

Australians were 'forthright, stolid and almost rude in their directness'; and the country itself, other than the glorious natural wonders, was 'artistically a barren land of bad taste, so far behind the times (she is still bedecking herself with crinolined doll tea cosies and telephone covers and gilded wastepaper baskets wreathed in the wax flowers of the twenties) that by the time she is ready to appreciate her young painters they will have established themselves abroad and won't want to return.'

The book, which balanced its stinging critique of almost everything man-made in his mother's homeland with its wonder at the country's natural splendours, caused an understandable stir when it was published, although not as much as one might have thought. The local reviews mostly praised his fearless appraisal and writing ability: 'In an age of hail-fellow-well-met reporters at large, and cafe columnists turned international observers, it is a welcome change to find a travel book written by an author with a cultured mind,' said the *Women's Weekly*.

For Enid, it was undoubtedly a vindication of her decision to take her young son away from small-town Sydney and its provincial expectations, and expose him to Europe's struggles and opportunities. Independent wealth had not dulled his natural curiosity.

There was one shock for her, though, when Rory revealed to her that he was gay. After numerous relationships with women, many of them older, he had decided that he preferred men. A casual glance at his photographic albums of La Fiorentina reveals his sexual proclivity, but Elvira de la Fuente insisted that Enid had not considered the possibility. 'She never suspected. It was a shock to her but a shock she overcame in a day or two. She was the mother I would like to have had. She never, never did what family people can do; criticise and mumble about their children.'

Enid also had to hold her tongue when Pat married for a second time in 1957, yet again in a rush and this time to a young man she had met in a Nassau nightclub. Count Aymon de Roussy de Sales was a budding artist, several years her junior. His late father, Raoul, had been a well-known French journalist and 'mouthpiece' of Charles de Gaulle as he led the French Resistance during the war—a nobleman with a mountaintop castle and a descendant of François de Sales, a former Bishop of Geneva and Catholic saint.

Pat would write with great flourish about their love-life, including his marriage proposal aboard a yacht during a tornado: 'I could hardly hear him above the screaming of the wind. He was laughing as he bent to kiss me. I knew I wanted to spend the rest of my life with this wonderful man.'

But the flame would die quickly, the marriage lasting barely a year, complicated yet again by Pat's reluctance to leave her mother's side and an ectopic pregnancy which left her unable to ever have children. This time, however, it was her husband who wanted to end the marriage: 'I received a *Dear Jane* letter asking for a divorce. He had met someone in Mexico. Quite naturally, I replied that he should go ahead with his romantic plans and I would not try and stop him.'

In truth, his request probably came as some relief.

Enid's marriage to Marmaduke Furness may have been troubled but if there was one positive legacy it was the love that she and the children would develop for the wild freedom of Africa. Caryll was now firmly ensconced on a property a two-hour trek north of Nairobi, and visits became a regular part of Enid's annual travels. If the Riviera was the epitome of social luxury and excess, then the central highlands of Kenya were its natural equivalent.

The bumpy drive from Nairobi to the so-called White Highlands was almost biblical in its splendour. At first there was a series of lush rolling hills and valleys covered in giant croton trees and hillsides smothered in the contrasting shades of the emerald coffee plantations and the yellow-green of the tea bushes. There was a spot on the road where Enid and Pat would stop to gaze in awe at the distant snow-clad peaks of Kilimanjaro to the south and Mount Kenya to the north.

Then came a steep descent into the Rift Valley, the 35-million-year-old tectonic fault line. The road down into the valley had been built by Italian prisoners of war, who followed old elephant trails to carve a thoroughfare through the dense forest. Spread out below was a spectacle of extinct volcanos and lakes, bordered to the east by the Aberdare mountain range and to the west by the Mau escarpment and Loita Hills. The dusky plains between teemed with game; the lakes were crimson with the dense flocks of flamingos on their shores.

Equator Farm, named because the equator ran through the centre of the house Caryll had built when his mother bought the 12,000 acres for him in celebration of his return to civilian life, was set into a 10,000-foot high escarpment of the Aberdares. He ran dairy cattle and maize crops on the upper levels of the tiered landscape, which was surrounded by dense forest and a waterfall that cascaded thousands of feet to the valley below.

Caryll had also married on a whim but, unlike his older sister's commitment difficulties, it was a union that would last. In the spring of 1950, during a trip back to La Fiorentina from his new home in Kenya, Caryll had stopped in Paris for a few days. One evening, he was invited to a cocktail party by neighbours, none of whom spoke more than a few words of English. In an attempt to make the young man feel more comfortable, they also invited the daughter of a friend, who had been studying languages at the Sorbonne and was a fluent English speaker.

It seemed obvious to those who attended the party that it was love at first sight for young Lord Waterpark, who promptly invited Danièle Guirche, daughter of a well-to-do Parisian textile manufacturer, to spend some time with him that summer at La Fiorentina.

They were married less than a year later. Danièle was happy to move to Kenya with her new husband, whose interest in farming had been sparked by having spent time at the Royal Agricultural University at Cirencester after he graduated from

Eton. There would be three children—Caroline in 1952 and Juliet a year later. Roderick arrived in 1959.

In the fifties, the end of white colonialism in Kenya loomed large. Just as Caryll and Danièle were settling into their new life, the so-called Mau Mau Uprising began, an eight-year guerrilla campaign by rebels against the white establishment they accused of stealing their land. Although most of those killed would be African, there would also be white victims such as the Ruck family—Roger, Esme and their six-year-old son Michael—who were hacked to death when a mob of thirty rebels raided their property, along the road to Equator Farm.

Caryll would sit at the dinner table each evening with a Barretta sub-machine gun in his lap, conscious of the Mau Mau tactic of making sudden raids at homes of white settlers. He slept for six years with a box of hand grenades under his bed and frequently chased away gang members lying in wait at the bottom of the grounds.

By 1959 they'd had enough. The dangers were too great, particularly with a young family, so Caryll and Danièle packed up and returned to London. 'Some nights we could see the smoke of their campfires,' Danièle, now a spritely ninety years old, recalls. 'It was very unsettling with young children. That's why we left in the end. The fighting might have been over but you could never be quite sure what might happen.'

But for Pat and Enid, it was just the beginning of their affair with Africa, undeterred by the violence even when they were confronted one year with the sight of torture victims buried alive, head-first in aardvark holes, by the side of the road.

Despite the concerns of their driver, Enid insisted on stopping as she and Pat dug frantically to save the men, but they were long dead from suffocation.

The visit in 1958 was supposed to be a holiday to help Pat recover physically from the trauma of her ectopic pregnancy and psychologically from the failure of her second marriage, but everything changed at the airport when a friend who had come to meet them gave Pat an orphaned lion cub.

Tana, as Pat called the barely week-old animal that sat in the palm of her hand, had been found next to her dead mother, who had been shot by poachers on the banks of the Tana River. Unable to take the animal back to France, Pat had a choice to make—give up the cub or give up La Fiorentina. She chose the latter.

The holiday turned into a property hunt and, with her mother's support, Pat found a farm at Karen, north of Nairobi, near where the Danish author Karen Blixen had written her 1937 memoir, *Out of Africa*.

'It was the same view that she described so lovingly in the book,' Pat would write. 'With binoculars I could see the grave of her lover, the hunter Denys Finch Hatton, on the lower ridges of the Ngong Hills. As Tana grew up, she would wander off there and lie under its shadow.'

The property was called Ol Orion, a rambling colonial bungalow overlooking the Rift Valley. It was framed by giant bougainvillea hedges, flat-topped acacias, daturas with their heavily scented devil's trumpet flowers, and wild olives. It would be her home for the next seven years, during which time she would collect a menagerie of rescued animals, including a cheetah, a baboon, bushbuck, warthogs, genet cats, monkeys by the score, two cranes and a chimpanzee she named Joseph.

Pat had no doubts about her choice. For all its wonders, the life at Cap Ferrat was Rory and Enid's world; it was a place in which she had always felt inadequate. Her only concern was leaving Enid, who was beginning to show signs of fragility: her usual energy was waning and there were the first signs of osteoarthritis.

Her ageless mother suddenly seemed in danger. When Pat, on one of her frequent trips back to La Fiorentina, found Enid motionless in bed one morning, she thought the worst. Pat burst out crying, and this wakened Enid, who embraced her daughter in a sea of silk and scent. 'Oh my darling,' she soothed. 'If I look that old I had better go and get another facelift.'

It was a typical response from a woman who never made a fuss, but Pat remained worried: 'I realised that Mummy, for all her beauty and glamour and attentive lovers and ex-lovers was, in fact, vulnerable and insecure in an alien world. All my life I had felt an urge to protect her from people who surrounded her and who understood her so little.'

35

THE RACING GAME

Beryl Markham was a pioneering aviator, the first woman to fly solo, non-stop across the Atlantic from east to west. She achieved this feat in 1936 in a heroic twenty-hour flight, during which her fuel tanks froze, forcing her to crash-land in a Nova Scotia bog to complete the crossing.

In doing so she matched the achievement of America's darling flyer Amelia Earhart, who, four years before, had crossed the Atlantic in the opposite direction although history would regard the two women very differently, one feted in her mysterious death and the other largely forgotten until late in a long and controversial life.

British-born but raised unconventionally in Kenya, Beryl was taught to fly by Tom Campbell Black when he was managing an aviation company in Africa. The pair became lovers, even though she was married with a young child, causing a scandal that ultimately caused Campbell Black to accept the role of Marmaduke Furness's private pilot and to move to England.

It was under these circumstances that Beryl Markham first met Enid, then the new Lady Furness, and began a friendship that would last, on and off, for the best part of three decades.

Both were strong-willed, tall, sleek and exotic women, who commanded the attention of men and courted controversy. Pat would recall when Beryl and Campbell Black flew into Burrough Court one day when she was nine years old: 'Mummy said "Today you are going to see a very beautiful lady" and I did. She was dressed in a white flying suit and looked so glamorous and beautiful—and she remained so long as I knew her.'

Beryl was not only an adventurous pilot but a successful racehorse trainer. Learning from her father, she became Kenya's youngest and first female trainer at the age of eighteen and over the next few years she won most of Kenya's main races. It was in this capacity that she reconnected with Enid almost thirty years after their first meeting.

In the intervening years Beryl had married three times, the first to a man twice her age, and taken numerous lovers, including a very public affair with Henry, Duke of Gloucester, until the Royal Family intervened. She was a tomboy in attitude but feminine in expectation and desire, striking with blue eyes, blonde hair and long, long legs. She once said: 'A life has to move or it stagnates. Even this life, I think. Every tomorrow ought not to resemble every yesterday.'

One might have been describing Enid, the only difference being that Beryl divorced her husbands while Enid buried hers.

'Beryl has a very masculine attitude to sex,' Enid once remarked to Pat, by way of explanation of her 'loose' ways and without a hint of irony.

❦

In the early sixties, Enid was spending more and more time each year in Africa with Pat. Tiring of the social demands of the Riviera, she luxuriated in an environment where she could paint all day, surrounded by her beloved animals without the need for human company. Yet she would dress formally for dinner at the Muthaiga Club, still the centre of white social life.

Many of their friends from the Riviera would visit, among them Solange Herter, who watched one day as the lion Tana dragged Enid through the living room and out of the French doors into the yard. 'She was unperturbed by her plight,' she said later. 'There was blood on her arms, but she was not remotely frightened. Pat told me later that it happened all the time.'

One day in 1962 Enid was invited to the East African Turf Club, where its most important race of the year, the East Africa Derby, was to be run. Despite being invited by a leading horse owner named Tubby Block, Enid was denied entry to the stables.

'What do I need to get into this bloody place,' she demanded.

'A horse,' her host replied.

'Well buy me one,' Enid retorted.

And so began Enid's investment in the thoroughbred industry and her renewed friendship with Beryl, who happened to train Tubby's horses. Within two seasons, Enid and Beryl had won the Derby, the very race from which Enid had been excluded, with a horse named Lone Eagle (named after Beryl's hero, the pilot Charles Lindbergh).

Six months later Beryl convinced Enid to buy a property in South Africa on the outskirts of Cape Town, more than 5000 kilometres south of Nairobi, where Beryl believed they had the opportunity to develop one of Africa's biggest thoroughbred studs.

The property earmarked by Beryl was called Broadlands, once the last outpost from Cape Town before settlers ventured across the treacherous passes of the Hottentots Holland Mountains into the centre of the country. A tree-lined drive from the main road led to a white-walled Cape Dutch house built in the late eighteenth century. There was a huge block of stables set among four hundred acres of green paddocks, orchards and vineyards positioned between the steep face of Table Mountain and the rocky, white-capped coastline of False Bay.

Enid was smitten and bought Broadlands on the spot. The cheque was signed and presented on the same day, with plans to move twenty-two horses from Beryl's tiny farm over the winter.

At first there was general amusement in the South African thoroughbred community; first that horses reared in Kenya were being shipped out and expected to compete against their finer thoroughbreds, but also because the operation was being run by women. But the first meeting of the 1965 season changed that perception when Enid and Beryl landing a winning double, including one of the Cape's main races, the Durbanville Cup.

The victories continued and, when Beryl convinced a jockey named Ryan 'Buster' Parnell, who had ridden for her in Kenya, to move down to Cape Town, it seemed that success was assured. Parnell, who would later become an Irish flat race champion, quickly established himself as a leading rider in southern Africa.

But there was trouble brewing behind the scenes. Beryl was as erratic and difficult as she was brilliant. She had ignored the advice of the previous property owners and rid the stables of all horses other than her own, stripping the business of valuable income from boarders who had previously paid to keep an extra forty or fifty horses on the property for breeding purposes.

At the same time, she had doubled the wages bill and was spending money hand over fist on her own projects, such as improvements to the training track, in a risky strategy that required spectacular success on the track to be financially worthwhile.

Beryl's manner was also a problem. She once told a female groom who'd broken her arm that she was a 'bloody fool', before riding away and leaving her writhing in agony on the ground. To top it off, she also had a reputation of being light-fingered, as Pat, who was visiting Broadlands, found out one day when staff wages she'd left in a handbag went missing. Beryl was the obvious culprit; when confronted, she replied: 'If you are stupid enough to leave it lying around, then I would be stupid not to avail myself of it.'

Enid's bank manager, fearing the worst, tried to intervene. 'The company, as such, must make up its mind whether it is to be run on business-like and profitable lines or whether it is to become a hobby and a residence for the directors who are quite prepared to pay in the necessary money for the privilege. Something must be done and done quickly as in my opinion it represents a ship without a captain heading for the rocks.'

Enid was at the end of her tether, writing to a friend: 'It is absolute hell working anywhere near Beryl because she fights with everybody and unless one is working for her the entire time and getting nothing done on the farm, that is all that matters to her. My interest is in the farm and not the horses, and I don't care a damn if I sell every one of the horses because I certainly will not go on like this.'

The clash of two strong personalities played out in the strangest of ways—beneath the dining table. It was witnessed several times by Buster Parnell, who was astounded by the parties Enid would host, often attended by 'dukes and archbishops; you never really knew who was going to be there'.

'Beryl was always the last to arrive,' he told author Mary Lovell who was writing a biography of Beryl called *Straight on Till Morning*. 'She'd sail in, usually after everyone else had sat down, looking marvellous with her two boxers, Circe and Caesar, trailing her. Enid habitually allowed her two pugs to join her at dinner and the four dogs created absolute havoc. It would always start well, but after a while there would be stirring and murmurs from under the table. Then little growls. Eventually the diners would be politely holding onto their wine glasses and pretending they hadn't noticed that the whole table literally shook from the minor war occurring around their feet. Eventually Beryl would say plaintively, "Enid, I do wish you would control your dogs darling." Enid would smile sweetly and raise her glass, which never contained anything stronger than water or Coca-Cola.'

By 1967 the situation had become untenable. Not only was the farm leaking money like a sieve, but Beryl's promise of big race wins to compensate was falling well short of expectations. Something had to give and eventually Beryl quit, taking her remaining horses and returning to Kenya. Enid, relieved, was left to pick up the pieces. And there was a price to pay: she would have to move permanently to South Africa.

Pat always feared that her mother had been seduced and duped by Beryl Markham into buying Broadlands, particularly as the proposal was initially supposed to have been a partnership with Beryl's then boyfriend, a businessman named Jorgen Thrane, only to have him walk away from the deal.

It wasn't that Enid couldn't afford the property—of course she could—but she couldn't manage it by herself, which meant that Pat would be forced to help, turning her own life in Kenya upside down, even giving up Ol Orion and leaving most of her animals behind.

Her biggest concern was Tana, who was now fully grown. It was one thing to have a tame lioness on a secluded property outside Nairobi and entirely another to move her to a new country and a property where horses and people roamed freely.

It was hard not to be resentful about the turn of events, but Pat had held her tongue after initially expressing doubt about the move to buy Broadlands. And when the family doctor told her that the higher altitudes of Kenya were causing problems for her mother's health, specifically her heart, she felt compelled to accept the inevitable.

For the first few years, while Beryl was in charge, Pat only travelled to South Africa when Enid was visiting there from France. Basically she stayed in Kenya, where she built a game lodge on a property further into the mountains, partly as a business venture offering walking safaris for tourists but also to give Tana more freedom as civilisation began to encroach on the boundaries of Ol Orion. It seemed to be a race against time to return her beloved lioness to the wild.

But when Beryl left in a huff, Pat packed her bags and moved south permanently. It was the last she would see of Tana who had, by now, found a mate and was nursing cubs of her own. Pat's heartache even thirty years later was clear as she penned her autobiography.

'I can still see her as I went to say goodbye, lying on her back, surrounded by her family, content and at peace. Or was this how I wanted to remember her? I don't know anymore. I didn't truly realise I would never see her again, and if I had known that, would I have had the courage to leave? What fate befell this golden creature that was my other self?'

Pat's arrival at Broadlands sparked immediate interest in her among the local South African media, which homed in on the story of her raising, loving and finally releasing Tana back into the wild, the narrative so similar to the *Born Free* story of Joy Adamson and her lioness, Elsa. Pat, blonde and square-jawed, even looked like Adamson.

The subsequent story was quickly picked up around the world, including in Australia, where Frank O'Neill read it and decided to make contact with his former wife. They hadn't seen each other in almost seventeen years, and yet within months they would be reunited and planning to remarry.

Frank had thrived in the years since their marriage collapsed. No longer a dental assistant and swim coach, he was now the most successful builder of swimming pools in Australia, at a time when the country was enjoying an economic boom. But, despite his success, Frank was still Frank: a quiet man in his early forties, who seemed almost embarrassed by his sporting fame. He clearly still held a flame for the woman who had married and then abandoned him, perhaps because he saw a person equally uncomfortable in her own, luxurious, surroundings.

For her part, Pat was undecided. She was on the rebound after an eight-year love affair with a safari guide: Stan Lawrence Brown. Stan was married and would never leave his wife, so when she moved to Cape Town the relationship petered out. He was too possessive anyway, she had decided.

Frank's reappearance had, understandably, thrown her but it seemed as if it was meant to be, particularly when a faith healer told Enid that a man was coming to see her daughter from a faraway land starting with *A*—'like an old coat that becomes new'. It was as if their marriage had been cut short before it had had time to flourish, although both of them realised that their relationship could never be conventional. And perhaps that was the answer. Why did they need to be conventional? Frank would always live in Australia and spend time in Africa, and she could do the reverse. They each had their own lives and would spend time together when either visited the other.

That was Caryll's view when Pat suddenly had cold feet a few days before the wedding. Sensing her doubts, he put his sister in a boat and rowed her out onto Lake Naivasha, where they spent several hours paddling among the hippos and flamingos while he reassured her that Frank was the right man for her. A few days later, Pat and Frank were remarried in a low-key ceremony in Nairobi.

Enid had stemmed the financial bleed at Broadlands by reopening the deserted stables to boarders, but it had been a struggle to find a new trainer after Beryl's tempestuous departure. They had only a handful of racehorses left and prospective trainers didn't fancy their chances of success.

A solution came one morning when Enid suggested that Pat take on the role. The idea at first seemed ludicrous but the more she thought about it, the more Pat liked the idea of the challenge. She had grown up with horses and had an affinity with animals. Perhaps she could combine the two and find someone to teach her the finer skills of thoroughbred training.

But they also needed horses, and a trip to Sydney by the two women in the autumn of 1968 happened to coincide with the Sydney Easter horse sales. Pat pestered her mother into attending the sales. Here was an opportunity to buy some decent thoroughbreds, she argued, so they bought a number of yearlings, which were shipped back to Broadlands.

There would be another fortuitous meeting while they were in Sydney, when Pat and Enid were introduced to Tommy Smith, the country's leading thoroughbred trainer, who warmed to their story of Broadlands and agreed to help and guide their purchase of fillies and colts for racing and breeding. He even visited the stud, and cast an eye over its facilities and made suggestions about feed and stabling.

At Smith's suggestion, they swam the horses each morning in the surf at False Bay and, rather than stabling them in the afternoons, removed their hind shoes and let them loose in the paddocks. A medical room was added to incorporate techniques being developed by Smith's vet, an Englishman named Percy Sykes, who was revolutionising the industry by using haematology—blood counts—to measure condition and performance.

Pat was granted a training licence, albeit reluctantly by dubious race officials, and the combination of canny purchases, new training techniques and individual diets for each horse based on Sykes's theories began to produce results when My Lovely, one of the fillies paraded around the auction ring at Randwick that year, became South Africa's champion three-year-old.

They had hit on a winning formula and returned to Australia for more horses. Enid warmed to the auction ring, treating the experience as if she was at the chemin de fer table in a Riviera casino, bidding fiercely for the horses identified by Pat and Tommy Smith.

Many were named for their links to Australia and the family. First came a 'bold but ugly' filly named Miss Lindeman, bought for just $500, with hindquarters like a tank and an attitude like Queen Boadicea's, who proved a sprinting sensation and won ten of her eighteen starts.

Swan River, named after their Perth stopover on the flight from South Africa, was as refined as Miss Lindeman was broad and quickly showed promise as a racer with eccentric habits, like travelling to races with the ducks and geese that occupied her stable. She would twice win the Durban Oaks and a dozen other races at distances from 1000 to 2400 metres.

Her half-sister Rose Bay, named after the Sydney landmark, would win the Cape and Durban Guineas while Miss International won eight consecutive races and Lady Kenmare ten, before all were retired to be brood mares among sixty that roamed the Broadlands pastures by 1972.

Enid—who had become something of a racing celebrity by accepting trophies with a meerkat on her shoulder—and Pat had turned a likely financial disaster into a personal success in just five years.

36

HOME

It had been more than half a century since Enid had taken her infant son Rory and left Sydney 'to ride the international whirl', but her arrival back in her home city in April 1969 still created media attention.

'Australia's famous and wealthy countess might move to Sydney', the *Sydney Morning Herald* announced, pointing to Enid's declaration that the city had finally 'come of age'.

'It compares with London, Paris, any city you can name,' she insisted, flashing an extravagant watch. 'It is exciting and alive. I wish I had known sooner.

'I left Sydney because it was so provincial . . . but now it has gone ahead tremendously. Such buildings, and art galleries and shops and restaurants. And the atmosphere is so different. I would like to sell my properties in South Africa, all but one of my farms in Kenya, my London and US properties and all of my six French homes, except La Fiorentina, and come to Sydney.'

The interview unfolded as the reporter would have hoped, with stories of wealth and splendour: how Brigitte Bardot had wanted to buy La Fiorentina, but was rebuffed and had to settle for a lesser property in St Tropez; about the treasure trove of paintings, antiques and silver in the villa—'There's a Rodin in the hallway'—and her neighbour Somerset Maugham, who had included her as a character in one of his books. Richard Burton and Elizabeth Taylor were currently renting the villa for $4000 a week.

But there were also hints of fragility. Enid was struggling again with the back injury caused in the riding accident so many years before; it had come back to haunt her in old age. This time Enid endured the pain rather than relying on morphine, which had almost ruined her life. Now aged in her late seventies, the injury had bowed her back noticeably and made a woman who once glowed and paraded for the cameras wary about being photographed. Finally she consented, sitting rather than standing in the lounge room of her brother Grant's Rose Bay house, but still, according to the cooing journalist, 'a poised and impressive woman' who had added a faint tint to her silver hair to match her pale blue eyes.

What was left unsaid was that behind the stories—'we have seven servants in the house and fourteen stable boys'—and the tributes, Enid was struggling to make sense of her scattered finances. The heavy investment at Broadlands was beginning to reap dividends but her financial advisers had been warning about the need to consolidate and perhaps cash in a few assets, hence her comments about selling houses.

It might have been different if Bernard Baruch had still been around, but the last of Enid's lovers and admirers had died a few years before, just as she was being pushed by an enthusiastic Beryl Markham into the Broadlands deal.

Beyond the façade of ridiculous wealth, Enid struggled with the demands of managing various fortunes across three continents. Money had never been her strong suit—a detail for others to deal with as she made her way through life, wars and husbands.

Enid gave banknotes away to strangers without counting them, stashed diamond necklaces in tissue boxes and bought houses, farms, boats and planes for her children. She entertained lavishly and hired staff to attend to the whims of her guests; she gambled without a care, and travelled often and in luxury.

But in the twilight years of her life it was becoming obvious that the money tree had been shedding leaves: the Furness and Cameron fortunes were still bountiful, but they now could be counted in the tens, rather than hundreds, of millions.

The first to go would be La Fiorentina, the villa that had defined her outrageously extravagant life; it was put on the market for the unprecedented asking price of over $US3 million. (In 2014 it was again on the market, this time for a rumoured $US525 million, making it one of the most expensive houses in the world.)

And that was just for the main house and immediate grounds. The price for Le Clos was $US1 million with $US750,000 each for La Florida and La Maison Blanche. The decision to sell La Fiorentina was an emotional wrench; less so the house in Lees Place in London which had mostly stood empty in recent years as her visits to the city became fewer and fewer. The house on Nassau would also go, the days of beachfront summers long gone.

Among the few records kept by her family is a file of correspondence between Enid and her financial and legal advisers in Sydney, London and New York. These documents give an insight into the complications she faced.

There was evidence of splendour, like the list of her jewellery (for insurance purposes) that included a necklace of thirty-four diamonds totalling 140 carats, two cabochon emerald brooches set in layers of diamonds, a necklace of 163 pearls set in platinum, and dozens of brooches, bracelets, rings, earrings and necklaces featuring sapphires, rubies, topaz and aquamarine. In total, the collection was worth more than £100,000 (£2 million today) and, as one letter noted, most of it was sitting in a locked cupboard, the key to which had been lost.

Her shopping receipts, neatly folded and pressed, revealed a conspicuous consumption that today would appear outrageous but in the context of her life it was perfectly acceptable, if not expected. Among the chits was a clip totalling $1173 for dozens of items of cosmetics, perfumes and lingerie bought in one day alone from Elizabeth Arden in New York. Two days later she bought seven dresses from Bloomingdales and a gold Cartier clock; as well, she visited Saks Fifth Avenue, where she fell in love with a matching tortoise-shell and gold bracelet and clip, and added eight dozen pairs of Nina Ricci stockings. At a nearby luxury leather goods shop she bought a box of poker chips and a gold corkscrew.

There were bills for limousines and hotels and an insurance claim for the theft of some of her luggage while travelling aboard the *Queen Mary*. The latter itemised more purchases, including another trip to Elizabeth Arden, four Venetian glass ashtrays and a vase from a St Regis boutique, even bedspreads from Macy's, a leopard-print mackintosh, rolls of Thai silk and a $300 bottle of perfume.

Her stockbrokers in Sydney anxiously tried to reach her to make decisions about selling shares she'd held in the family company, Lindemans, which they believed had reached a zenith and should be sold and diverted into other blue chip stocks. 'I realise that the family affiliation to the company is such that these things cannot be done lightly,' observed one broker, his eagerness smacking of a financier wanting to take his cut. 'It's a pity we cannot keep in closer touch with each other because your interests in this country are very large.'

At times the banking system struggled to keep up with Enid's travels. With share deals held up because she was buying in one country and selling in another, there was confusion between the Bank of NSW and Barclays about where in the world money was needed and an uncashed cheque for $300 from the Chemical Bank of New York.

Most poignant was a letter from the Co-operative Winegrowers Association of South Africa. It was a thank you to Enid for entertaining a delegation in Cape Town during one of her early visits, when negotiations to buy Broadlands were being finalised. The reason for the dinner was clear from an offer made by one official, a Miss van Rensburg, who wrote: 'As promised, I am sending you under separate cover some information about viticulture in the Cape. Please do not hesitate to approach us if any other information is required.'

Enid was planning a vineyard, which seemed odd, considering that she never touched alcohol. But her life had come full circle: her decision to leave the Riviera, and to move to an inland farming property, echoed her grandfather's journey to establish Cawarra more than a century before.

EPILOGUE

There was no Christmas cheer at Broadlands in 1972.

Enid had been ill most of the year, her back pain exacerbated by a hiatus hernia that she was reluctant to dull with painkillers because of fears about her previous morphine addiction. Travel had been minimal; instead, she had been confined to bed, sometimes for a week or more, and at times struggling to get to the races, where her namesake, Miss Lindeman, was in the midst of a winning streak of ten races.

It was not surprising, even in the heat of an African summer, that Enid developed pneumonia. She was confined to bed in early December and a nurse was hired. But Enid resisted; ever true to her maxim about never admitting illness, she was found up a ladder one morning looking for her meerkat, frantic that it was not on her bed.

Pat refused to believe that her energetic mother would not

recover but, as the New Year arrived, she began spending nights in Enid's bed to watch over her. It seemed just a matter of time.

On 5 January 1973, Pat was woken by the dawn light through window slats. Outside, one of the workmen was watering the lawn before the heat of the day set in. Her mother stirred a few minutes later.

Ignoring Pat, Enid rolled slowly over to the edge of the bed and sat up. Looking to her right, she whispered, 'Oh mother' and stretched out her arms as if reaching for someone, before she lay back down on the bed. She died a few moments later, three days short of her eighty-first birthday.

Pat could not remember the funeral, only that Rory came out from France and took her ashes back to La Fiorentina, where he built a tombstone at the point of Cap Ferrat. When he moved to the town of Ménerbes at the foot of the French Alps a few years later, Rory took her ashes again and created another tombstone in his garden.

And when Rory died in 1985 from an AIDS-related illness, aged seventy-one, Caryll took both their ashes back to England, where they were buried in the churchyard next to the family home in the town of Bletchingdon, Oxfordshire. There is a stained-glass window in the church, depicting Enid surrounded by her animals.

Caryll was buried alongside them when he died in 2013 at the age of eighty-seven.

After her mother died, Pat fell into financial difficulties but friends ensured that she could stay at Broadlands, where she continued to care for her ever-increasing menagerie. Frank would spend three months of the year in Africa until he became too old to travel. He still lives in Manly.

Pat died in 2019, a few weeks before her ninety-fourth birthday, in the same room as her mother. She was broke, the great fortunes of Roderick Cameron and Marmaduke Furness whittled away on fabulous lives of excess and fed by Enid Lindeman's creed—'Never be afraid, never be jealous and never complain when you are ill.'

AFTERWORD & ACKNOWLEDGEMENTS

The idea of a biography of Enid Lindeman was proposed during a pleasant dinner several years ago at the home of my British publisher and friend, Clare Drysdale. Among the guests that day was Andrew Stuart-Robertson, who listened attentively as Clare and I discussed the recent publication of another of my books, *Sheila: The Australian beauty who bewitched British society*. 'Have you heard of Enid Lindeman?' Andrew exclaimed after listening to the adventures of Sheila Chisholm. 'She had four husbands who all died and walked a cheetah in Hyde Park on a diamond collar.'

Talk about an elevator pitch. I was hooked, so thank you, Andrew.

While it took some years to get around to researching and writing about Enid. I have written several other books since that dinner, each a study of a person (in one case a family) who had achieved much in their chosen field and led fascinating lives in doing so.

Maverick Mountaineer tells the story of George Ingle-Finch, originally from Orange in New South Wales, who was not only a climber on the first Everest expedition in 1922 but also an incredible scientist who, among other feats, helped save London from the Blitz by teaching brigades how to suffocate a chemical fire.

Miss Muriel Matters was a book about the life of the dazzling suffragist from Adelaide, who in 1908 at the height of the suffrage battle in England became the first woman to make a speech in the House of Commons at Westminster. The following year she climbed into a rickety airship and flew over London dropping *Vote for Women* leaflets.

Then there was the family behind the iconic Australian confectionary company, Darrell Lea, whose success from hard work and a canny business acumen was offset by the darkness of their private lives, particularly Valerie Lea who raised four natural and three adopted children.

Enid is a different kind of journey, a woman of undoubted spirit and character whose life of unimagined riches and adventures was smothered in a celebration of individuality amid controversy, hardship and tragedy, alongside enormous wealth and privilege.

I would like to thank Clare Drysdale, firstly for having hosted the dinner referred to above but also as my British publisher who manages to combine encouragement, nous and practicality in a way that inspires me to keep going.

I am also indebted to Richard Walsh, one of the legends of Australian publishing, who has supported, encouraged and occasionally admonished me throughout by career as an author. Long may it continue.

Equally, my amazing wife Paola has always been my biggest supporter through the frequent doubts that are part and parcel of attempting to earn some sort of living out of writing books.

It must be quite confronting when a stranger telephones out of the blue and announces they are writing a biography of a beloved member of their family, and yet Enid's daughter-in-law Danièle and her children Caroline, Juliet and Rory have been very accommodating and helpful during the process, including Caroline agreeing to interview her aunt Pat on my behalf during a trip to South Africa. It was timely, sadly, given that Pat passed away last September at the age of 93.

Pat's memoir *A Lion in the Bedroom* was an invaluable reference. Her tales about Enid were refreshingly forthright, although I frequently found myself forming perhaps a more generous view of her mother's antics than she. Memory can often play tricks, if unintentionally, so I searched for corroborating sources where possible.

Rory Cameron's various books were also important sources, particularly about the rebuilding of La Fiorentina and his mother's early life in Paris, as well as her visits to Australia.

One of the frustrations of recreating lives from the early years of the twentieth century is that the subject and most of their friends have long since passed away, so first-hand testimony is difficult to find. The archived interview notes of

American journalist Dominick Dunne were a godsend (even if I did disagree with his frequent acceptance of mythology as fact) because back in the late 1980s he had interviewed a number of the visitors to La Fiorentina.

Others who have helped include Lyndsy Spence, fellow author and admirer of Enid, who wrote a chapter about her life in her 2019 book *She Who Dares: Ten trailblazing society women*. Lyndsy also wrote a biography on Doris Delevingne, *The Mistress of Mayfair*, published in 2016, which was my main source for the chapter 'The Storekeeper's Daughter'.

Last but not least, I owe a great deal to senior executives at Allen & Unwin. I feel privileged to have a career writing books. It is a notoriously difficult industry and I have always had amazing support from people including Patrick Gallagher, Annette Barlow and Tom Gilliatt, not to mention my in-house editor, Tom Bailey-Smith, and my copyeditor, Deonie Fiford, who have helped turn faulty scribble into my thirteenth book.

London, January 2020

SELECTED BIBLIOGRAPHY

Baruch, B., *Baruch: My own story*, New York: Henry Holt and Company, 1957

Cameron, R., *Australia: History and horizons*, London: Weidenfeld and Nicolson, 1971

Cameron, R., *Equator Farm*, New York: Roy Publishers, 1956

Cameron, R., *The Golden Haze: With Captain Cook in the South Pacific*, Cleveland: World Publishing Company, 1964

Cameron, R., *The Golden Riviera*, London: Weidenfeld and Nicolson, 1975

Cameron, R., *My Travel's History*, London: Hamish Hamilton, 1950

Cameron, R., *Shells*, London: Octopus, 1972

Castlerosse, V., *Valentine's Days*, London: Methuen, 1934

Castlerosse, V., untitled manuscript, (unpublished)

Cavendish O'Neill, P., *A Chimpanzee in the Wine Cellar*, Jonathan Ball: Johannesburg, 2012

Cavendish O'Neill, P., *A Lion in the Bedroom*, Jonathan Ball: Johannesburg, 2004

Chisholm, A. and Davie, M., *Beaverbrook: A life*, London: Hutchinson, 1992

Dunne, D., *Fatal Charms and the Mansions of Limbo*, New York: Ballantine Books, 1999

Lees-Milne, J., *Prophesying Peace*, London: Chatto and Windus, 1977

Lovell, M.S., *Straight on till Morning: The life of Beryl Markham*, London: Abacus, 2009

Lovell, M.S., *The Riviera Set*, London: Little, Brown, 2016

Maugham, W. Somerset, *Strictly Personal*, London: William Heinemann, 1942

Mosley, L., *Castlerosse*, London: Arthur Barker, 1956

Norrie, P., *Lindeman: Australia's classic winemaker*, Sydney: Apollo Books, 1993

Smollett, T., *Travels through France and Italy*, Oxford: Oxford University Press, 1979

Spence, L., *The Mistress of Mayfair*, Cheltenham: The History Press, 2017

Spence, L., *She Who Dares: Ten trailblazing society women*, Cheltenham: The History Press, 2019

Thompson, G.M., *Lord Castlerosse*, London: Weidenfeld and Nicolson, 1973

Vanderbilt, G. and Furness, T., *Double Exposure: A twin autobiography*, London: F. Muller, 1959

Robert Wainwright has worked as a journalist for 30 years and is the author of thirteen books, including *Sheila* and *The Maverick Mountaineer*, which won *The Times* Biography of the Year prize at the British Sports Book Awards in 2017. He lives in London.